Odisha Judicial Services Examination

Previous Years Solved MCQs

OJS (Civil Judge) Exam
Previous Year Prelims Question Papers with Answer Key

WITH EXPLANATIONS

2011-2024

Fourth Edition

2026

Compiled by
Abhishek Choudhary
Advocate, Supreme Court of India
Gold Medalist, B.Sc. LL.B (Hons.), L.L.M.

A work of

LEGIS ORBIS

(A Micro Enterprise registered with Ministry of MSME, Government of India)

In case of any query, please write to us at
support@legisorbis.com

2026

This book is a publication of Legis Orbis

First Edition	2022
Second Edition	2024
Third Edition	2025
Fourt Edition (Reprint)	2026

Legis Orbis
(A Micro Enterprise registered with Ministry of MSME, Government of India)
Website: www.legisorbis.in | E-mail: contact@legisorbis.in

MRP ₹ 399/-

ISBN: 9798886066333

Disclaimer

Printed by: Notion Press Media Private Limited
For: **Legis Orbis**

Table of Contents

PREFACE

The Odisha Judicial Services (OJS) Examination is a prestigious and highly competitive exam conducted for the recruitment of Civil Judges in the state of Odisha. As aspirants gear up to face this challenging examination, having the right study material is crucial for success. The path to clearing the OJS (Civil Judge) Prelims requires not only a solid understanding of law but also an efficient approach to practice and revision.

This book, Odisha Judicial Services Examination: OJS (Civil Judge) Exam Previous Year Prelims Question Papers with Answer Key, aims to provide a comprehensive resource for candidates preparing for the OPSC Civil Judge Exam. Compiled meticulously from the previous years (2011-2024), this compilation of solved question papers is designed to assist aspirants in familiarizing themselves with the structure and nature of the examination.

What makes this book an invaluable resource is its detailed answer key that not only provides the correct answers but also offers clear, concise, and accurate explanations, ensuring that candidates understand the rationale behind each solution. The book's inclusion of previous years' question papers helps candidates practice under actual exam conditions, boosting their confidence and improving their time-management skills.

In addition to extensive coverage, this book remains aligned with the latest exam trends and syllabus, ensuring its relevance in the ever-evolving landscape of the OJS (Pre.) Exam. As the most updated resource available in the market, it equips candidates with the tools they need to approach the examination with confidence and clarity.

We hope that this book proves to be a trusted companion in your journey towards success in the Odisha Judicial Services Examination. May it guide you towards your goal of becoming a Civil Judge in the state of Odisha.

Best of luck in your preparation!

Legis Orbis

Legis Orbis

FROM THE FOUNDER'S DESK

It is with great pride and a deep sense of responsibility that we present this comprehensive guide to your preparation for the Odisha Judicial Services (OJS) Examination. As educators and publishers, we understand the importance of reliable, accurate, and up-to-date resources when preparing for such a crucial milestone in your career. Our mission at Legis Orbis has always been to provide students with the highest quality study material that not only helps them prepare effectively but also inspires them to achieve their highest potential.

The OJS Examination, being one of the most sought-after exams for aspiring legal professionals in Odisha, requires rigorous preparation and a clear understanding of the exam pattern. With this book, we have endeavored to make your preparation journey smoother by compiling a rich collection of previous year's question papers (2011-2024) along with detailed and precise answer keys. Each question is carefully explained to ensure that you not only know the answer but also understand the underlying concepts, which will help you tackle a wide variety of questions in the exam.

This book stands out for its extensive coverage, clear explanations, and focus on providing the most current and relevant content, in line with the evolving exam syllabus. It is our sincere hope that this resource empowers you, boosts your confidence, and provides you with a competitive edge as you prepare for the OJS (Pre.) Exam.

We firmly believe that with dedication, the right guidance, and persistent hard work, you can turn your dream of becoming a Civil Judge into a reality. We wish you all the best in your endeavors and trust that this book will play a key role in your success.

Happy studying, and may your journey towards judicial excellence be fulfilling and victorious!

Abhishek Choudhary
Founder, Legis Orbis

ABOUT EDITOR IN CHIEF

Abhishek Choudhary, recipient of the prestigious University Gold Medal for excellence in the five-year integrated B.Sc. LL.B (Hons) program, is a distinguished member of the Bar Council of Delhi.

With over eight years of legal practice, he has established himself as a proficient advocate at the Hon'ble Supreme Court of India, various High Courts, and National and State Commissions. Abhishek's expertise spans a broad range of legal fields, with a particular focus on dispute resolution and alternative dispute resolution mechanisms. As a member of the Supreme Court Bar Association (SCBA), he has consistently demonstrated his ability to lead and manage complex legal projects.

In addition to his professional accomplishments, Abhishek holds an LL.M. in Corporate and Commercial Laws, further enriching his knowledge and capabilities in these specialized areas. His academic and professional journey reflects a commitment to excellence and a dedication to advancing the practice of law.

ACKNOWLEDGEMENT

We would like to extend our sincere gratitude to all those who have contributed to the creation of this book, Odisha Judicial Services Examination: OJS (Civil Judge) Exam Previous Year Prelims Question Papers with Answer Key.

First and foremost, we are deeply grateful to the esteemed faculty members, legal experts, and subject matter specialists whose invaluable insights, knowledge, and guidance have shaped the content of this book. Their expertise has been instrumental in ensuring the accuracy, relevance, and clarity of the explanations provided in this compilation.

We also wish to express our heartfelt thanks to the candidates who have shared their experiences, feedback, and suggestions over the years. Your inputs have been a constant source of motivation for us to refine and improve this book to better serve your needs.

A special mention goes to our editorial team, designers, and production staff, who have worked tirelessly to ensure that this book is presented in the most effective, user-friendly manner. Their attention to detail, dedication, and commitment to excellence have played a pivotal role in bringing this resource to life.

We also acknowledge the support of our family and friends for their constant encouragement, understanding, and belief in our vision to provide top-quality study material for aspirants.

Lastly, we extend our gratitude to the Odisha Public Service Commission (OPSC) for conducting the OJS Examination and providing an opportunity for bright legal minds to contribute to the judiciary.

This book is dedicated to every aspirant working hard to fulfill their dreams of becoming a Civil Judge. We hope that it serves as a valuable tool in your preparation and helps you achieve success in the OJS (Civil Judge) Examination.

Thank you for trusting us as your guide on this important journey.

With humility and gratitude,

Legis Orbis Team

2011

1. Under the Indian Penal Code, abetment is constituted ___.

(a) By instigating a person to commit an offence
(b) By engaging in a conspiracy to commit an offence
(c) By intentionally aiding a person to commit an offence
(d) All of the above

2. The distinction between Sections 299 and 300 I. P. C. was made clear by ___.

(a) Marshall, J. in R. V. Govinda
(b) Melvill, J. in Govinda V. R.
(c) Melvill, J. in R. V. Govinda
(d) Marshall, J. in Govinda V. R.

3. Which Section deals with dowry death?

(a) 304-A of I. P. C.
(b) 498-A of I. P. C.
(c) 489-A of I. P. C.
(d) 304-B of I. P. C.

4. Grievous Hurt means ___.

(a) Emasculation
(b) Disfiguration
(c) Any hurt which endangers life
(d) All of the above

5. Whoever voluntarily obstructs any person so as to prevent that person from proceeding in any direction in which that person has a right to proceed is ___.

(a) Wrongful confinement
(b) Force
(c) Wrongful restraint
(d) Defamation

6. Whoever by force compels or by any deceitful means induces any person to go from any place is ___.

(a) Abduction
(b) Kidnapping
(c) Slavery
(d) Forced Labour

7. The solemn resolution in the Preamble of our Constitution is made in the name of ___.

(a) Constituent Assembly of Free India
(b) Constitution of India
(c) Indian Independence Act
(d) People of India

8. One of the remedies for the false imprisonment is ___.

(a) Habeas Corpus
(b) Mandamus
(c) Certiorari
(d) Prohibition

9. Every citizen of India has a right to contest in election unless disqualified is ___.

(a) An Ordinary Civil Right
(b) An Important Constitutional Right
(c) A Fundamental Right
(d) A Fundamental Duty

10. Article 39A of the Constitution of India deals with ___.

(a) Free Legal Aid
(b) Free and Compulsory Education
(c) Free Housing to the Poor
(d) Free Medical Aid to the Citizen

11. The members of the UPSC are appointed by ___.

(a) The Cabinet
(b) The Chief Justice of India
(c) The Prime Minister of India
(d) The President of India

12. Which one of the following amendment accorded precedence to Directive Principles over Fundamental Rights?

(a) 44th Amendment
(b) 24th Amendment
(c) 39th Amendment
(d) 42nd Amendment

13. The Oath is administered to the President of India by ___.

(a) Speaker of the Lok Sabha
(b) Prime Minister of India
(c) Attorney General of India
(d) Chief Justice of India

14. The special provisions to Finance Bills is provided under the Constitution of India in ___.

(a) Article 114
(b) Article 115
(c) Article 116
(d) Article 117

15. Suspension of provisions of Article 19 during Emergency is dealt in ___.

(a) Article 352

(b) Article 355
(c) Article 358
(d) Article 361

16. Provisions as to the administration and control of Scheduled Areas and Scheduled Tribes are in ___.

(a) Ninth Schedule
(b) Seventh Schedule
(c) Fifth Schedule
(d) Third Schedule

17. Section 89 of the C. P. C. was inserted in ___.

(a) 1993
(b) 1998
(c) 1999
(d) 2009

18. For instituting a suit against the Government, notice should be given before ___.

(a) Two months
(b) Three months
(c) One month
(d) Six months

19. Decision on question of limitation ___.

(a) Operates as res judicata
(b) Does not operate as res judicata
(c) Operates as res judicata, if not erroneous
(d) None of the above

20. The Code of Civil Procedure ___.

(a) Applies to whole of India
(b) Applies to whole of India except Jammu and Kashmir
(c) Applies to the whole of India except Jammu and Kashmir and Nagaland
(d) Applies to whole of India except Jammu and Kashmir, Nagaland and Tribal Areas

21. Choose the most appropriate answer.

A judgement debtor ___.

(a) Cannot be arrested
(b) Can be arrested
(c) Can be arrested and detained if certain conditions are fulfilled
(d) Can be arrested and detained if certain conditions are fulfilled only in Civil Prison

22. Choose the most appropriate answer.

Movable property not in possession of the judgement debtor ___.

(a) Cannot be attached
(b) Can be attached by actual seizure
(c) Can be attached by an order prohibiting the person in possession thereof from giving it to the judgement debtor
(d) By leaving the same in the custody of respectable person as custodian

23. Precept means ___.

(a) Command
(b) Order
(c) Writ
(d) All of the above

24. Garnishee means ___.

(a) Judgement Debtor
(b) Judgement Creditor
(c) Judgement Debtor's Debtor
(d) Guarantor

25. Suo Motu means ___.

(a) In the matter
(b) Suit filed
(c) Of its own motion
(d) Small matter

26. Actus curiae neminem gravabit means ___.

(a) The act of court shall harm no one
(b) Grave acts cannot be pardoned
(c) Remedy must cure the act
(d) All acts cannot be sued in a Court

27. Section 75 of the Indian Evidence Act, 1872 deals with ___.

(a) Public Documents
(b) Private Documents
(c) Certified Copies of Public Documents
(d) Proof of Other Official Documents

28. The term 'Admission' is defined in the Indian Evidence Act, 1872 in ___.

(a) Section 17
(b) Section 18
(c) Section 19
(d) Section 20

29. Section 23 of the Indian Evidence Act, 1872 deals with ___.

(a) Relevance of Admissions in Civil Cases
(b) Relevance of Oral Admissions as to Contents of Documents
(c) Relevance of Oral Admissions as to Contents of Electronic Records

(d) None of the above

30. According to Section 141 of the Indian Evidence Act, 1872, any question suggesting the answer which the person putting it wishes or expects to receive, is called a ___.

(a) Answerable Question
(b) Convenient Question
(c) Suggestive Question
(d) Leading Question

31. The term 'Examination-in-Chief' has been defined in the Indian Evidence Act, 1872 in ___.

(a) Section 137
(b) Section 138
(c) Section 139
(d) Section 140

32. The Examination of a Witness by the Adverse Party shall be called his ___.

(a) Examination-in-Chief
(b) Cross-Examination
(c) Re-Examination
(d) Examination on Facts

33. Section 115 of the Indian Evidence Act, 1872 deals with ___.

(a) Estoppel
(b) Estoppel of Tenant
(c) Estoppel of Acceptor of Bill of Exchange, Bailee or Licensee
(d) Evidence as to Affairs of State

34. A Witness who is unable to speak is called as ___.

(a) Deaf Witness
(b) Dumb Witness
(c) Hostile Witness
(d) Unreliable Witness

35. 'Actus me invito factus non est mens actus' means ___.

(a) The act itself does not make a man guilty unless his intentions were so
(b) An act done by me against my will is not my act at all
(c) The intent and the act both must
(d) None of the above

36. Robbery is an aggravated form of ___.

(a) Theft
(b) Extortion

(c) Both (a) and (b)
(d) All of the above

37. Person who may be said to be of unsound mind is ___.

(a) An idiot
(b) A madman
(c) One who is drunk
(d) All of the above

38. When two or more persons by fighting in a public place disturb the public peace is ___.

(a) Affray
(b) Riot
(c) Assault
(d) Curfew

39. The Court of a Magistrate of first class may pass a sentence of imprisonment for a term not exceeding ___.

(a) Three years
(b) Five years
(c) Seven years
(d) Four years

40. Under which Section of Cr. P. C. a police officer can arrest a person without an order from a Magistrate and without warrant?

(a) Section 42
(b) Section 40
(c) Section 51
(d) Section 41

41. Power to search a place is provided under ___.

(a) Section 45
(b) Section 46
(c) Section 47
(d) Section 48

42. Which of the following is process to compel the appearance of persons before the Criminal Courts?

(a) Summons
(b) Warrants
(c) Attachment and sale of property
(d) All of the above

43. Under which Section of Cr. R C. a person who is avoiding execution of a warrant may be proclaimed absconder?

(a) Section 81
(b) Section 83

(c) Section 82
(d) Section 84

44. Any dispute relating to possession of immovable property is decided by ___.

(a) Judicial Magistrate
(b) Executive Magistrate
(c) Either by Executive or by Judicial Magistrate
(d) Neither by Judicial nor by Executive Magistrate

45. The recording of the statements by a police officer during investigation is provided by ___.

(a) Section 161(1)
(b) Section 161(2)
(c) Section 161(3)
(d) Section 162(1)

46. Under Sec. 167, the Magistrate can order detention in ___.

(a) Police Custody
(b) Judicial Custody
(c) Jail
(d) Any Custody as he thinks fit

47. Which of the following Sections does not provide for joinder of charges?

(a) Section 219
(b) Section 221
(c) Section 222
(d) Section 225

48. Which Section is based on the maxim "Nemo debet bis vexari pro eadem causa" i.e. a man shall not be twice vexed for one and the same cause?

(a) Section 300
(b) Section 301
(c) Section 302
(d) Section 303

49. Chapter V of the Indian Evidence Act, 1872 deals with ___.

(a) Oral Evidence
(b) Documentary Evidence
(c) Burden of Proof
(d) Witnesses

50. Section 62 of the Indian Evidence Act, 1872 deals with ___.

(a) Primary Evidence
(b) Secondary Evidence

(c) Proof of Documents by Primary Evidence
(d) Cases in which Secondary Evidence relating to Documents may be given

51. Which of the following is transferable property?

(a) Actionable claim
(b) Pension
(c) Right of way
(d) Chance of legacy

52. Where mortgagee is entitled to enjoy the benefits of the mortgaged property in lieu of interest on debt, the mortgage is called ___.

(a) Simple Mortgage
(b) Equitable Mortgage
(c) Usufructuary Mortgage
(d) English Mortgage

53. Which of the following is not a duty of the seller?

(a) To produce title deeds
(b) To disclose patent defects
(c) To execute conveyance
(d) To pay the outgoings

54. Consideration for lease is ___.

(a) License
(b) Price
(c) Debt
(d) Premium

55. A person who projects himself to be the owner when he is not is called ___.

(a) Ostensible owner
(b) Co-owner
(c) Equitable owner
(d) None of the above

56. Section 14 of the T. P. Act deals with ___.

(a) Conditional Transfer
(b) Vested Interest
(c) Rule Against Perpetuity
(d) Restricted Covenant

57. The period of limitation for filing of a suit on the basis of a promissory note from the date of its execution is ___.

(a) One year
(b) Two years
(c) Three years
(d) Six years

58. The limitation period in a suit by a surety against a co-surety when the surety pays anything in excess of his own share is ___.

(a) One year
(b) Three years
(c) Six years
(d) Twelve years

59. What is the limitation period in a suit by a landlord to recover possession from a tenant after the date the tenancy is determined?

(a) One year
(b) Three years
(c) Six years
(d) Twelve years

60. For a review of judgement by a Court other than the Supreme Court, from the date of the decree or order, the limitation is ___.

(a) One year
(b) Three years
(c) Six years
(d) Twelve years

61. In computing the period of limitation for an appeal, a review or revision, the time requisite for obtaining a copy of the decree or the order appealed against shall be excluded under ___.

(a) Section 11(1)
(b) Section 12(2)
(c) Section 13(3)
(d) Section 14(4)

62. 'Time requisite' under Section 12(2) of the Limitation Act means ___.

(a) Absolutely necessary time
(b) Actual time taken
(c) Maximum time
(d) Minimum time

63. Section 17 of the Limitation Act takes within its ambit ___.

(a) Concealments
(b) Frauds
(c) Mistakes
(d) All of the above

64. Section 17 of the Limitation Act does not take within its ambit ___.

(a) An appeal

(b) An execution application
(c) A suit
(d) All of the above

65. The period of limitation for setting aside a sale on execution of a decree, is ___.

(a) 30 days
(b) 60 days
(c) 90 days
(d) 180 days

66. Which of the following amount to presenting civil proceedings with 'due diligence and in good faith' within the meaning of Section 14 of the Limitation Act?

(a) Failure to pay the requisite court fee found deficient
(b) Error of judgement in valuing a suit
(c) Both (a) and (b)
(d) Neither (a) nor (b)

67. In which of the following cases the Court by going negatively with women's right to property, disqualified the daughter-in- laws right to father-in-laws property on the ground that the son had murdered his own father?

(a) Vallikannu Vs R. Sengaperumal, A. I. R. 2005
(b) Narashimha Murthy Vs Sushilabai, A. I. R. 1996
(c) Gurupad Vs Heerabai, A. I. R. 1978
(d) Shyama Devi Vs Manju Shukla (1994) 6 S. C. C.

68. Presumption that the younger survived the elder under Section 21 of the Hindu Succession Act, 1956 is a ___.

(a) Presumption of fact
(b) Presumption of fact and law
(c) Rebuttable presumption of law
(d) Irrebuttable presumption law

69. Which Section of the following of the Indian Succession Act, 1925 treats agnates and cognates and male and female heirs equally?

(a) Section 27(a)
(b) Section 27(b)
(c) Section 33-A
(d) Section 26

70. 'A' who is governed by Indian Succession Act, executes an instrument purporting to his will, but he does not understand the nature of the instrument, nor the effect of its provision. This instrument is ___.

(a) Valid
(b) Invalid
(c) Voidable
(d) None of the above

71. In which Section of the following of the Indian Succession Act, 1925 it is provided that where a bequest is made to a person by a particular description, and there is no person in existence at the testator's death who answers the description, the bequest is void under:

(a) Section 111
(b) Section 112
(c) Section 114
(d) Section 116

72. 'A' by his will, bequeaths to 'B' the sum of Rs. 5,000 and afterwards in the same will repeats the bequest in the same words. 'B' is entitled to ___.

(a) One legacy of Rs. 5,000
(b) Both legacy of Rs. 5,000
(c) Legacy becomes invalid
(d) None of the above

73. Schedule V of the Indian Succession Act, 1925 deals with ___.

(a) Form of Certificate
(b) Form of Caveat
(c) Form of Probate
(d) Form of Letters of Administration

74. Section 14 of the Hindu Succession Act, 1956 applies to ___.

(a) Movable property
(b) Immovable property
(c) Both movable and immovable property
(d) None of the above

75. A suit for Possession under Section 5 of the Specific Relief Act, can be filed within ___.

(a) 3 years
(b) 6 years
(c) 9 years
(d) 12 years

76. Under the Specific Relief Act, a suit for Recovery of Possession can be filed ___.

(a) Only in respect to movable property
(b) Only in respect to immovable property

(c) Both (a) and (b)
(d) None of the above

77. Section 26 of the Specific Relief Act fixes the time limit for discovery of mistake or fraud to be ___.

(a) Six months
(b) Three months
(c) One year
(d) None of the above

78. A claim for damages in suit for injection can be laid down ___.

(a) Under Section 38 of the Specific Relief Act
(b) Under Section 39 of the Specific Relief Act
(c) Under Section 40 of the Specific Relief Act
(d) Under Section 37 of the Specific Relief Act

79. Section 11 of the Specific Relief Act, 1630 provides for ___.

(a) Specific Performance of a part of the contract
(b) Defence respecting suits for Relief based on Contract
(c) Specific Performance of Contracts connected with Trusts
(d) Circumstances in which Specific Performance of a Contract is enforceable

80. Obligation under Specific Relief Act ___.

(a) Is a right in rem
(b) Is a right in personam
(c) Both (a) and (b)
(d) None of the above

81. Under the Specific Relief Act, the declaratory decree can ___.

(a) Be declined
(b) Not be declined
(c) Be commuted
(d) Be withheld

82. Under Section 12(2) of the Specific Relief Act, 1963, part performance of a Contract can be enforced by ___.

(a) The Promisor
(b) The Promisee
(c) Both (a) and (b)
(d) None of the above

83. Section 8 of the Specific Relief Act can be invoked ___.

(a) Against a person who has possession or

control over the property
(b) Against the person who is the owner of the article claimed
(c) By the person not entitled to the possession of the article
(d) In respect of the ordinary article

84. In a suit under 6 of the Specific Relief Act, the Court can ___.

(a) Adjudicate on the title
(b) Direct the defendant(s) to remove the structure
(c) Permit the plaintiff to pull down the structure
(d) None of the above

85. The term 'donatio mortis causa' refers to ___.

(a) Death bed gift
(b) Actionable claims
(c) Universal donee
(d) None of the above

86. Right of redemption arises in the case of ___.

(a) Gifts
(b) Mortgage
(c) Lease
(d) Exchange

87. Which of the following is a doctrine of equity?

(a) Doctrine of redemption
(b) Doctrine of consolidation
(c) Doctrine of lis pendens
(d) Doctrine of marshalling

88. Which of the following deals with the doctrine of election?

(a) Section 45
(b) Section 15
(c) Section 53-A
(d) Section 35

89. To convert a proposal into a promise, the acceptance must be ___.

(a) Absolute and qualified
(b) Absolute and unqualified
(c) Unusual and reasonable
(d) Usual and qualified

90. Contracts of Adhesion are ___.

(a) Unfair contracts
(b) Unlawful contracts
(c) Contracts of adults
(d) Standard form contracts

91. A agrees with B to discover treasure by magic. The agreement is ___.

(a) Void
(b) Voidable
(c) Illegal
(d) Unnatural

92. If the goods are bailed for hire, the bailor is responsible for damages for the faults in the bailed goods which ___.

(a) He is aware
(b) He is not aware
(c) He is aware and unaware
(d) He is reasonably aware

93. A contract of guarantee may be ___.

(a) Oral
(b) Written
(c) Oral or Written
(d) None of the above

94. If the promisor absolutely repudiates the contract prior to the promised date of performance, it is ___.

(a) Frustration
(b) Impossibility of performance
(c) Final breach
(d) Anticipatory breach

95. If a person is employed by and acting under the control of the original agent in the business of agency, he is known as ___.

(a) Sub-agent
(b) Substituted Agent
(c) Del-credere Agent
(d) Mercantile Agent

96. A contracts to pay B Rs. 20,000 if B's house is burnt. It is a ___.

(a) Wagering Contract
(b) Quasi Contract
(c) Contingent Contract
(d) Illegal Contract

97. To create an agency ___.

(a) Consideration is necessary
(b) Consideration is not necessary
(c) Some consideration is necessary
(d) Adequate consideration is necessary

98. Every agreement, of which the object or consideration is unlawful, is ___.

(a) Void
(b) Voidable
(c) Illegal
(d) Unfair

37	A	77	D
38	A	78	C
39	A	79	C
40	D	80	B

99. 'Heir' has been defined under___.
(a) Section 3(d) of the Hindu Succession Act
(b) Section 3(e) of the Hindu Succession Act
(c) Section 3(f} of the Hindu Succession Act
(d) Section 3(g) of the Hindu Succession Act

100. Hindu Succession Amendment Act, 2005 came into effect on ___.

(a) 9th June, 2005
(b) 9th August, 2005
(c) 9th July, 2005
(d) 9th September, 2005

ANSWERS

1	D	41	C	81	A
2	C	42	D	82	C
3	D	43	C	83	A
4	D	44	B	84	D
5	C	45	C	85	A
6	A	46	D	86	B
7	D	47	D	87	C
8	A	48	A	88	D
9	B	49	B	89	B
10	A	50	A	90	D
11	D	51	A	91	A
12	D	52	C	92	C
13	D	53	D	93	C
14	D	54	D	94	D
15	C	55	D	95	A
16	C	56	C	96	C
17	C	57	C	97	B
18	A	58	B	98	A
19	D	59	D	99	C
20	D	60	-X-	100	D
21	B	61	B		
22	C	62	A		
23	D	63	D		
24	C	64	B		
25	C	65	B		
26	A	66	C		
27	B	67	A		
28	A	68	C		
29	A	69	A		
30	D	70	D		
31	A	71	B		
32	B	72	A		
33	A	73	B		
34	B	74	C		
35	B	75	D		
36	C	76	C		

2012

1. R. C. Cooper vs. Union of India is commonly known as ___.

(a) Privy Purse Case
(b) Fundamental Right Case
(c) Bank Nationalization Case
(d) Mandal Commission Case

2. Number of fundamental rights guaranteed only to citizens are ___.

(a) 5
(b) 6
(c) 9
(d) 10

3. Following Schedule relates to the Municipality ___.

(a) VII
(b) IX
(c) XI
(d) XII

4. Presidential satisfaction for imposing President Rule is ___.

(a) Subject to judicial review on the ground of malafide
(b) Subject to judicial review
(c) Not subject to judicial review
(d) Subject to judicial review after the rule ends

5. The current Lokpal Bill was introduced under ___.

(a) Article 248
(b) Article 252
(c) Article 253
(d) Article 246

6. The Legislature of a State may impose restrictions on trade, commerce and intercourse under ___.

(a) Article 302
(b) Article 303
(c) Article 304
(d) Article 305

7. Article 245 has been interpreted on the basis of ___.

(a) Doctrine of Territorial Nexus
(b) Doctrine of Colourable Legislation
(c) Doctrine of Eclipse
(d) Doctrine of Pith and Substance

8. By the 42nd Amendment Act the Preamble of the Constitution has been amended at ___.

(a) One Place
(b) Two Places
(c) Three Places
(d) None of the above

9. The following state has two Houses ___.

(a) Orissa
(b) Karnataka
(c) Chhattisgarh
(d) Arunachal Pradesh

10. The provisions dealing with the Supreme Court can be amended ___.

(a) By absolute majority
(b) By absolute majority and ratification
(c) By special majority and ratification
(d) By special majority

11. A suit is bad for non-joinder of a necessary party, as provided ___.

(a) Under Order 1, Rule 10 of CPC
(b) Under Order 1, Rule 9 of CPC
(c) Under Order 1, Rule 1OA of CPC
(d) Under Order 1, Rule 11 of CPC

12. Legal representative under Section 2(11) of CPC means a person who is a ___.

(a) Relative of parties to the suit
(b) Co-sharer of the benefits assuming to the parties
(c) Close neighbour
(d) Who in law represents the estate of the deceased person

13. Court can direct the parties to opt for any one mode of alternative dispute resolution under ___.

(a) Order X, Rule 1A of CPC
(b) Order X, Rule 1B of CPC
(c) Order XI, Rule 1 of CPC
(d) Order XII, Rule2 of CPC

14. Discovery by interrogatories and inspection has been provided ___.

(a) Under order X of CPC
(b) Under order XI of CPC
(c) Under order XV of CPC
(d) Under order XVI of CPC

15. Clerical or arithmetical mistakes in judgements, decrees or orders etc. can be corrected ___.

(a) Under Section 152 of CPC

(b) Under Section 153 of CPC
(c) Under Section 151 of CPC
(d) Under Section 153A of CPC

16. Compensatory costs in respect of false or vexations claims or defences are imposed ___.

(a) Under Section 34 of CPC
(b) Under Section 35 of CPC
(c) Under Section 35A of CPC
(d) Under Section 35B of CPC

17. Abetment of proceedings is governed ___.

(a) By order XXI of CPC
(b) By order XXII of CPC
(c) By order XXIV of CPC
(d) By order XX of CPC

18. A temporary injunction can be granted to a party establishing ___.

(a) That there is prima facie case in his favour
(b) Irreparable injury to him in case injunction is not granted
(c) Balance of convenience in his favour
(d) All of the above

19. Right to appeal from original decree has been provided under ___.

(a) Section 94 of CPC
(b) Section 95 of CPC
(c) Section 96 of CPC
(d) Section 100 of CPC

20. Adjournment can be granted ___.

(a) Under Order XIV Rule 1 CPC

(o) Under Order XV Rule 2 CPC
(c) Under Order XVI Rule 3 CPC (d) Under Order XVII Rule 1 CPC

21. Non-Cognizable offence means ___.

(a) A police officer has authority to arrest without warrant
(b) A police officer cannot arrest without warrant
(c) It depends upon the discretion of the police officer
(d) On request of complainant, arrest can be made

22. Under which Section of Cr.P.C., the Assistant Public Prosecutor is appointed?

(a) Section 20
(b) Section 24
(c) Section 13
(d) Section 25

23. Which of the following can make the arrest?

(a) A Police Officer
(b) A Magistrate
(c) A Private Person
(d) All of the above

24. Under Section 50, Cr.P.C. it is not mandatory to inform the arrested person that he is entitled to be released on bail ___.

(a) With warrant
(b) Without warrant
(c) With warrant for bailable offence
(d) Without warrant for non-bailable offence

25. A summons issued by a Court must be in ___.

(a) Duplicate
(b) Triplicate
(c) Writing and Duplicate
(d) Writing and Triplicate

26. An Executive Magistrate is empowered to grant remand under Section 167, Cr.P.C. for a maximum period of ___.

(a) 15 days
(b) 7 days
(c) 60 days
(d) 90 days

27. Which Section provides for joint trial for several persons?

(a) Section 220
(b) Section 221
(C) Section 222
(d) Section 223

28. Power of the Court to convert Summons- cases into Warrant-cases is provided under ___.

(a) Section 258
(b) Section 259
(c) Section 260
(d) Section 261

29. Which Section empowers the Court to examine the accused?

(a) Section 312
(b) Section 313
(c) Section 314
(d) Section 315

30. Under Section 357, an order of compensation can be passed by the ___.

(a) Trial Court
(b) Appellate Court I High Court or Sessions Court
(c) Both (a) and (b)
(d) Only (b)

31. The object of Indian Evidence Act, 1872 asset out in the Preamble is ___.

(a) To repeal certain parts and to consolidate, define and amend the Law of Evidence
(b) To consolidate, define and amend the Law of Evidence
(c) To define and amend the Law of Evidence
(d) To repeal certain parts and to define and amend the Law of Evidence

32. Law of Evidence is ___.

(a) A Substantive Law
(b) An Adjective Law
(c) Both (a) and (b)
(d) Neither (a) nor (b)

33. Under the Indian Evidence Act, 1872, the relevant fact ___.

(a) Must be legally relevant
(b) Must be logically relevant
(c) Must be logically and legally relevant
(d) Must be logically and legally relevant and admissible

34. Confession of one accused is admissible against co-accused ___.

(a) If they are tried jointly for different offences
(b) If they are tried for the same offence but not jointly
(c) If they are tried for different offences and not jointly
(d) If they are tried jointly for the same offence

35. A dying declaration la relevant in India ___.

(a) Only in criminal proceeding
(b) Only in summary proceeding
(c) Only in civil proceeding
(d) In civil as well as criminal proceeding

36. The opinion of an expert can be on the question of ___.

(a) Foreign Law
(b) Indian Law
(c) Both (a) and (b)
(d) Only (b) and not (a)

37. Secondary evidence is admissible ___.

(a) Where the non-production of primary evidence has not been accounted for
(b) Irrespective of whether the non-production of primary evidence has been accounted for or not
(c) Where the non-production of primary evidence has been accounted for
(d) Beth (a) and (b) are correct

38. A is charged with travelling on a railway without a ticket ___.

(a) The burden of proving that he did not have the ticket is on the prosecution
(b) The burden of proving that he did not have the ticket is on the party who asserts it
(c) The burden of proof is on railway authorities
(d) The burden of proving that he had a ticket i1on him

39. When document creating an obligation is in the hands of the obligor, the obligation has been discharged ___.

(a) It is a presumption of Law
(b) It is a presumption of Fact
(c) It is an irrebuttable presumption of Law
(d) It is a mixed presumption of Law and Fact

40. The husband and wife are competent witnesses for or against each other ___.

(a) In civil proceedings
(b) In criminal proceedings
(c) Both in civil and criminal proceedings
(d) These are privileged communications, cannot be disclosed

41. Fraudulently has been defined as doing anything with intent to defraud ___.

(a) Section23
(b) Section 25
(c) Section24
(d) Section 26

42. Section 34 of IPC ___.

(a) Creates a substantive offence
(b) Is a rule of evidence
(c) Both (a) and (b)
(d) Neither (a) nor (b)

43. The maxim "ignorantia juris non excusat" means ___.

(a) Ignorance of Law is no excuse
(b) Ignorance of Fact is no excuse
(c) Ignorance of Law is an excuse

(d) Ignorance of Fact is an excuse

44. Section 84 of IPC provides for ___.

(a) Medical insanity
(b) Legal insanity
(c) Moral insanity
(d) All of the above

45. The right to private defence is based on the natural instinct of ___.

(a) Self Preservation
(b) Self Respect
(c) Self Sufficiency
(d) Self Reliance

46. Chapter XX of IPC deals with ___.

(a) Offences related marriage
(b) Defamation
(c) Offences against property
(d) None of the above

47. The essential ingredients of a crime are ___.

(a) Motive, mens rea and actus reus
(b) Motive, intention and knowledge
(c) Actus reus and mens rea
(d) Knowledge, intention and action

48. In which case Supreme Court held that the defence of drunken can be availed of only when intoxication produces such a condition as the accused loses the requisite intent.ion for the offence ___.

(a) Appa Salved vrs State of Maharashtra, AIR 2007 SC 763
(b) Mubarak Hussain vrs State of Rajasthan, AIR 2007 SC 697
(c) Neetu vrs State of Punjab, AIR 2007 SC 758
(d) Kamala Devi vrs K. Kanwar, AIR 2007 SC 663

49. Sex with a girl through fraudulent consent, amounts to ___.

(a) Simple physical assault
(b) Molestation
(c) Attempt to rape
(d) Rape

50. Every murder is culpable homicide but not vice-versa. The statement ___.

(a) Is true
(b) Is false
(c) Depends upon the circumstances
(d) Depends upon the degree of probability

51. The Limitation Act and the Code of Civil Procedure are to be read together because both are statutes relating to procedure and they are in ___.

(a) Pari Materia
(b) Modus Operandi
(c) Colourable Legislations
(d) Doctrine of Acquiescence

52. For the balance due on a mutual, open and current account where there have been reciprocal demands between the parties the period of limitation is ___.

(a) 3 years
(b) 12 years
(c) 4 years
(d) 30 years

53. For possession of immoveable property when the plaintiff has become entitled to possession by reason of any forfeiture or breach of condition the period of limitation is ___ when the forfeiture is incurred or the condition is broken.

(a) 3 years
(b) 12 years
(c) 9 years
(d) 1 year

54. Where the period of limitation for filing a suit expired on 28th May, 1961; but no judge or officer could enter into the court premises due to picketing of the Civil Court from 19th to 29th May, the presentation of the plaint on 30th May, was held to be ___.

(a) Delayed
(b) In time since Section 4 is an exception to general rule laid down in Section 3 of the Act
(c) Inordinate delay
(d) None of the above

55. Where the prescribed period for any suit, appeal or application expires on a day when the court is closed, the suit, appeal or application may be instituted, preferred or made on the day ___.

(a) When the court reopens within 30 days
(b) According to the advocate wishes
(c) Before closing of the court
(d) When the court reopens

56. Appeal from an order of acquittal under Section 417(1) or (2) of the Code of Criminal

Procedure is ___ from the date of the order appealed.

(a) 30 days
(b) 90 days
(c) 60 days
(d) 12 months

57. The acquisition of easementary right is acquired by prescription after ___ uninterrupted with the person.

(a) 30 years
(b) 20 years
(c) 15 years
(d) 5years

58. To set aside a sale in execution of a decree including any such application by a judgment ___ of sale.

(a) 60 days
(b) 30 days
(c) 90 days
(d) 3 years

59. The Law of Limitation bar a action in the Court but not ___.

(a) Plea of change of law
(b) Plea of defence
(c) Plea of Ignorance
(d) Plea of estoppel

60. Any suit for which no period of limitation is provided elsewhere in this schedule the period of limitation is ___ when the right to sue accrues.

(a) 9 years
(b) 6 years
(c) 1 year
(d) 3 years

61. Attached to the earth means ___.

(a) Things rooted in the earth
(b) Thing embedded in the earth
(c) Things attached to what is embedded in the earth
(d) All of the above

62. A transfers Rs. 5,000 to Bon condition that B resides with A, otherwise to C. The transfer in favour of C is ___.

(a) Collateral Transfer
(b) Condition Precedent
(c) Ulterior Transfer
(d) None of the above

63. Restrictive covenants are ___.

(a) Such contracts which restrict the use or enjoyment
(b) Condition imposed by transferor restricting use or enjoyment
(c) Both of the above
(d) None of the above

64. Feeding the estoppel by grant is a doctrine of ___.

(8) Section 42
(b) Section 43
(c) Section 44
(d) Section 45

65. Mahomed Musa vrs. Aghore Kumar Ganguli (42 I. A 1) is the leading case of ___.

(a) Lis Pendens
(b) Fraudulent Transfer
(c) Doctrine of Election
(d) Part Performance

66. English mortgage means ___.

(a) Mortgagor should bind himself to repay mortgage money
(b) Property mortgage should be absolutely transferred to mortgagee
(c) On the payment of mortgage money mortgagee will reconvey the property
(d) All of the above

67. Where two persons mutually transfer the ownership of one thing for the ownership of another, the transaction is ___.

(a) Sale
(b) Actionable claim
(c) Exchange
(d) Charge

68. A lease can be determined ___.

(a) By merger
(b) By forfeiture
(c) By surrender
(d) By all of the above

69. Redeem up, foreclose down is the rights of a ___.

(a) Assignee
(b) Mortgagee
(c) Mesne mortgagee
(d) Donee

70. No mortgagee paying off a prior mortgage shall thereby acquire any priority in

respect of his original security. It is ___.

(a) Rules of Marshalling
(b) Rules against tacking
(c) Rules of subrogation
(d) None of the above

71. Law of Contracts is ___.

(a) The whole law of agreements
(b) The whole law of obligations
(c) The law of agreements creating obligations
(d) The law of obligations arising out of con-tracts

72. Announcement of Auction Sale without reserve is an ___.

(a) Invitation to offer
(b) Offer
(c) Incomplete offer
(d) Inchoate offer

73. Consideration may be ___.

(a) Present or past or future
(b) Present or future
(c) Present or past
(d) Past or future

74. Obligations resembling those created by contract are known as ___.

(a) Contingent contracts
(b) Wagering contracts
(c) Quasi-contracts
(d) Irregular contracts

75. The right of subrogation in a contract of guarantee is available to the ___.

(a) Creditor
(b) Principal Debtor
(c) Surety
(d) Indemnifier

76. General lien is available to ___.

(a) Bailee
(b) Bailor
(c) Pawnee
(d) Banker

77. 'S' said to a shop keeper..."Let 'P' have the goods, I will see you paid." This is a ___.

(a) Contract of Guarantee
(b) Contract of Indemnity

(e) Contract of Wager
(d) Contingent Contract

78. When consent is caused by fraud or misrepresentation, the contract is ___.

(a) Voidable at the option of the aggrieved party
(b) Void
(c) Unenforceable
(d) Irregular

79. The foundation of law of damages for breach of contract is laid down in ___.

(a) Tinn vrs Hoffman
(b) Taylor vrs Gladwell
(c) Addis vrs Gramaphone Co.
(d) Hadley vrs Baxandale

80. Acceptance of lesser sum in full satis-faction of the debt ___.

(a) Discharges the debt
(b) Discharges only the paid part of the debt
(c) Discharges the paid part and interest thereon
(d) Gives a right to sue for the balance amount

81. Under the Hindu Succession Act, the property of a male Hindu dying intestate shall devolve according to the provisions of ___.

(a) Section 8
(b) Section 9
(c) Section 6
(d) Section 14

82. A dies after the commencement of the Hindu Succession Act, leaving behind three sons, B. C and D. The interest in the property passes to by ___.

(a) Sapind relationship
(b) Testamentary succession
(c) Survivorship
(d) Limited estate

83. Any property possessed by a female Hindu whether acquired before or after the commencement of the Act shall be held by her as ___.

(a) Limited owner
(b) Ancestral property
(c) Stridhana property
(d) Full owner

84. One who is related by blood to the de-ceased through female is known as ___.

(a) Agnate
(b) Cognate

(c) Sapindas
(d) Dependant

85. A Hindu dies leaving behind father and son's daughter's son. They are ___.

(a) Class I heirs
(b) Class II heirs
(c) Preferential heirs
(d) None of the above

86. The Indian Succession Act applies only to the cases of ___.

(a) Self acquired property
(b) Ancestral property
(c) Survivorship
(d) Intestate and testamentary succession

87. To manage the estate of the deceased an Administrator is appointed by ___.

(a) Testator
(b) Government
(c) Court
(d) Family of the deceased

88. A Holograph Will is a will written by the ___.

(a) Coparcener
(b) Advocate
(c) Successor
(d) Testator

89. A legacy is bequeathed to A and in case of his death to B. If A survives the testator, the legacy to B ___.

(a) Does not take effect
(b) Becomes vested
(c) Takes effect
(d) Representatives of 8 takes

90. A copy of the will certified under the seal of the Court, with a grant administration to the estate of the testator is known as ___.

(a) Letter of administration
(b) Probate
(c) Executor
(d) Privileged will

91. The following Section of the Specific Relief Act deals with contracts with specific performance with variation ___.

(a) Section 21
(b) Section 32
(c) Section 18

(d) Section 19

92. The principle in which Section 12 of the Specific Relief Act is based on ___.

(a) "Equity looks to the substance rather than to the mere letter of a contract"
(b) "Equity looks to the substance of the contract and requires substantial compliance with its conditions rather than its literal fulfilment"
(c) Both (a) and (b)
(d) None of the above

93. The principle 'Doctrine of Specific Performance' is based on ___.

(a) Specific performance will not be granted where damages are an adequate remedy
(b) The granting of specific performance is within the discretion of the court
(c) Specific performance would be refused where the contract was wanting mutuality at the time when it was entered into
(d) All of the above

94. One of the following statements is not applicable according to Section B of the Specific Relief Act ___.

(a) No suit can be bought against the owner
(b) A person having a special right to present possession may bring the suit even against the owner of the property
(c) A decree is for the return of movable property
(d) A decree is for the money value against a movable property

95. According to Section 15 one of the following persons cannot enforce the Specific Performance of a contract ___.

(a) The representative-in-interest or the principal
(b) A reversioner in possession
(c) A reversioner in reminder
(d) A reminder man for tenant not for life

96. Contracts which cannot be enforced under Section 14 of the Specific Relief Act ___.

(a) Where compensation is adequate remedy
(b) Contracts involving personal skill
(c) Contracts of Determinable Nature
(d) All of the above

97. One of the following is a contract which has been held not 'indivisible' ___.

(a) A contract for the sale of property in one lot

(b) A contract for the sale of plot of land cannot be regarded as separate contract for selling different portion of the plot
(c) Where property is sold in distinct lots, with separate contract for each lot
(d) Where a person enter into a mutual contract for sale or purchase

98. In a suit for Specific Performance the defendant may set up the following grounds ___.

(a) Uncertainty and Excess of power
(b) Hardship and Unfair Advantage
(c) Both (a) and (b)
(d) None of the above

99. Rectification of an instrument under the Specific Relief Act is allowed when Fraud or Mutual Mistake of the parties to a contract is allowed under ___.

(a) Section 26 (1)
(b) Section 27
(c) Section 22
(d) None of the above

100. Refuse to rescind a contract by a court is laid down in one of the following Sections of the Specific Relief Act ___.

(a) Section 26 (2)
(b) Section 27 (2)
(c) Section 28
(d) Section 29

20	D	50	A	80	A
21	B	51	A	81	A
22	D	52		82	C
23	D	53	A	83	D
24	D	54	B	84	B
25	C	55	B	85	B
26	B	56	D	86	D
27	D	57	B	87	C
28	B	58	B	88	D
29	B	59	A	89	A
30	C	60	A	90	B

ANSWERS

1	C	31	B	61	D	91	C
2	A	32	B	62	B	92	C
3	D	33	A	63	C	93	D
4	B	34	D	64	B	94	A
5	C	35	D	65	D	95	D
6	C	36	A	66	D	96	D
7	A	37	C	67	C	97	C
8	B	38	D	68	D	98	D
9	B	39	B	69	B	99	A
10	D	40	C	70	B	100	B
11	B	41	B	71	C		
12	D	42	B	72	A		
13	A	43	A	73	A		
14	B	44	B	74	C		
15	A	45	A	75	C		
16	C	46	A	76	D		
17	B	47	D	77	A		
18	D	48	B	78	A		
19	C	49	D	79	C		

2013

1. Which one of the following doctrines is not related to Article 13 of the Constitution?

(a) Doctrine of Eclipse
(b) Doctrine-of colourable legislation
(c) Doctrine of waiver
(d) Doctrine of severability

2. Which one of the following is not a state under Article 12 of the Constitution?

(a) Berhampur University Student Union
(b) C. S. I. R.
(c) Municipal Corporation, Bhubaneshwar
(d) Union Public Service Commission

3. Which Fundamental Right is available to citizens only?

(a) Right to equality
(b) Protection against arrest and detention
(c) Freedom of speech and expression
(d) Protection of life and personal liberty

4. Which Fundamental Right is available to all persons?

(a) Right to form Union
(b) Protection of life and personal liberty
(c) Right to assemble peaceably.
(d) Right to move freely throughout the territory of India

5. Which Article of the Indian Constitution is related to Doctrine of self incrimination?

(a) Article 20(1)
(b) Article 22
(c) Article 20(3)
(d) Article 20(2)

6. Which one of the following is a Directive Principle of State Policy?

(a) Right to Education
(b) Right to Die
(c) Right to move Supreme Court
(d) To organise Village Panchayats

7. Which one of the following is not a Directive Principle of State Policy?

(a) Uniform Civil Code
(b) Organisation of Village Panchayats
(c) Right to Education
(d) Free Legal Aid

8. Which one of the following is not a fundamental duty?

(a) To protect Sovereignty
(b) To defend the Country
(c) To respect National Anthem
(d) To promote Indian Culture

9. In which case the doctrine of prospective overruling was evolved by the Supreme Court?

(a) Shankari Prasad vs. Union of India
(b) I. C. Golak Nath vs. State of Punjab
(c) Sajjan Singh vs. State of Rajasthan
(d) Keshava Nand Bharti VS. State of Kerala

10. Which case is related to constitutionality of 'right to die'?

(a) Maneka Gandhi vs. Union of India
(b) Gian Kaur vs. State of Punjab
(c) A. K. Gopalan vs. Union of India
(d) Kharak Singh vs. State of U.P.

11. Preliminary decree can be passed in a suit ___.

(a) For partition
(b) Of partnership
(c) For possession and Mesne profit
(d) All of the above

12. Pecuniary jurisdiction of the court has been dealt with in ___.

(a) Section 2 of CPC
(b) Section 6 of CPC
(c) Section 9 of CPC
(d) Section 15 of CPC

13. Set-off can be ___.

(a) Legal set-off
(b) Equitable set-off
(c) Both (a) and (b)
(d) Either (a) or (b)

14. Remedies available against an ex-parte decree include ___.

(a) Appeal
(b) Review
(c) Application for setting aside ex-parte decree
(d) Application

15. Nemo debet bis vexari pro una et eadem causa means ___.

(a) It is in the interest of state that there should be an end to litigation
(b) A judicial decision must be accepted as correct
(c) No one shall be vexed twice for one and the

same cause of action.
(d) Where there is a right there is a remedy

16. In execution of decree for the maintenance, salary of a person can be attached to the extent of ___.

(a) One fourth
(b) One third
(c) Two third
(d) One half

17. Under section 100 CPC, a second appeal lies to the ___.

(a) Supreme Court
(b) High Court
(c) Tribunal
(d) Court of District Judge

18. Section 89 CPC provides for ___.

(a) Settlement of dispute by High Court only
(b) Settlement of dispute by Supreme Court or High Court
(c) Settlement of dispute through Village Panchayat
(d) Settlement of dispute outside the Court

19. Section 115 of CPC applies only when ___.

(a) There is error of law
(b) There is error of fact
(c) There is jurisdictional error
(d) There is erroneous decision

20. If an indigent person's suit abates on the death of the plaintiff, under Order XXXIII; Rule 11A of CPC, the fee payable on plaint shall be recoverable from ___.

(a) The estate of deceased plaintiff
(b) The defendant
(c) The State Government
(d) Either (a) or (b) or (c)

21. Warrant case means a case ___.

(a) In which a police officer cannot arrest without warrant
(b) In which the court in first instance, shall issue a warrant of arrest against the accused
(c) Relating to an offence punishable with imprisonment for a term not exceeding 2 years
(d) Relating to an offence punishable with death, for life or for a term exceeding two years

22. The Court of Magistrate First Class may pass a sentence for maximum term of imprisonment awardable in a summary trial is ___.

(a) Three months
(b) One year
(c) Two years
(d) Six years

23. The Section under Cr. P. C. for 'Order for maintenance of wives, children and parents' is ___.

(a) Section 135
(b) Section 125
(c) Section 145
(d) Section 124

24. Section 304 of Cr. P. C. deals with ___.

(a) Protection to accused against double prosecution for the same offence
(b) Withdrawal from prosecution
(c) Legal aid to the accused at State expenses
(d) Order to release on probation of good conduct

25. Which Section of the Cr. P. C. provides that a person once convicted or acquitted cannot be tried again for the same offence?

(a) Section 304
(b) Section 300
(c) Section 321
(d) Section 302

26. Under Section 39 of Cr.P.C. every person has to give information to Magistrate or Police Officer about the commission of an offence punishable under ___.

(a) Sections 121 to 126 of I PC
(b) Sections 489A to 489E of IPC
(c) Sections 302 and 304 of IPC
(d) All of the above

27. Who is given protection from arrest under Section 45 of Cr.P.C.?

(a) Members of Armed Forces
(b) Judicial Officers
(c) President of India
(d) Members of Parliament

28. Under Section 416 of Cr.P.C., the High Court can postpone capital sentence on ___.

(a) Unsound person
(b) Old person
(c) Pregnant woman
(d) Politician

29. Under Section 366 of Cr.P.C., the sentence of death to be submitted by Court of Session for confirmation by ___.

(a) High Court
(b) Governor
(c) Supreme Court
(d) President

30. Under Section 354 of Cr.P.C., the language and content of the judgement ___.

(a) Shall be written in the language of the Court
(b) Shall contain the paint or points for determination, the decision thereon and the reasons for the decision
(c) Shall specify the offence of which and the Section of the IPC or other law under which the accused is convicted
(d) All of the above

31. According to Section 141 of the Indian Evidence Act, 1872, any question suggesting the answer which the person putting it wishes or expects to receive, is called ___.

(a) Answerable Questions
(b) Convenient Questions
(c) Suggestive Questions
(d) Leading Questions

32. Section 115 of the Indian Evidence Act, 1872 deals with ___.

(a) Doctrine of Estoppel
(b) Presumption as to the Commission of a Crime
(c) Presumption as to Dowry Death
(d) Presumption as to Abetment of Suicide by a Married Woman

33. Section 125 of the Indian Evidence Act, 1872 deals with ___.

(a) Information as to Commission of Offences
(b) Confidential Communications
(c) Official Communications
(d) Professional Communications

34. A witness who is unable to speak is called as ___.

(a) Dumb Witness
(b) Deaf Witness
(c) Unreliable Witness
(d) Hostile Witness

35. Section 75 of the Indian Evidence Act, 1872 deals with ___.

(a) Public Documents

(b) Certified Copies of Public Documents
(c) Proof of Other Official Documents
(d) Private Documents

36. Under the provisions of the Indian Evidence Act, 1872, when an accused says that he did not ma.ke confession, it is called ___.

(a) Extra-Judicial Confession
(b) Judicial Confession
(c) Retracted Confession
(d) Retracted Extra-Judicial Confession

37. Opinion of an expert under Section 45 of the Indian Evidence Act, 1872 ___.

(a) Is sometimes a conclusive proof and sometimes an inconclusive proof
(b) Is corroborative in nature
(c) Is supportive in nature
(d) Is corroborative as well as supportive in nature

38. Section 8 of the Indian Evidence Act, 1872 deals with ___.

(a) Conduct
(b) Motive
(c) Preparation
(d) All of the above

39. Section 47A of the Indian Evidence Act, 1872 deals with ___.

(a) Relevance of Opinion Relating to Electronic Signatures
(b) Relevance of Opinion Relating to Existence of Right or Custom
(c) Relevance of Opinion Relating to Usages and Tenets
(d) Relevance of Opinion Relating to Relationship

40. The term 'Admission' is defined in the Indian Evidence Act, 1872 in ___.

(a) Section 20
(b) Section 19
(c) Section 18
(d) Section 17

41. According to ____ "a crime is a violation of public rights and duties due to the whole community".

(a) Sir William Blackstone
(b) Prof. Glanville Williams
(c) Sir Kenny
(d) Sir Russell

42. Crime which do not require intention, recklessness or even negligence as to one or more elements in the actus reus are known as ___.

(a) Vicarious liability
(b) Strict liability
(c) Act of God
(d) Force majeure

43. Section 304B in Chapter XVI of IPC deals with ___.

(a) Rape
(b) Cruelty
(c) Dowry death
(d) Insult to modesty of woman

44. The Hon'ble Supreme Court of India in one of the following cases held that the general principles of criminal jurisdiction is that, jurisdiction is determined by the locality of the offence irrespective of the nationality or any other similar attributes of the offender ___.

(a) State of Bombay vs. L. Apte
(b) State of Bombay vs. Kathikala Oghad
(c) State of Maharashtra vs. M. H. George
(d) Mubarak Ali vs. State of Bombay

45. According to the Hon'ble Supreme Court. if a particular offence carries mandatory sentence of imprisonment, a company ___.

(a) Cannot be prosecuted for such offence
(b) Can be convicted t however can't be imprisoned
(c) Can be convicted and can be fined
(d) Can be convicted and directors can be imprisoned

46. "They also serve who only stand and wait." This observation formed part of the judgement of the Hon'ble Supreme Court in one of the following cases ___.

(a) Nanda Rasool vs. State of Bihar
(b) Ramnath vs. State of Madhya Pradesh
(c) Ramashish Yadav vs. State of Bihar
(d) Pandurang vs. State of Hyderabad

47. Section 377 of IPC provides for ___.

(a) Robbery
(b) Public nuisance
(c) Theft
(d) Unnatural offences

48. 'Qui facit per alium per se' is the essence of one of the following principles of criminal liability ___.

(a) Joint Criminal Liability
(b) Vicarious liability
(c) Corporate criminal liability
(d) Strict liability

49. In which case the Hon'ble Supreme Court of India has struck down mandatory death penalty under Section 303 of I. P. C. as unconstitutional?

(a) Machhi Singh vs. State of Punjab
(b) Bachan Singh VS. State of Punjab
(c) Santa Singh VS. State of Punjab
(d) Mithu vs. State of Punjab

50. The two-judge bench of Hon'ble Supreme Court in one of the following cases held that long delay by the President of India or Governor of State in disposing mercy petitions from the convicted person under Anti-Terrorism laws or similar status can't be ground for communication of death penalty into life imprisonment ___.

(a) Shersingh vs. State of Punjab (1983)
(b) People Union for Democratic Rights VS. Union of India (2013)
(c) Trivenibin VS. State of Punjab (1989)
(d) Jagmohan Singh vs. State of Uttar Pradesh (1973)

51. The intention of Law of Limitation is ___.

(a) Not to give a right where there is none
(b) To interpose a bar after a certain period to a suit to enforce an existing right
(c) Both (a) and (b)
(d) None of the above

52. For an account and a share of profits of a dissolved partnership, the period of limitation is ___ from the date of dissolution.

(a) 2 years
(b) 3 years
(c) 12 years
(d) 30 years

53. The extension of a prescribed period in certain cases on sufficient cause of being shown for the delay under Section 5 of the Limitation Act is known as ___.

(a) Doctrine of extension
(b) Doctrine of condonation
(c) Doctrine of sufficient cause
(d) All of the above

54. Subject of limitation is dealt within ___ of the Constitution.

(a) Entry 12, List II
(b) Entry 12, List III
(c) Entry 13, List II
(d) Entry 13, List III

55. Under Section 25 of the Limitation Act, 1963, the right to access and use of light or air, way, watercourse, use of water, or any other easement which have been peaceably enjoyed without interruption for ___ years if the property, belongs to government shall be absolute and indefeasible ___.

(a) 20 years
(b) 30 years
(c) 12 years
(d) 3 years

56. Choose the right answer.

(i) The Law of Limitation bars the remedy in a court of law only when period of limitation has expired.

(ii) The Law of Limitation does not extinguish the right that it cannot be enforced by judicial process.

(iii) If a claim is satisfied outside the court of law after the expiry of period of limitation, that is not illegal.

(iv) If a claim is satisfied outside the court of law after the expiry of period of limitation, that is illegal.

(a) (i), (ii), (iii)
(b) (ii) and (iv)
(c) (ii), (iii), (iv)
(d) None of the above

57. Under the Code of Civil Procedure, 1908 the period of limitation to file an appeal to a High Court from decree or order is ___ from the date of decree or order.

(a) 30 days
(b) 60 days
(c) 90 days
(d) 3 years

58. The Limitation Act, 1963 came into force on ___.

(a) 1st January, 1964
(b) 5th October, 1963
(c) 1st January, 1963
(d) 1st October, 1963

59. The specific performance of a contract shall be sought within ___ from the date fixed for the performance, or, if no such date is fixed, when the plaintiff has noticed that performance is refused.

(a) 1 year
(b) 3 years
(c) 12 years
(d) 20 years

60. Continuous running of time refers to ___.

(a) Where once time has begun to run, no subsequent disability or inability to institute a suit or make application stops it
(b) Where once time has begun to run, subsequent disability or inability to institute a suit or make application stops it
(c) Where once time has begun to run, subsequent disability or inability to institute a suit or make application stops it, provided the court grant leave
(d) Where once time has begun to run, subsequent disability or inability to institute a suit or make application stops it, provided there is bonafide cause in view of the court

61. 'Nemo dat quod non habet' means ___.

(a) One can transfer what he doesn't possess
(b) Possession is nine points in law
(c) Transfer without consideration is invalid
(d) One cannot transfer what he doesn't possess

62. 'A' transferred a land to 'B' with a condition that if 'B' sold it, he must sell it to 'C' and nobody else. The condition is ___.

(a) Void
(b) Voidable
(c) Legal
(d) Voidable at the option of 'C'

63. Section 52 of the Transfer of Property Act contains the doctrine of ___.

(a) Lis Pendens
(b) Part performance
(c) Feeding the grant by estoppel
(d) Notice

64. A suit to obtain a decree that a mortgagor shall be absolutely debarred of his right to redeem the mortaga.ged property is called a suit for ___.

(a) Part performance
(b) Election
(c) Foreclosure
(d) Estoppel

65. For the purpose of making a gift of immovable property, the transfer must be effected by ___.

(a) Delivery of possession
(b) A registered instrument signed by or on the behalf of the donor and duly attested
(c) By simple instrument
(d) By simple instrument accompanied by delivery of possession

66. A mortgage by deposit of title deed is called ___.

(a) Anomalous mortgage
(b) English mortgage
(c) Equitable mortgage
(d) Usufructuary mortgage

67. A lease of immovable property from year to year, can be made by ___.

(a) Oral agreement
(b) Oral agreement accompanied by delivery of possession
(c) Simple instrument
(d) Only by a registered instrument

68. Which one of the following statement is not correct in the context of transfer of property?

(a) It means an act by which a living person conveys property
(b) He conveys property in present or in future
(c) He conveys to one or more other living person
(d) He cannot transfer property to himself and one or more other living persons

69. Which of the following is not an actionable claim?

(a) A claim to mesne profits
(b) A claim for arrears of rent
(c) A claim for return of earnest money
(d) A claim to money under insurance policy

70. Which of the following is not an essential requirement for a gift made by a Mohammedan?

(a) Declaration of the gift by the donor
(b) Acceptance of the gift by the donee
(c) Delivery of possession to the donee
(d) The gift must be effected through a registered instrument

71. An offer made to the public at large is called ___.

(a) Valid offer
(b) Specific offer
(c) General offer
(d) None of the above

72. "Past consideration is no consideration". This statement is ___.

(a) Correct under Indian Law of Contract
(b) Correct under English Law of Contract
(c) Correct both under Indian and English Law of Contract
(d) Not correct under both, Indian and English Law of Contract

73. The display of articles in a show-room indicating their prices amounts to ___.

(a) Offer
(b) Counter offer
(c) Invitation to an offer
(d) Mere advertisement

74. Which one of the following does not render a contract void after it has been made?

(a) Commercial impossibility
(b) Physicar impossibility
(c) Legal impossibility
(d) Practical impossibility

75. Hadley V. Baxendare is related to ___.

(a) Quasi-contract
(b) Contingent Contract
(c) Damages for Breach of Contract
(d) None of the above

76. M. C. Chako vs. State Bank of Travancoret AIR 1970 SC 504 case is related to ___.

(a) Breach of Contract
(b) Privity of Contract in India
(c) Restitution
(d) None of the above

77. Under the Indian Contract Act, 1872, a contract of 'Indemnity' is defined in Section ___.

(a) 126
(b) 127
(c) 128
(d) 124

78. 'A' saves 'B' from drowning in a river. 'B' promises to pay 'A' Rs. 10,000 for this kind of act. The contract is ___.

(a) Void for want of consideration
(b) Voidable
(c) Unenforceable because it is immoral
(d) Enforceable as it covered by exceptions to consideration

79. The Commissioner of Wealth Tax, Mysore vs. Vijayaba Dowger Maharani Saheb, Bhavnagar and Others, AIR 1970 SC case is related to ___.

(a) General damages
(b) Special damages
(c) Wagering agreement
(d) Contingent Contract

80. A continuing guarantee may be revoked ___.

(a) By notice to the creditor
(b) By surity's death
(c) By both (a) and (b)
(d) None of the above

81. On which date the Hindu Succession Act, 1956 came into force?

(a) 17th May
(b) 17th June
(c) 17th July
(d) 17th April

82. A dies intestate and is survived by a son of predeceased half-blood brother, S and a daughter of a full blood predeceased sister D. How S and D will succeed the property?

(a) D will get entire property
(b) S will get entire property
(c) D and S both will get equal property
(d) D will get 3/4th share and S will get 1/4th share

83. The Hindu Succession Act does not have territorial jurisdiction over ___.

(a) Only Hindus of Jammu and Kashmir
(b) Only Hindus of Goa, Daman and Diu
(c) Only Hindus of Renocants of Pondicherry
(d) Hindus of all the above areas

84. A Hindu female W dies and is survived by her husband H, one son S, two unmarried daughters D1 and D2. How the property of W will be divided?

(a) Into four equal parts

(b) 1/2 to husband and remaining 1/2 to son and daughters
(c) 1/2 to son and remaining 1/2 to husband and daughters
(d) 1/3 to husband, 1/3 to son and remaining 1/3 to daughters

85. Which one of the following cannot be a ground for disqualification under Hindu Succession Act, 1956?

(a) Mental Infirmity
(b) Physical defects
(c) Conversion to other religion
(d) Diseases

86. The term 'Codicil' under Indian Succession Act relates to instruments made in relation to ___.

(a) Intestate
(b) Probate
(c) Will
(d) Gift

87. The degree of kindred are computed under Indian Succession Act in the manner set forth in the table of kindred set out in ___.

(a) Schedule 2
(b) Schedule 1
(c) Schedule 3
(d) Schedule 4

88. A legacy is bequeathed to A on condition that he shall marry with the consent of B, C, and D. A marries with F without consent but obtains consent afterwards. The legacy is ___.

(a) Valid as A has fulfilled the condition of vesting legacy
(b) Not valid as A has not fulfilled the condition of vesting legacy
(c) Both (a) and (b)
(d) The condition is void ab-initio hence no question of challenging legacy

89. A person taking no benefit directly under a will but deriving a benefit under it indirectly is nut put to his election, has been provided under which section of Indian Succession Act?

(a) Section 185
(b) Section 186
(c) Section 187
(d) Section 184

90. The deceased has made a specific bequest of part of his property. The executor not having assented to the bequest sells the subject of it. The sale is ___.

(a) Valid
(b) Void
(c) Voidable
(d) Voidable at the discretion of executor only

91. Under Section 31 of the Specific Relief Act, the essential conditions under which cancellation of an instrument may be ordered are ___.

(a) That the written instrument is void or voidable against the plaintiff
(b) That the plaintiff has reasonable apprehension of serious injury from the instrument is left outstanding
(c) That in view of the circumstances the court considers it as reasonable and necessary to cancel the document
(d) All of the above

92. A relief against parties and persons claiming under them by subsequent title, for specific performance of a contract may be enforced under ___.

(a) Section 12
(b) Section 19
(c) Section 18
(d) Section 8

93. In a simple suit for specific performance of contract for sale, a person who is not a party to the Agreement for Sate is neither a necessary, nor proper party. The exemptions available under Specific Relief Act are as follows ___.

(a) Cases of novation
(b) Interest arising out of prior contracts
(c) Where it is necessary to join parties for avoiding multiplicity of proceedings
(d) All of the above

94. Where a person is in settled possession of property, even on the assumption that he had no right to remain on the property, he cannot be dispossessed by the owner. This relief is available in the Specific Relief Act under ___.

(a) Section 6
(b) Section 11
(c) Section 9
(d) Section 8

95. A person is entitled to possession of specific immovable property may recover it by suit filed under the provisions of the Civil Procedure Code. This relief is provided in Specific Relief Act under ___.

(a) Section 11
(b) Section 4
(c) Section 5
(d) Section 9

96. Any person having the possession or control over the article of movable property, of which he is not the owner, may be compelled to deliver it to the person entitled to the immediate possession in the following case ___.

(a) When the possession of the thing claimed has been wrongfully transferred from the plaintiff
(b) When the thing claimed is held by the defendant as the agent or trustee of the plaintiff
(c) Both (a) and (b)
(d) None of the above

97. Injunction can be granted under Specific Relief Act in the following ___.

(a) Protection of intellectual properties
(b) A wife can restrain her husband from• contracting a second marriage
(c) Passing-off and like action
(d) All of the above

98. One of the following Sections under Specific Relief Act deals with Specific Performance with variation ___.

(a) Section 18
(b) Section 19
(c) Section 20
(d) Section 21

99. To obtain a mandatory injunction under Section 39 of the Specific Relief Act, the plaintiff must show that there has been a breach of obligation in the nature of ___.

(a) Legal obligation
(b) It is necessary to maintain status quo
(c) None of the above
(d) Both (a) and (b)

100. Where an instrument is evidence of different rights or different obligations, the Court may, in a proper case, cancel it in part and allow it to stand for the residue. This provision is provided in the Specific Relief Act under ___.

(a) Section 21
(b) Section 32
(c) Section 42
(d) Section 40

ANSWERS

1	B	31	D	61	D	91	D
2	A	32	A	62	A	92	B
3	C	33	A	63	A	93	D
4	B	34	A	64	C	94	A
5	C	35	D	65	B	95	C
6	D	36	D	66	C	96	C
7	C	37	D	67	D	97	C
8	D	38	D	68	D	98	A
9	B	39	A	69	A	99	A
10	B	40	D	70	D	100	B
11	D	41	A	71	C		
12	B	42	A	72	B		
13	C	43	C	73	C		
14	C	44	D	74	A		
15	C	45	D	75	C		
16	B	46	B	76	B		
17	B	47	D	77	D		
18	D	48	B	78	D		
19	C	49	D	79	D		
20	A	50	A	80	C		
21	D	51	C	81	B		
22	C	52	B	82	B		
23	B	53	C	83	A		
24	C	54	D	84	A		
25	B	55	B	85	D		
26	D	56	A	86	C		
27	A	57	C	87	B		
28	C	58	A	88	B		
29	A	59	B	89	D		
30	D	60	A	90	A		

2014

1. Indian Constitution was enacted and adopted on ___.

(a) 26th January, 1950
(b) 26U1 November, 1949
(c) 15th August, 1947
(d) 14th August, 1947

2. The Constitution (9th Amendment) Act, 2011 inserted under Art. 19 (1)(c) ___.

(a) Associations
(b) Unions
(c) Organisations
(d) Co-operative Societies

3. Supreme Court of India permitted passive euthanasia subject to certain guidelines in the case of ___.

(a) Aruna Ramachandra Shanbaugh v. Union of India
(b) Gian Kaur v. State of Punjab
(c) P. Rathinam v. Union of India
(d) Maruti Sripati Dubal v. State of Maharashtra

4. The case of Jaya Bachchan v Union of India relates to ___.

(a) Territorial Constituencies
(b) Membership in Rajya Sabha
(c) Office of Profit
(d) Dissolution of Lok Sabha

5. New States are formed under Art. 3 of the Constitution by ___.

(a) A Law of the Parliament
(b) By Constitutional Amendment under Art. 368
(c) By a Law of the State Legislature concerned
(d) By a Law of the State Legislature concerned and Law of the Parliament

6. Art. 123 deals with ___.

(a) Power of the President to dissolve Lok Sabha
(b) Power of the Governor to promulgate ordinances
(c) Power of the President to promulgate ordinances
(d) Power of the Parliament to pass the bills

7. Doctrine of Pith and Substance relates to ___.

(a) Interpretation of statutes to solve the problem of competing legislature in the same field
(b) Serve the objectionable portions of the statute that violate Fundamental Rights
(c) Interpretation of statutes to solve problems arising out of territorial nexus
(d) Interpretation of statutes to solve problems of waiver of Fundamental rights

8. Provision for imposing the President's rule in case of failure of constitutional machinery in the states is provided under ___.

(a) Art. 353
(b) Art. 360
(c) Art. 352
(d) Art. 356

9. Removal or suspension of a member of Public Service Commission shall be done in accordance with ___.

(a) Art. 316
(b) Art. 317
(c) Art. 350
(d) Art. 351

10. According to Art. 233 the appointment of a district judge shall be done by ___.

(a) The President in consultation with the High Court of the State concerned
(b) The Governor of the State concerned in consultation with the High Court of the State concerned
(c) The Governor in consultation with the Chief Justice of India
(d) The collegium of the High Court

11. Existence of two suits, by parties litigating under same title, one previously instituted which is pending at present and the other filed later, wherein a matter in issue in the subsequently filed suit is directly and substantially in issue in the other and the relief claimed in the subsequent suit can effectively be passed by the court of previous instance. Which Section of CPC decides the fate of the subsequently filed suit and its proceeding?

(a) S. 11
(b) S. 9
(c) S. 10
(d) S. 12

12. Where there are mutual debts between the plaintiff and the defendant, one debt may be settled against another. This can be a statutory defence to a plaintiff's action and it is called as ___.

(a) Cross-claim
(b) Set-off
(c) Cross-demands
(d) Cross-decrees

13. An attachment before judgement order takes away ___.

(a) Right to ownership
(b) Right to file suit
(c) Power to alienate the property
(d) Capacity of execution of a decree

14. The three pillars on which foundation of every order of injunction rests ___.

(a) Prima facie case, injury with damage and balance of inconvenience
(b) Prima facie case, reparable injury and balance of convenience
(c) Prima facie case, irreparable injury and balance of convenience
(d) Prima facie case, damage without injury and balance of convenience

15. ___ is to enable subordinate courts to obtain in non-appealable cases the opinion of the High Court in the absence of a question of law and thereby avoid the commission of an error which could not be remedied later on.

(a) Review
(b) Reference
(c) Appeal
(d) Revision

16. Which of the propositions are correct?

(i) Legal set off requires a court fee, but no court-fee is required in the case of an equitable set off.

(ii) In a legal set off amount claimed can be time barred and in an equitable set off claim cannot be allowed if it is time barred.

(iii) In a legal set off it is not necessary that cross demands arise out of same transaction and in an equitable set off cross demands must arise out of same transaction.

(iv) Legal set off can be for any amount not ascertained and an equitable set off may be allowed only for an unascertained amount.

(a) Only (i) is correct
(b) Only (i) and (iii) are correct
(c) Both (i) and (iv) are correct
(d) None of the above

17. Where a party to a suit requires information as to facts from the opposite party, he may administer to his adversary a series of questions. It is called as ___.

(a) Question petition
(b) Question pamphlet
(c) Interrogatories
(d) Discovery

18. ____ is a suit filed by or against one or more persons on behalf of themselves and others having the same interest in the suit.

(a) Joint suit
(b) Representative suit
(c) Collusive suit
(d) Collective suit

19. A person appointed by the court to protect, preserve and manage the property during the pendency of the litigation ___.

(a) Amicus curiae
(b) Preserver
(c) Protector
(d) Receiver

20. A, a railway company, is in possession of goods as a consignee. It does not claim any interest in the goods except lien of wharfage, demurrage and freight but rival claims have been made by Band C adversely to each other. A can institute ___.

(a) An application to decide the same
(b) An interpleader suit
(c) Friendly suit
(d) None of the above

21. Find out the correct remainder of the statement. "The object of investigation is"

——.

(a) To collect evidence that aids the court in finding out the truth
(b) To collect information that helps in punishing the person
(c) To collect the information to arrest the person
(d) None of the above

22. Any Police Officer may arrest without warrant any person ___.

(a) Who has been concerned in any cognizable offence
(b) Who has been proclaimed as an offender
(c) Who is reasonably suspected of being a deserter from any armed forces

(d) All of the above

23. Under Section 37 of Cr.P.C., every person is bound to assist a Magistrate or Police Officer in the taking or preventing the escape of any other person whom such Magistrate or Police Officer is authorized to arrest ___.

(a) In the prevention or suppression of a breach of peace
(b) In the prevention of any injury to be committed to any railway, canal, telegraph or public property
(c) In all the above cases
(d) None of the above

24. ____ shall establish a Court of Session for every Sessions division.

(a) State Government
(b) Central Government
(c) Supreme Court
(d) President of India

25. F. I. R. under Section 154 of the Cr. P. C. is not a substantive piece of evidence. Its only use is to contradict or corroborate the matter thereof. Held in ___ case.

(a) Shambhu Dass v. State of Assam, AIR 2010 SC 3300
(b) Ravishwar Manjhi v. State of Jharkhand, AIR 2009 SC 1262
(c) State of Karnataka v. K. Yarappa Reddy, 1999 (8) SCC 715
(d) Sheelam Ramesh v. State of Andhra Pradesh, 1999 (8) SCC 369

26. ____ Section of the Cr. P. C. deals with medical examination of the victim of rape.

(a) Section 164
(b) Section 164 A
(c) Section 166
(d) Section 166 B

27. Whenever a charge is altered or added to by the court after the commencement of the trial, the prosecutor and the accused ___.

(a) Shall be allowed to recall or resummon and examine with reference to such alteration or addition, any witness who may have been examined
(b) Shall be allowed to recall or resummon and examine with reference to such alteration or addition, any witness who may have been examined, unless the Court, for reasons to be recorded in writing, considers that the prosecutor or the accused, as the case may be, desires to recall or re-examine such witness for the purpose of vexation or delay or for defeating the ends of justice
(c) Shall not be allowed to recall or resummon and examine with reference to such alteration or addition, any witness who may have been examined
(d) Shall not be allowed to recall or resummon and examine with reference to such alteration or addition, any witness who may have been examined, because such witness may be vexed or trial gets delayed or is defeated

28. What persons may be charged jointly?

(i) Persons accused of the same offence committed in the course of the same transaction

(ii) Persons accused of an offence and persons accused of abetment of, or attempt to commit, such offence

(iii) Persons accused of different offences committed in the course of the same transaction

(iv) Persons accused of more than one offence of the same kind, within the meaning of Section 219 committed by them jointly within the period of twelve months

(a) i, ii and iii
(b) i, iii and iv
(c) All of the above
(d) None of the above

29. Causing miscarriage, an offence punishable under the Indian Penal Code (45 of 1860), with the permission of the Court before which any prosecution for such offence is pending, be compounded by ___.

(a) The person who caused miscarriage
(b) The husband of the woman to whom miscarriage is caused
(c) The woman to whom miscarriage is caused
(d) The caretaker of the woman

30. ___ confers the power upon the High Court to transfer cases and appeals.

(a) Section 406
(b) Section 407
(c) Section 405
(d) Section 404

31. Propositions regarding confession of a co-accused, not required to be on oath and cannot be tested by cross examination are

___.

(i) Is no evidence within the meaning of S.23 of Evidence Act and cannot be the foundation of a conviction

(ii) The only limited use which can be made of a confession of a co-accused is by way of furnishing an additional reason for believing such other evidences as exists

(iii) Is a weak type of evidence and is much weaker than the evidence of an approver

(a) Only (ii) and (iii) are correct
(b) Only (i) and (iii) are correct
(c) Only (i) and (ii) are correct
(d) (i), (ii) and (iii) are correct

32. Original document is the best evidence – Exception to this rule is contained in ___.

(a) Indian Evidence Act
(b) Criminal Procedure Code
(c) Bankers Book Evidence Act
(d) None of the above

33. Reliability of Multiple dying declarations came for discussion under which case?

(a) Vimal v. State of Maharashtra, 2006 AIR SGW 5953
(b) Pratap Mishra v. State of Orissa, AIR 1977 SC 1307
(c) State of Maharashtra v. Dr Praful B Desai (2003) 4 SCC '601
(d) None of the above

34. "The doubt, the benefit of which the accused is entitled, must be such' as, rational thinking, sensible man may fairly and reasonably entertain, not the doubts of a vacillating mind that has not the moral courage to decide but shelters itself, in a vain and idle skepticism. There must be doubt which a man may honestly and conscientiously entertain."

(a) Cockburn
(b) Lord Halsbury
(c) Lord Black
(d) None of the above

35. "The DNA test cannot rebut the conclusive presumption envisaged under S. 12 of the Indian Evidence Act. The parties can avoid the rigor of such conclusive presumption only by proving non-access which is a negative proof." It was so held in which case ___.

(a) Shaik Fakruddin v. Shaik Mohammed Hasan AIR 2006 AP 48
(b) Siddaramesh v. State of Karnataka (2010) 3 SCC 152
(c) Kailash v. State of Madhya Pradesh AIR 2007 SC 107
(d) Somwanti v. State of Punjab, AIR 1963 SC 151

36. An accomplice is unworthy of credit unless he is corroborated in material particulars is a ___.

(a) Presumption of fact
(b) Presumption of law
(c) Conclusive proof
(d) None of the above

37. A dispute regarding handwriting can be proved by ___.

(a) Calling an expert
(b) Examining a person acquainted with the handwriting of the writer of the questioned document
(c) Both (a) and (b)
(d) None of the above

38. 'The time-tested rule is that acquittal of a guilty person should preferred to conviction of an innocent person. Unless the prosecution establishes the guilt of the accused beyond reasonable doubt a conviction cannot be passed on the accused. A criminal court cannot afford to deprive liberty of the appellants, lifelong liberty, without having at least a reasonable level of certainty that the appellants were the real culprits." In which case Supreme Court held so ___.

(a) Rang Bahadur Singh v. State of U.P. AIR 2000 SC 1209
(b) Ramanath v. State, AIR 1953 SC 420 (Supreme Court)
(c) Sardul Singh Caveeshar v. State of Bombay, AIR 1957 SC 747 (Supreme Court)
(d) State v. Nalini, AIR 1999 SC 2640 (Supreme Court)

39. Section ____ of the Evidence Act provides that where a security procedure has been applied to an electronic record at a specific time, the record is deemed to be a secure electronic record from such time until the time of verification.

(a) 85A
(b) 85B

(c) 67A
(d) 65B

40. A subsequent case which referred to the principles of Praful Desai judgement ___.

(a) Dr. Kumar Saha v. Dr. Sukumar Mukherjee
(b) Nivrutti Pandurang Kokate v. Maharashtra
(c) Goutham Kundu v. State of West Bengal
(d) Mohd. Kalam v. Bihar

41. A, being a public servant directed by law to take property in execution, in order to satisfy a decree pronounced in B's favour by a court of law, knowingly disobeys that discretion of law, with the knowledge that he is likely thereby to cause injury to B. A has committed the offence defined in Section ___.

(a) 166
(b) 167
(c) 157
(d) 158

42. Which of the following does not form part of Actus Reus?

(a) Thought of conduct
(b) Result of conduct
(c) Circumstances as are specified by law
(d) Conduct

43. Under which of the cases can a statute exclude mens rea?

(a) Public nuisance
(b) Cases in public interest
(c) Both of the above
(d) None of the above

44. A with a view to murdering D enters D's bedroom at night when D is out of station. A is guilty of ___.

(a) House trespass
(b) Attempt to murder
(c) Murder
(d) No offence

45. Criminal conspiracy is defined by ___.

(a) Section 120
(b) Section 120-B
(c) Section 120-A
(d) Section 120-0

46. X meets Z on the National Highway, shows a knife and demands money, and gold ornaments found on the body of Z. He has committed ___.

(a) Theft
(b) Dacoity
(c) Extortion
(d) Robbery

47. Dacoity can cover ___.

(a) Robbery based on extortion
(b) Robbery based on theft
(c) Both of the above
(d) None of the above

48. Use of violence by a member of unlawful assembly, in furtherance of their common object will constitute offence of ___.

(a) Rioting
(b) Assault
(c) Affray
(d) None of the above

49. The defence of consent has no application in cases of ___.

(a) Causing grievous hurt
(b) Causing death
(c) Both (a) and (b)
(d) None of the above

50. The essence of sedition under the Indian Penal Code is/are ___.

(a) Result
(b) Intention
(c) Both intention and result
(d) Benefits or gain of the accused

51. All instruments for the purpose of limitation shall be deemed to be made with reference to ___.

(a) Gregorian calendar
(b) English calendar
(c) Roman calendar
(d) Nanak Shahi calendar

52. Section 3 of the Limitation Act does not apply to ___.

(a) Suits
(b) Applications
(c) Executions
(d) None of the above

53. Which of the claims under S.3 of the Limitation Act is treated as a separate suit?

(a) Set off
(b) Counter claim
(c) Both (a) and (b)

(d) Neither (a) nor(b)

54. Section 3 of the Limitation Act is applicable to the period prescribed by any ___.

(a) Local Law
(b) Special Law
(c) Both (a) and (b)
(d) Neither (a) nor (b)

55. Time barred debt can be claimed as ___.

(a) Set off
(b) Counter claim
(c) Afresh suit
(d) None of the above

56. In order to attract Section 4 of the Limitation Act, the court should be closed ___.

(a) For the whole of the day
(b) During any part of normal working hours
(c) For substantial part of the day
(d) For more than half of the normal working hours

57. Under the Limitation Act, legal disabilities are ___.

(a) Minority
(b) Insanity
(c) Idiocy
(d) All of the above

58. Acknowledgement made by a person other than a person under liability is good if the person making it is ___.

(a) A relative of the person under liability
(b) An agent of the person under liability
(c) A servant of the person under liability
(d) Is the master of the person under

59. Under Section 19 for the extended period of limitation the part payment must be ___.

(a) In the handwriting of the person making the payment
(b) In the writing signed by the person making the payment
(c) Either (a) or (b)
(d) Neither (a) nor (b)

60. An Ex parte decree can be set aside within 30 days from ___.

(a) The date of the Ex parte decree
(b) The knowledge of the Ex parte decree where summon or notice was not duly served
(c) Both (a) and (b)

(0) Neither (a) nor (b)

61. Under the Transfer of Property Act, instrument means ___.

(a) Non testamentary instrument
(b) Testamentary instrument
(c) Both (a) and (b)
(d) Neither (a) nor (b)

62. Under the Transfer of Property Act, attached to the earth means ___.

(a) Rooted in the earth as trees and shrubs
(b) Embedded in the earth as walls and buildings
(c) Attached to what is so embedded for the beneficial enjoyment of that to which it is attached
(d) All of the above

63. Which Section of the Transfer of Property Act explains, "He who accepts the benefit under the instrument must adopt the whole of it"?

(a) S.52
(b) S.41
(c) S.35
(d) S.53A

64. Actionable claim means ___.

(a) Unsecured debt
(b) Any debt
(c) Claim recognized by civil courts to grant relief
(d) All of the above

65. To create an interest for the benefit of an unborn person which of the following requirements should be there?

(a) No direct interest
(b) Prior interest
(c) Absolute interest
(d) All of the above

66. Which conditions apply to create a vested interest?

(a) It is not defeated by the death of the transferee before he obtains possession
(b) It is transferable and heritable
(c) It accrues in the present and immediately, even though the enjoyment is postponed
(d) All of the above

67. The act of transferring property during the pendency of a proceeding makes the transfer ___.

(a) Void
(b) Voidable
(c) Neither void nor voidable
(d) Illegal

68. X sells a property to Z with a condition that he must live in it. The condition is ___.

(a) Void
(b) Voidable
(c) Legal
(d) None of the above

69. Which of the following is not a transfer of property?

(a) Sale
(b) Mortgage
(c) Lease
(d) Partition

70. How can a transfer of property be made?

(a) Orally
(b) Bya registered instrument
(c) Both (a) and (b)
(d) Neither (a) nor (b)

71. Where the proposal made is to be accepted by letters sent through post, the contract is completed, the moment ___.

(a) The letter accepting the proposal is posted
(b) When the letter reaches the proposer
(c) The postman delivers the letter to the proposer
(d) The postman delivers the letter to a person other than the proposer

72. A revokes by telegram his proposal to B, before its acceptance by B, to sell his house at a certain price. The revocation is complete against A when ___.

(a) The telegram is dispatched
(b) The telegram is returned undelivered
(c) The telegram is sent to a friend of A
(d) B learns that the telegram has been received by A

73. In an unconscionable contract the burden of proving that the contract was not induced by undue influence lies on ___.

(a) The person who is in a position to dominate the will of another
(b) The person who accepted the proposal
(c) The friend of the acceptor
(d) The friend of the proposer

74. A contract is voidable if consent to an agreement ___.

(a) Is based on a mistake as to law
(b) One of the parties was under a mistake of fact
(c) Both the parties are under a mistake as to a matter of fact essential to the agreement
(d) Consent is caused by coercion, fraud or misrepresentation

75. A businessman enters into an agreement with a Chartered Accountant to pay him fees and commission for the tax saved by so arranging the accounts as to conceal the true income of the business. Any dispute between the Businessman and the Chartered Accountant on the fee and commission is to be settled by arbitration. The agreement is ___.

(a) Void
(b) Voidable
(c) Voidable in part
(d) Void in part

76. Under an agreement sells to B his skin bleaching products business "Intimate Whitener" and the goodwill of the business with the condition that A will not carry on such similar business throughout India so long as B carries it on anywhere in India. The agreement records that this condition is reasonable and that no court will have jurisdiction to examine this condition. The agreement is ___.

(a) Void
(b) Voidable
(c) Voidable in part
(d) Void in part

77. A agrees to pay B Rs. 1 Lakh if X is not made the Prime Minister after he wins in the general election for choosing members of Parliament. According to the Contract Act, this is a contingent contract under ___.

(a) S.35
(b) S. 34
(c) S. 33
(d) S. 32

78. Where the order, in which reciprocal promises are to be performed is not expressly fixed by the contract, they shall be performed in that order which ___.

(a) The nature of the transaction requires
(b) Is required by the acceptor

(c) Is required by the proposer
(d) Is required by the arbitrator appointed by the proposer and acceptor

79. A bailor is liable for damages arising to the bailee from the faults in the goods, if he did not disclose to the bailee his awareness of all ___.

(a) The faults
(b) The faults which interfere with the use of the goods
(c) The faults which materially interfere with the use of the goods
(d) The faults which make them valuable for some other use

80. An agent has to pay compensation to his principal for his misconduct which results in losses that are ___.

(a) An indirect result of the misconduct
(b) Remotely caused by the misconduct
(c) Indirectly and remotely caused by the misconduct
(d) Directly caused by the misconduct

81. One person is deemed to be an agnate of another if they are related to each other ___.

(a) By blood or adoption wholly through a male
(b) Not wholly through males
(c) Wholly through a female
(d) Not wholly through females

82. The general rules of succession of a Hindu male dying intestate are contained in Section ___ of the Hindu Succession Act, 1956.

(a) S. 7
(b) S. 8
(c) S. 14
(d) S. 15

83. Husband in Entry (a) of Section 15(1) of the Hindu Succession Act, 1956 includes ___.

(a) Husband of a subsisting marriage
(b) A divorced husband
(c) Both (a) and (b)
(d) Neither (a) nor (b)

84. Under S. 19 of the Hindu Succession Act, 1956, if two or more heirs succeed together to the property of an intestate, they shall take the property as ___.

(a) Tenants in common

(b) Joint tenants
(c) Either (a) or (b)
(d) Neither (a) nor (b)

85. The right of a child in the womb at the time of the death of the Hindu intestate are provided under the Hindu Succession Act in ___.

(a) S. 19
(b) S. 20
(c) S. 21
(d) S. 22

86. An Indian Christian under the Indian Succession Act, 1925 means ___.

(a) Native of India
(b) A native of India who is or in good faith is of unmixed Asiatic descent
(c) A native of India who is or in good faith professes the Catholic religion
(d) A native of India who is or in good faith claims to be of unmixed Asiatic descent and who professes any form of the Christian religion

87. The domicile of a wife under the Indian Succession Act, 1925 is ___.

(a) The place of her birth
(b) The place of her education
(c) The place where her family last resided
(d) That of her husband

88. Under Section 20 of the Indian Succession Act, 1925 a husband on marriage ___.

(a) Acquires an interest in the wife's property
(b) Does. not acquire an interest in the wife's property
(c) Becomes the trustee of the wife's property
(d) Becomes the guardian of the wife's property

89. The property of an intestate where he has left no lineal descendants can be distributed under the Indian Succession Act, 1925 only after deducting the share of ___.

(a) His widow
(b) His children
(c) His step children
(d) His parents

90. Privileged Wills are those made by ___.

(a) Any person above 18 years of age
(b) Soldiers
(c) Soldiers or airmen engaged in warfare or a mariner at sea
(d) A mariner at land

91. No suit for the recovery of possession can be filed under S. 6 of the Specific Relief Act, after the expiry of ___.

(a) Six months from the date of dispossession
(b) Nine months from the date of dispossession
(c) Twelve months from the date of dispossession
(d) Eighteen months from the date of dispossession

92. A contract can be specifically enforced ___.

(a) Where compensation is adequate relief for the non-performance of the contract
(b) Where the contract by its nature is determinable
(c) Where it involves the performance of continuous duty which the court cannot supervise
(d) None of the above

93. Which of the following can be specifically enforced?

(a) A contract for sale of property under allotment
(b) Mere agreement to enter into a contract
(c) Contract to marry
(d) None of the above

94. A defendant can take any of the following defences in a suit for specific performance ___.

(a) Money is adequate compensation
(b) Uncertainty of the terms of the contract
(c) Contract made in excess of power
(d) All of the above

95. Anyone of the following grounds will prevent a plaintiff from seeking specific enforcement ___.

(a) Plaintiff has violated an essential term of the contract
(b) Plaintiff has acted fraudulently
(c) Plaintiff has acted at variance
(d) All of the above

96. Relief of specific performance can be granted for enforcing ___.

(a) Civil rights
(b) Penal laws
(c) Both civil rights and penal laws
(d) Neither civil rights nor penal laws

97. A suit for possession under Section 5 of the Specific Relief Act can be filed within ___.

(a) Three years
(b) Six years
(c) Twelve years
(d) Thirty years

98. Section 13 of the Specific Relief Act, has no application when the transfer has been affected in respect of property whose ___.

(a) Vendor has no title to the property
(b) Vendor has title to the property
(c) Vendor has imperfect title
(d) None of the above

99. Relief of Rescission is granted in cases where ___.

(a) Contract is void
(b) Contract is voidable
(c) Contract is both voidable and void
(d) Contract is neither void nor voidable

100. A declaration under S. 34 of the Specific Relief Act can be sought by ___.

(a) A stranger having no interest in the property
(b) A person whose legal character or a right to property is denied
(c) A person whose legal character or right to property is not denied
(d) All of the above

ANSWERS

1	B	31	D	61	A	91	A
2	D	32	A	62	D	92	D
3	A	33	D	63	C	93	D
4	C	34	A	64	D	94	D
5	A	35	A	65	B	95	D
6	C	36	A	66	D	96	A
7	A	37	C	67	C	97	C
8	D	38	A	68	A	98	B
9	B	39	B	69	D	99	B
10	B	40	A	70	C	100	B
11	A	41	A	71	B		
12	B	42	D	72	A		
13	C	43	A	73	A		
14	C	44	A	74	D		
15	B	45	C	75	A		
16	B	46	D	76	A		
17	C	47	C	77	D		
18	B	48	A	78	A		
19	D	49	C	79	C		
20	B	50	B	80	D		
21	A	51	A	81	A		
22	D	52	D	82	B		
23	C	53	C	83	A		

24	A	54	C	84	A
25	A	55	D	85	B
26	B	56	B	86	D
27	B	57	D	87	D
28	C	58	B	88	B
29	C	59	C	89	A
30	B	60	C	90	C

2015

1. In 42nd Amendment which of the following words were Inserted to Preamble of the Constitution?

(a) Justice
(b) Liberty of thought, expression
(c) Equality of status
(d) Unity and integrity of the nation

2. By which Amendment of the Constitution was Bodo, Dogri and Maithili inserted In Eighth Schedule of the Constitution?

(a) Ninety Second Amendment
(b) Seventy Second Amendment
(c) Forty Third Amendment
(d) Forty Sixth Amendment

3. Which Article of the Constitution States that 'there shall be a Council of Ministers at the head to aid and advise the President who shall, in exercise of, his functions, act in accordance with such evidence'?

(a) Article 74
(b) Article 73
(c) Article 80
(d) Article 75

4. What does Article 14 prohibit?

(a) Reasonable classification
(b) Class legislation
(c) Both (a) and (b) of the above
(d) Promotions

5. Which of the following provisions defines 'State'?

(a) Article 12 of the Indian Constitution
(b) Article 14 of the Indian Constitution
(c) Article 15 of the Indian Constitution
(d) Article 20 of the Indian Constitution

6. Strength to Panchayati Raj in India was given by___.

(a) 42nd Amendment 1976
(b) 44th Amendment 1978
(c) 73rd Amendment 1992
(d) 86th Amendment 2002

7. In which of the following cases the Supreme Court held that, the BCCI was not financially, functionally or administratively dominated by the Government nor was it under the control of Government? Therefore it was not a State___.

(a) Lena Khan V. Union of India, AIR 1987 SC 1515
(b) Tekraj V. Union of India, AIR 1988 SC 469
(c) Zee Telefilms Ltd. V. Union of India, AIR 2005 SC 2677
(d) None of the above

8. Which of the following provisions of the Constitution of India relates to doctrine of 'Level playing field'?

(a) To assemble peaceably and without arms
(b) To form Associations or Unions
(c) To freedom of speech and expression
(d) To practice any profession or to carry on any occupation, trade or business

9. The provision that men and women have right to an adequate means of livelihood is a part of___.

(a) Fundamental Rights
(b) Directive Principles of State Policy
(c) Fundamental Duties
(d) Preamble

10. Which of the following provisions of Constitution of India mandates that State shall provide free and compulsory education to all children of the age of 6 to 14 years in such manner as the State may, by Law, determine?

(a) Article 19
(b) Article 21
(c) Article 21-A
(d) Article 29

11. Which order is not included in definition of "Decree"?

(a) Order allowing relief to Plaintiff
(b) Order as to rejection of Plaint
(c) Order of dismissal of suit for default
(d) Order as to determination of any question within Section 144 of C.P.C.

12. Where you will file suit for partition of immovable property of worth Rs.12,000/-?

(a) The Court of Civil Judge (Jr Divn.)
(b) The Court of Civil Judge (Sr. Divn.)
(c) The Court of Additional District Judge
(d) The Court of District Judge

13. No Second Appeal shall lie from any decree when the subject matter of the original suit is for recovery of money not exceeding ___.

(a) Rs.50,000/-

(b) Rs.1,00,000/-
(c) Rs.25,000/-
(d) Rs.75,000/-

14. The rule of conclusiveness of Judgment which is partly based on the maxim 'interest reipublicae ut sit finis litium' is found in which section of the Code of Civil Procedure?

(a) Section 12
(b) Section 11
(c) Section 24
(d) Section 13

15. Under which of the following situations suit will be defeated?

(a) Mis-joinder of parties
(b) Mis-joinder of necessary parties
(c) Non-joinder of necessary parties
(d) Non-joinder of proforma party

16. Constructive res-judicata is contained in___.

(a) Explanation III of Section 11 of CPC
(b) Explanation IV of Section 11 of CPC
(c) Explanation VI of Section 11 of CPC
(d) Explanation VII of Section 11 of CPC

17. Which of the following circumstances does not ordinarily allow amendment of pleadings?

(a) After appearance of defendants
(b) After issues are settled
(c) After the trial has commenced
(d) After judgment is over

18. How many adjournments may be allowed to parties to suit during hearing of the suits?

(a) Four
(d) Ten
(c) Three
(d) Five

19. Which of the following facts is not required to be proved to grant Temporary Injunction?

(a) Prima-facie case
(b) Balance of inconvenience
(c) Irreparable loss or injury
(d) Balance of convenience

20. Which of the following Sections of the CPC deals with the power of the Supreme Court to transfer suits or appeals or other proceeding from a High Court in one State to a High Court in any other State?

(a) 25
(b) 24
(c) 26
(d) 27

21. FIR is not a substantive evidence, it can be used during trial___.

(a) To corroborate the informant
(b) To contradict the informant
(c) Both (a) and (b)
(d) None of the above

22. No member of the Armed Forces of the Union shall be arrested for anything done or purported to be done by him in the discharge of his official duties except after obtaining the consent of ___.

(a) High Court
(b) Supreme Court
(c) State Government
(d) Central Government

23. Within the meaning of the provisions of Section 2(d) of the Cr.P.C. "Complaint"___.

(a) Does not include police report
(b) Includes police report
(c) Includes police diary
(d) Includes court summons

24. How much maintenance a Judicial Magistrate can award under Section 125 of the Code of Criminal Procedure?

(a) Upto Rs.1,000/- per month
(b) Upto Rs. 5,000/- per month
(c) Such monthly rate as such Magistrate think fit
(d) Upto Rs.10,000/- per month

25. Warrant case has been defined under Section 2(x) Cr.P.C. as a case relating to offence punishable with death, Imprisonment for life or Imprisonment for a term___.

(a) Exceeding two years
(b) Exceeding three years
(c) Exceeding one year
(d) Exceeding one year but less than two years

26. Under the Scheme of Cr.P.C, the original jurisdiction to take cognizance of an offence is vested in___.

(a) The Court of Session
(b) The Court of Magistrate
(c) The High Court

(d) All of the above

27. How many offences of same kind committed in a year by a person can be charged together?

(a) Six
(b) Eight
(c) Four
(d) Three

28. The cases in which the inherent powers of the High Court may be exercised under Section 482 Code of Criminal Procedure are___.

(a) Where the allegations are absurd and inherently improbable
(b) Where the allegations do not disclose a cognizable offence
(c) Where a proceeding is instituted with an ulterior motive
(d) All of the above

29. What is the period of remand of an accused person to custody at a time during trial by the Magistrate under Section 309 of Cr.P.C.?

(a) 30 days
(b) 15 days
(c) 21 days
(d) 28 days

30. Which Section of the Code of Criminal Procedure, 1973 creates an obligation on a person to give Information to the nearest Magistrate with regard to commission of certain offences?

(a) Section 43
(b) Section 29
(c) Section 39
(d) Section 224

31. Section 113A of the Evidence Act was inserted by which amendment?

(a) Act No. 43 of 1986
(b) Criminal Act No. 45 of 1985
(c) Act No. 46 of 1983
(d) Terrorist Affected Areas (Special Courts) Act, 1984

32. Presumption___.

(a) Is an evidence
(b) Is a proof
(c) Shows on whom the burden of proof lies
(d) All of the above

33. In which case motive is important to prove guilt of accused?

(a) Case based on direct evidence of occurrence witness
(b) Case based on circumstantial evidence
(c) Case based on Judgment of another Court
(d) Case based on relevant fact

34. Which provision of Indian Evidence Act relates to Test Identification Parade of person?

(a) Section 3
(b) Section 8
(c) Section 9
(d) Section 26

35. The main principle underlying law of Evidence is___.

(a) All evidences, oral or documentary, must be admitted
(b) Evidence need not be confined to facts in issue
(c) Hearsay evidence may be relevant in circumstances
(d) The best evidence must be given in all cases

36. Alibi is governed by___.

(a) Section 6 of Evidence Act
(b) Section 8 of Evidence Act
(c) Section 12 of Evidence Act
(d) Section 11 of Evidence Act

37. What is the nomenclature of the Examiner of Electronic Evidence under Indian Evidence Act?

(a) Government Examiner
(b) Expert
(c) Invigilator
(d) Scientist

38. Which of the following documents is not presuJ11ed as primary, document which could be proved only by leading secondary evidence?

(a) Carbon copy of permits, written by hand under uniform carbon process
(b) F.I.R.
(c) Registered Sale Deed
(d) Certificated copy of Will

39. Which of the following provisions enshrines about presumption as to dowry death?

(a) Section 113A of Indian Evidence Act
(b) Section 1138 of Indian Evidence Act
(c) Section 114A of Indian Evidence Act
(d) Section 88A of Indian Evidence Act

40. What is the nomenclature of witness who is required to be cross-examined by the party who has called said witness in his or her behalf?

(a) Chance witness
(b) Occurrence witness
(c) Hostile witness
(d) Official witness

41. Which of the following is not "person" under Indian Penal Code?

(a) Individual
(b) Company
(c) Association or body of persons
(d) State

42. The offences of Voyeurism are punishable under which Section of the Indian Penal Code?

(a) Section 376
(b) Section 354B
(c) Section 354C
(d) None of the above

43. Chapter V of IPC deals with____.

(a) Abetment
(b) Attempt
(c) Election
(d) Religion

44. Under what provision of Indian Penal Code a person is found punishment of murder under the doctrine of transferred malice?

(a) Section 301
(b) Section 304
(c) Section 304A
(d) Section 307

45. A man committing physical contact and advances involving unwelcome and explicit sexual overtures shall be punishable by ____.

(a) Imprisonment for two years
(b) Rigorous imprisonment for three years
(c) Imprisonment for life
(d) Simple Imprisonment for six months

46. The right of private defence is based on the natural instinct of____.

(a) Self-preservation
(b) Self-respect
(c) Self-sufficiency
(d) Self-reliance

47. A man is said to commit rape when he does sexual intercourse with a woman with or without her consent when she is under ____ of age.

(a) 16 years
(b) 17 years
(c) 18 years
(d) 20 years

48. The expression 'harm' is used in Section 81 of Indian Penal Code in the sense of____.

(a) Hurt
(b) Injury or damage
(c) Physical injury
(d) Moral wrong or evil

49. 'A' voluntarily throws into a river, a ring belonging to 'Z' with the intention of thereby causing wrongful loss to 'Z'. What offence is committed by 'A'?

(a) Section 427 of IPC
(b) Section 426 of IPC
(c) Section 379 of IPC
(d) Section 406 of IPC

50. 'A' puts 'z' into fear of hurt and dishonestly induces 'Z' to sign a blank cheque and delivers it to 'A'. 'Z' signs the cheque and delivers it to 'A'. 'A' is guilty of____.

(a) Theft
(b) Extortion
(c) Robbery
(d) Attempt to commit extortion

51. Section 3 of Limitation Act, 1963 does not apply to____.

(a) Suits
(b) Appeals
(c) Applications
(d) Execution proceedings

52. Where a suit Is based on fraud, the period of limitation begins only after the fraud is discovered under____.

(a) Section 15
(b) Section 20
(e) Section 17
(d) Section 16

53. Which of the following Sections of limitation Act empowers Court to receive Appeal after condoning delay?

(a) Section 3
(b) Section 5
(c) Section 7
(d) Section 8

54. A time barred debt can be claimed___.

(a) As a set off
(b) As a counter claim
(c) As a fresh suit
(d) None of the above

55. The requisite under Section 12(2) of Limitation Act means___.

(a) Minimum time
(b) Maximum time
(c) Actual time taken
(d) Absolutely necessary time

56. The period of limitation for a suit, to redeem or recover possession of immovable property mortgaged, by a mortgagor, is___.

(a) 12 years
(b) 30 years
(c) 6 years
(d) 3 years

57. Condonation of delay is dealt with under___.

(a) Section 5 of Limitation Act
(b) Section 7 of Limitation Act
(c) Section 9 of Limitation Act
(d) Section 10 of Limitation Act

58. Where after filing of a suit, a new plaintiff or defendant is substituted or added as a party to the suit, the suit shall be, for the purpose of limitation___.

(a) Deemed to be brought on the date, the addition was made
(b) Deemed to be instituted on the earlier date
(c) Deemed to be on such date as the Court decides
(d) Either (b) or (c)

59. The period of limitation for Suit relating to money lent under an agreement that it shall be payable on demand is ___ since the loan is made.

(a) Five years
(b) Four years
(c) Three years

(d) Six years

60. In the matters of condonation of delay under Section 5 of Limitation Act, 1963, public institution like bank should___.

(a) Be treated at par with private individuals
(b) Be treated at par with private institutions
(c) Be treated at par with corporate bodies
(d) Neither be treated at par with (A), nor (B) nor (C)

61. Which of the following properties cannot be defined as immovable property?

(a) Building
(b) Standing brick wall
(c) Standing timber
(d) Earth on the ground

62. Which of the following properties may be transferred?

(a) A public officer
(b) Salary of a public office
(c) Paddy land
(d) A right to future maintenance in whatsoever manner arising, secured

63. A covenant for pre-emption cannot be considered void in law because ___.

(a) It is a written document
(b) It is a registered document
(c) It does not offend rule against perpetuities
(d) It is made for consideration

64. Which section of the Transfer of Property Act deals with the transfer for benefit of unborn person?

(a) Section 10
(b) Section 52
(c) Section 13
(d) Section 24

65. Which provision of Transfer of Property Act comes under Doctrine of lis pendens?

(a) Section 14
(b) Section 35
(c) Section 52
(d) Section 54

66. Where, on a transfer of property, an interest therein is created in favour of a person without specifying the time when it is to take effect, or in terms specifying that it is to take effect forthwith or on the happening of an event which must happen, such interest is___.

(a) Contingent interest
(b) Vested interest
(c) Perpetual interest
(d) Class interest

67. What is transferred to mortgagee by mortgage of immovable property?

(a) Transfer of title
(b) Transfer of an interest
(c) Transfer of money
(d) Transfer of name in ROR

68. What kind of suit is filed when party wants to enforce the right to redeem?

(a) Suit for foreclosure
(b) Suit for recovery of money
(c) Suit for redemption
(d) Suit for declaration of title

69. What is the period of notice to terminate lease from year to year?

(a) 15 days
(b) 30 days
(c) 6 months
(d) 9 months

70. Before the commencement of Transfer of Property Act, 1882, the transfer of immovable properties in India were governed by the___.

(a) Principles of English Law and Equity
(b) Indian Registration Act, 1908
(c) British State of Goods Act, 1880
(d) Indian Contract Act, 1872

71. What is reasonable time for the performance of contract?

(a) Is a question of fact
(b) Is a question of law
(c) Is a mixed question of fact and law
(d) Is a question of prudence

72. 'A' and 'B' being traders, entered upon a contract. 'A' has private information of a change in prices which would affect 'B's willingness to proceed with the contract___.

(a) A is bound to inform B
(b) A is not bound to inform B
(c) B is bound to be informed
(d) None of the above

73. All agreements are contract if they are made by the free consent of parties competent to contract, for lawful consideration and with ___.

(a) A regular object
(b) An unlawful object
(c) A lawful object
(d) A good object

74. In a valid contract, what comes first?

(a) Enforceability
(b) Acceptance
(c) Promise
(d) Proposal

75. Contract caused by mistake of one party as to matter of fact is___.

(a) Not voidable
(b) Voidable
(c) Valid
(d) Void

76. A's son forged B's name to a promissory note, B under threat of prosecuting A's son obtains a bond from A for the amount of the forged note. If B sues on this bond the court___.

(a) Has no jurisdiction in this case
(b) Must not set aside the bond
(c) May set aside the bond
(d) None of the above

77. In which of the following cases, the Supreme Court held that in a case of breach of contract, the proof of loss is not necessary when genuine pre-estimated loss is stipulated in contract?

(a) Roop Kumar V. Mohan Thedani, 2003
(b) ONGC Ltd. V. Saw Pipes Ltd., 2003
(c) Pawan Hans Ltd. V. UOI, 2003
(d) SBI V. United Commercial Bank, Delhi, 2003

78. Rama promises, for no consideration, to give Shyama Rs. 10,000/•. What's the nature of agreement?

(a) Voidable agreement
(b) Unlawful agreement
(c) Lawful agreement
(d) Void agreement

79. What is the time for performance of promise when a promisor is to perform his promise without application by the promisee a no time for performance is specified?

(a) Indefinite time
(b) One year

(c) Three years
(d) Within a reasonable time

80. 'A' contracts to repair 'B's house in a certain manner and receives payment of Rupees One Lakh in advance. 'A' repairs the house but not according to contract. What is the amount of costs that 'B'. Is entitled to recover from 'A'?

(a) As per market value
(b) The cost of making the repair conform to contract
(c) No amount can be recovered
(d) As per decision of Arbitrator

81. Where two persons are related by blood or adoption but not wholly through males, they are said to be___.

(a) Agnates
(b) Cognates
(c) Heir
(d) Kins

82. To whom the provisions of Hindu Succession Act are not applicable?

(a) Members of Scheduled Caste
(b) Members of Socially and Economically Backward Class
(c) Members of Scheduled Tribe
(d) Members of Brahmin Caste

83. To which properties Hindu Succession Act does not apply?

(a) Joint family property of members of Mitakshara School of Law
(b) Self-acquired property of Hindu male
(c) Self-acquired property of Hindu female
(d) Any property succession which is regulated by the Indian Succession Act by reason of provision contained in Section 21 of Special Marriage Act, 1954

84. Hindu Succession Act, 1956 came into effect from___.

(a) 15th June, 1956
(b) 16th June, 1956
(c) 17th June, 1956
(d) 18th June, 1956

85. Upon whom property of a Hindu male devolves when he dies intestate and there are no heirs of Class I and Class II?

(a) Upon the cognates of the deceased
(b) Upon the agnates of the deceased
(c) Upon the parents of the deceased
(d) None of the above

86. What does the word "possessed" occurring in Section 14(1) of Hindu Succession Act refer to?

(a) Right, title and interest
(b) Right to possession
(c) Actual or physical possession
(d) Possession as a tenant

87. The daughter of a coparcener shall by birth become a coparcener in her own right___.

(a) Hindu Succession Amendment Act, 2005
(b) Hindu Succession Act, 1956
(c) Hindu Succession Amendment Act, 2013
(d) No such provision exists in the law

88. An instrument made in relation to a Will, and explaining, altering or adding to its dispositions is known as___.

(a) Probate
(b) Will
(c) Codicil
(d) Executing document

89. The property of female Hindu under Section 14 of Hindu Succession Act, 1956 includes___.

(a) Movable and immovable property
(b) Stridhana
(c) Maintenance or arrears
(d) All of the above

90. When can the right of Executor or Legatee be established?

(a) Just after death of deceased
(b) After court of competent jurisdiction in India has granted probate of the Will
(c) After Succession Certificate is issued
(d) None of the above

91. What for Specific Relief can be granted?

(a) To enforce penal law
(b) To enforce individual civil rights
(c) To enforce political rights
(d) To obtain sanction

92. A suit for possession under Section 5 of Specific Relief Act can be filed within___.

(a) 3 years
(b) 6 months
(c) 12 years
(d) 30 years

93. What is the period of limitation for a suit for recovery of possession of Immovable property under Section 6 of the Specific Relief Act?

(a) After expiry of three months from date of dispossession
(b) After expiry of six months from date of dispossession
(c) After expiry of nine months from date of dispossession
(d) After expiry of twelve months from date of dispossession

94. The relief of specific performance can also be granted in___.

(a) Dissolution proceeding
(b) Arbitration proceeding
(c) Writ
(d) Winding up proceeding

95. What relief that Court can award when it decides that no Specific Performance ought to be granted although there has been contract broken by defendant___.

(a) Royalty
(b) Fine
(c) Compensation
(d) Civil imprisonment

96. What is the effect of declaration of right over a land under Section 34 of Specific Relief Act?

(a) In rem
(b) In personam
(c) Effective on adjoining land owners
(d) Binding on all persons of Society

97. How does the Court grant preventive relief?

(a) By Injunction
(b) By Declaration of Title
(c) By Pursuing the Parties
(d) By asking Police to do or not to do

98. In Specific Relief Act, relief would be provided under the following circumstances___.

(a) Sustenance of injury
(b) Compensation is not adequate relief
(c) Extremely impractical to ascertain damages
(d) Both (b) and (c)

99. What kind of injunction that Court may grant to prevent the breach complained of and also to compel the performance of requisite acts?

(a) Perpetual injunction
(b) Temporary injunction
(c) Mandatory injunction
(d) General sanction

100. When can Injunction be refused?

(a) To prevent a multiplicity of judicial proceedings
(b) To prevent defendant from dispossessing plaintiff
(c) To restrain any person from instituting or prosecuting any proceeding in a Court not subordinate to that from which the injunction is sought
(d) Where the invasion is such that compensation in money could not afford adequate relief

ANSWERS

No.	Ans	No.	Ans	No.	Ans	No.	Ans
1	D	31	C	61	C	91	B
2	A	32	C	62	C	92	C
3	A	33	B	63	C	93	B
4	B	34	C	64	C	94	D
5	A	35	D	65	C	95	C
6	C	36	D	66	B	96	B
7	C	37	B	67	B	97	A
8	D	38	D	68	C	98	D
9	B	39	B	69	C	99	C
10	C	40	C	70	A	100	C
11	C	41	D	71	A		
12	A	42	C	72	B		
13	C	43	A	73	C		
14	B	44	A	74	A		
15	C	45	B	75	A		
16	B	46	A	76	C		
17	C	47	C	77	B		
18	C	48	B	78	D		
19	B	49	B	79	D		
20	A	50	B	80	B		
21	C	51	X	81	B		
22	D	52	C	82	C		
23	A	53	B	83	D		
24	C	54	D	84	C		
25	A	55	C	85	B		
26	B	56	B	86	B		
27	D	57	A	87	A		
28	D	58	A	88	C		
29	B	59	C	89	D		
30	C	60	D	90	B		

2016

1. The structural part of Constitution of India is to a large extent derived from ___.

(A) Government of India Act, 1919
(B) Government of India Act, 1935
(C) Pitts Act, 1784
(D) Indian Independence Act, 1947

2. The Constitution of India describes India as ___.

(A) Quasi-federal
(B) A Union of States
(C) A Federation of States and Union Territories
(D) Partly unitary and partly federal

3. The provision of preventive detention is mentioned in ___.

(A) Article 20
(B) Article 22
(C) Article 23
(D) Article 24

4. A person who is not a member of Parliament can remain Minister only for ___.

(A) One Month
(B) Two Months
(C) Six Months
(D) None of the above

5. Who among the following is known as the guardian of public purse in India?

(A) Comptroller and Auditor General
(B) Parliament
(C) Finance Commission
(D) Finance Minister

6. The Proclamation of Emergency under Article 352 must be approved by both the houses of Parliament within ___ issue from the date of issue.

(A) One month
(B) Two months
(C) Three months
(D) Six months

7. By which Constitutional Amendment the numbers of Ministers have been limited to 15% of the total number of members of the Lower House?

(A) Ninetieth Amendment
(B) Ninety-first Amendment
(C) Ninety-second Amendment
(D) Ninety-third Amendment

8. Which of the following established Diarchy in India?

(A) Indian Council Act, 1909
(B) Government of India Act, 1919
(C) Government of India Act, 1935
(D) None of the above

9. Judicial Review of the 9th Schedule of the Indian Constitution has been made permissible by ___.

(A) Keshavananda Bharti Vs. State of Kerala
(B) M. Nagraj Vs. Union of India
(C) Minerva Mills Ltd. Vs. Union of India
(D) I. R. Coelho Vs. State of Tamil Nadu

10. The number of Articles and Schedules in original Indian Constitution were ___.

(A) 395 Articles and 8 Schedules
(B) 394 Articles and 8 Schedules
(C) 396 Articles and 10 Schedules
(D) 395 Articles and 7 Schedules

11. Section 115 of Code of Civil Procedure relates to ___.

(A) Error of fact
(B) Error of law
(C) Jurisdictional error
(D) Erroneous decision

12. Which of the following is not a rule of pleading?

(A) Pleadings should state fact and not law
(B) Facts stated should be material facts
(C) Pleadings should state the evidence
(D) Facts should be stated in concise form

13. The principle underlying is that where the parties have had an opportunity of controverting a matter, that should be taken the same thing as if matter had been actually controverted and decided.

(A) Explanation III, Section 11 CPC
(B) Explanation IV, Section 11 CPC
(C) Explanation VI, Section 11 CPC
(D) Explanation VII, Section 11 CPC KH-1A/13

14. Which of the following is not correct?

(A) Question of joinder of parties is a matter of procedure and not substantive right
(B) Objection as to non-joinder and mis-joinder of parties has to be taken at the earliest possible opportunity

(C) If necessary party is not joined, suit can be dismissed on that ground alone
(D) Where a defendant is added, plaint need not be amended

15. Where the suit abates on account of failure of the plaintiff to bring the legal representatives of the deceased defendant ___.

(A) Such abatement will operate as res judicata
(B) No fresh suit will lie on the same cause of action
(C) No application to set aside the dismissal can be filed
(D) All of the above

16. A decree should be drawn up within ___ days from the date of judgement.

(A) 15
(B) 30
(C) 45
(D) 60

17. Provision of Section 80 of the CPC is ___.

(A) Directory only
(B) Precautionary only
(C) Mandatory
(D) Depend on the nature of suit

18. Defendant is entitled to defend the suit as of right in ___.

(A) Summary suit
(B) Ordinary suit
(C) Both (A) and (B)
(D) None of the above

19. Order XI11 of CPC requires parties to produce the documentary evidence ___.

(A) On or before settlement of issues
(B) At any stage of proceedings
(C) At any stage of proceedings but before pronouncement of judgement
(D) When the Court directs

20. Order V of CPC deals with ___.

(A) Summons to witnesses
(B) Summons to defendant
(C) Both (A) and (B)
(D) Summons in general

21. Under which Section of Code of Criminal Procedure the term offence has been defined?

(A) Section 40

(B) Section 2(n)
(C) Section 2(m)
(D) Section 2(p)

22. A proclaimed person whose property has been attached can claim the property or sale proceeds on appearance within ___.

(A) 6 months of attachment
(B) 1 year of attachment
(C) 2 years of attachment
(D) 3 years of attachment

23. Minimum number of judges of High Court required to sign confirmation of death sentence ___.

(A) One
(B) Two
(C) Three
(D) Four

24. Transit remand means ___.

(A) Transfer of prisoner from one jail to another
(B) Transfer of criminal case from one court to another
(C) Taking accused by police from one state to another
(D) Taking accused from court to prison

25. Which one of the following Section of Cr.P.C. provides for free legal aid to the accused?

(A) Section 301
(B) Section 302
(C) Section 303
(D) Section 304

26. Classification of compoundable and non-compoundable offences has been provided under ___.

(A) First Schedule of Cr.P.C.
(B) Second Schedule of Cr.P.C.
(C) Section 320 of Cr.P.C.
(D) Section 321 of Cr.P.C.

27. Which Section of Cr.P.C. provides for compensation to groundlessly arrested persons?

(A) Section 356
(B) Section 357
(C) Section 358
(D) Section 359

28. The provisions of Cr.P.C. other than those relating to Chapter VIII, X and XI shall not apply in which of the following state?

(A) Tripura
(B) Sikkim
(C) Assam
(D) Nagaland

29. Which of the following is not an essential procedural requirement of Section 164 of Cr.P.C.?

(A) Confession to be made voluntarily
(B) Warning to the accused
(C) Recording of confession in presence of advocate of accused
(D) Memorandum at the foot of confession

30. The provision proving previous conviction is envisaged in which of the following Sections of Cr.P.C.?

(A) Section 295
(B) Section 296
(C) Section 297
(D) Section 298

31. Section 101 of Indian Evidence Act, 1872 illustrates the burden of proof in the sense of proving ___.

(A) A case
(B) A particular fact
(C) A fact to be proved to make evidence admissible
(D) All of the above

32. If the Court is satisfied with the trustworthiness of dying declaration ___.

(A) It can base conviction on it without corroboration
(B) It cannot base conviction on it
(C) It can be conviction on it but there must be corroboration with other evidences
(D) None of the above

33. Mark the correct option.

(A) It is necessary for the application of Section 18 of Evidence Act that there must be a formal agency
(B) Sections 18, 19 and 20 of Evidence Act are the exceptions of doctrine of privity
(C) Sections 17-20 of Evidence Act talk about judicial admissions
(D) Statements under Sections 17- 20 of Evidence Act should be regarding fact in issue only

34. Which of the following provisions of the Evidence Act corresponds to the proviso to rule 5(1) order VI11 of the CPC?

(A) Section 56
(B) Section 57
(C) Section 58
(D) Section 59

35. Under Section 14 of the Evidence Act, the facts showing the existence of state of mind, must be ___.

(A) Specific state of mind
(B) General state of mind
(C) Both (A) and (B)
(D) None of the above

36. Section 107 of Evidence Act relates to ___.

(A) Presumption of death
(B) Presumption of continuance of life
(C) Presumption of legitimacy
(D) Presumption of relationship

37. Previous good character is relevant in ___.

(A) Civil cases
(B) Criminal cases
(C) Both (A) and (B)
(D) None of the above

38. Under Section 165 of Evidence Act, judge may ask question about ___.

(A) Any relevant fact
(B) Any irrelevant fact
(C) Only those facts which disclose commission of offence
(D) Both (A) and (B)

39. Queen Empress Vs. Abdullah is a leading case on ___.

(A) Admissional FIR
(B) Confession
(C) Dying Declaration
(D) Admission

40. Which Section of Evidence Act defines public document?

(A) Section 72
(B) Section 74
(C) Section 75
(D) Section 76

41. Good faith is defined in Indian Penal Code under ___.

(A) Section 39
(B) Section 51
(C) Section 52

(D) Section 26

42. Maximum punishment the offence of theft in dwelling house is ___.

(A) 2 years
(B) 3 years
(C) 7 years
(D) 10 years

43. Which Section of IPC is based on the principle of "de minimis non curat lex"?

(A) Section 92
(B) Section 93
(C) Section 94
(D) Section 95

44. Disclosure of the identity of victim of rape is dealt under which Section of IPC?

(A) Section 354A
(B) Section 354C
(C) Section 229
(D) Section 228A

45. The offence of destruction of electronic record to prevent its production as evidence is punishable under which Section of IPC?

(A) Section 202
(B) Section 203
(C) Section 204
(D) Section 205

46. Who prepared the first draft of Indian Penal Code?

(A) Canning
(B) Stephen
(C) Bentinck
(D) Macaulay

47. Under which of the following Sections of IPC rash and negligent driving of vehicle on public way is an offence?

(A) Section 278
(B) Section 279
(C) Section 280
(D) Section 281

48. In Section 497 of IPC, actus reus relates to ___.

(A) Any person
(B) Time
(C) Place
(D) Married woman

49. Whether provocation was grave and sudden enough to mitigate the offence is a question of ___.

(A) Fact
(B) Law
(C) Law and Fact (mixed)
(D) None of the above

50. When a person monitors the use of internet, email or other form of electronic communication by a woman, he commits the offence of ___.

(A) Stalking
(B) Eve teasing
(C) Voyeurism
(D) None of the above

51. Extended period of limitation cannot stretch beyond ___ years from the cessation of disability.

(A) 2
(B) 3
(C) 5
(D) 6

52. Which of the following Sections of Limitation Act deals with exclusion of time in legal proceedings?

(A) 9
(B) 10
(C) 11
(D) 12

53. Section 6 of the Limitation Act covers ___.

(A) Persons en title to sue
(B) Persons entitle to apply for execution of decree
(C) Both (A) and (B)
(D) None of the above

54. Sections 6, 7 and 8 of Limitation Act are ___.

(A) Mutually exclusive
(B) Complementary
(C) Separated and not related
(D) Both (A) and (C)

55. The basic principle underlying Section ___ of Limitation Act is recognition of dictum "Once a trust, always a trust".

(A) 9
(B) 10
(C) 11
(D) 12

56. The period of limitation for compensation for infringing copyright is ___.

(A) 1 year
(B) 2 years
(C) 3 years
(D) 12 years

57. When a debt becomes time barred ___.

(A) It gets extinguished
(B) It becomes unenforceable in a court of law
(C) Both (A) and (B)
(D) None of the above

58. When a person is affected by one disability and another disability follows without leaving the gap, the suit may be filed ___.

(A) After the first disability has ceased
(B) After the either disability has ceased
(C) After both the disabilities have ceased
(D) Either (A), (B) or (C)

59. For the exercise of discretionary jurisdiction vested in the Court under Section 5 of Limitation Act, the proof of sufficient cause is a ___.

(A) Condition precedent
(B) Condition subsequent
(C) Either (A) or (B)
(D) Neither (A) nor (B)

60. The period of limitation is defined under which Section of Limitation Act?

(A) Section 2(h)
(B) Section 2U)
(C) Section 2(1)
(D) Section 2(n)

61. Section 12 of Transfer of Property Act, 1882 is not applicable to ___.

(A) Transfer by way of sale
(B) Transfer by way of exchange
(C) Transfer by way of gift
(D) Transfer by way of lease

62. Bellamy Vs. Sabine is related with which doctrine?

(A) Doctrine of lis pendens
(B) Doctrine of part performance
(C) Doctrine of election
(D) Doctrine of perpetuity

63. According to which one of the following Sections of Transfer of Property Act that in case of conflict between marshalling and contribution, former shall prevail?

(A) Section 80
(B) Section 81
(C) Section 82
(D) Section 83

64. Which of the following Section(s) deals with accession to the mortgaged property?

(A) Section 63
(B) Section 70
(C) Both Sections 63 and 70
(D) Section 61

65. Which of the following is not governed by Transfer of Property Act?

(A) Onerous gift
(B) Mortis Causa gift
(C) Universal gift
(D) Gift to disqualified person

66. Remedy of foreclosure is available in which one of the following mortgages?

(A) Usufructuary mortgage
(B) Simple mortgage
(C) Mortgage by conditional sale
(D) English mortgage

67. Rule against double possibilities was recognized in ___.

(A) Girijesh Dutt Vs. Data Din
(B) Whitby Vs. Mitchell
(C) Ardeshir Vs. Dadabhoy
(D) Sopher Vs. Administrator General of Bengal

68. The rule "redeem up foreclose down" is a combination of ___ Transfer of Property Act.

(A) Sections 89 and 91
(B) Sections 91 and 92
(C) Sections 92 and 93
(D) Sections 91 and 94

69. Which one of the following Sections of Transfer of Property Act defines charge?

(A) Section 100
(B) Section 101
(C) Section 104
(D) Section 105

70. Which Section of Transfer of Property Act provides against- condition restraining alienation?

(A) Section 9

(B) Section 10
(C) Section 11
(D) Section 12

71. Which of the followings amounts to discharge of contract?

(A) Performance of contract
(B) Frustration of contract
(C) Novation

(D.) All of the above

72. Hadley Vs. Baxandale is a leading case on ___.

(A) Anticipatory breach
(B) Remoteness of damages
(C) Breach of implied term
(D) None of the above

73. The test of intention to contract is ___.

(A) Objective
(B) Subjective
(C) Depends on case
(D) None of the above

74. It does not amount of counter proposal ___.

(A) Acceptance with a variation
(B) Inquiry into the terms of the proposal
(C) Partial acceptance
(D) Both (A) and (C)

75. The provisions as to consideration do not affect as between donor and donee, the validity of any gift which has actually been made. This is expressly provided in ___.

(A) Section 25(2) of Indian Contract Act
(B) Section 25(3) of Indian Contract Act
(C) Explanation 1 to Section 25 of Indian Contract Act
(D) Explanation 2 to Section 25 of Indian Contract Act

76. In case of alternative promises where one branch is legal and another illegal ___.

(A) The contract is void
(B) The legal branch can be enforced
(C) Neither legal nor illegal part can be enforced
(D) Both (A) and (C)

77. The Indian Contract Act, 1872 contains provision for the privity of contract under ___.

(A) Chapter I

(B) Chapter II
(C) Chapter III
(D) None of the above

78. Which of the following Sections of Indian Contract Act provides for gratuitous bailment?

(A) Section 158
(B) Section 159
(C) Section 160
(D) Section 161

79. Which one of the following Sections is an exception to Section 25 of Indian Contract Act?

(A) Section 183 of Indian Contract Act
(B) Section 184 of Indian Contract Act
(C) Section 185 of Indian Contract Act
(D) Section 186 of Indian Contract Act

80. Section 10 of Indian Contract Act requires ___ conditions for an agreement to become a contract.

(A) 3
(B) 5
(C) 6
(D) 7

81. Which Section of Hindu Succession Act deals with the concept of 'Escheat'?

(A) Section 27
(B) Section 28
(C) Section 29
(D) Section 30

82. Section 12 of Hindu Succession Act deals with order of succession among ___.

(A) Agnates
(B) Cognates
(C) Both (A) and (8)
(D) None of the above

83. Under the Hindu Succession Act, the presumption in case of simultaneous death is ___.

(A) The elder survived the younger
(B) The younger survived the elder
(C) There is no question of survival
(D) There is no such presumption

84. Under the Hindu Succession Act, if two or more heirs succeed together to the property of intestate, they shall take the property, save as expressly provided in the Act ___.

(A) As tenants in common
(B) As joint tenants
(C) Either (A) or (B)
(D) Both (A) and (B)

85. 'A' a Hindu has two wives W1 and W2 (both marriages took place before 1955) and one son S by W1 and four sons S1, S2, S3 and S4 from W2. On partition of coparcenary property W1 and W2 will get ___.

(A) No share as neither of them is a coparcenary
(B) 1/4 share each
(C) 1/5 share each
(D) 1/8 share each

86. Which one of the following Sections of Hindu Succession Act provides for notional partition?

(A) Section 6
(B) Section 18
(C) Section 10
(D) Section 14

87. Which Section of Indian Succession Act, 1925 defines probate?

(A) Section 2(e)
(B) Section 2(f)
(C) Section 2(g)
(D) Section 2(h)

88. Which of the following Chapter of Indian Succession Act deals with vesting of legacies?

(A) Chapter VI
(B) Chapter VII
(C) Chapter VIII
(D) Chapter IX

89. Which of the following is not Class I heir under Hindu Succession Act?

(A) Son
(B) Daughter
(C) Father
(D) Mother

90. Date of commencement of Hindu Succession (Amendment) Act, 2005 ___.

(A) 8th September, 2005
(B) 9th September, 2005
(C) 12th September, 2005
(D) 17h September, 2005

91. For the purpose of Section 7 of Specific Relief Act, right to present possession may be ___.

(A) Special
(B) Temporary
(C) Special but cannot be temporary
(D) Either (A) or (B)

92. When an instrument does not express the real intention of parties, the same may be rectified under which of the following Sections of the Specific Relief Act?

(A) Section 25
(B) Section 26
(C) Section 27
(D) Section 28

93. Section 28 of Specific Relief Act provides for recession of contract for sale or lease of immovable property in certain circumstances. The cost of proceedings under Section 28 shall be ___.

(A) Paid by the plaintiff
(B) Paid by the defendant
(C) In the discretion of the court
(D) None of the above

94. Under Section 12(2) of Specific Relief Act, 1963, where the contract part which remains unperformed is ___.

(A) Small proportion
(B) Considerable part
(C) Equal part
(D) None of the above

95. Which of the following Sections of Specific Relief Act provides circumstances where injunction cannot be granted?

(A) Section 38
(B) Section 39
(C) Section 40
(D) Section 41

96. Liquidation of damages is not a bar to specific performance in Specific Relief Act under ___.

(A) Section 20
(B) Section 22
(C) Section 23
(D) Section 24

97. Section 18(a) of Specific Relief Act dealing with non-enforcement except with variation uses the expression ___.

(A) Fraud
(B) Mistake of fact

(C) Misrepresentation
(D) All of the above

98. Detailed provisions about permanent injunctions are contained in ___.

(A) Order 39, CPC
(B) Sections 38-42 of Specific Relief Act
(C) Both (A) and (B)
(D) None of the above

99. Plaintiff can recover possession of immovable property without reference to title under which Section of Specific Relief Act?

(A) Section 5
(B) Section 6
(C) Section 7
(D) Both (A) and (B)

100. In case of breach of contract to transfer immovable property, ordinarily the courts are entitled to presume that ___.

(A) Compensation is not adequate relief
(B) Compensation is adequate relief
(C) Relief cannot be specific performance
(D) None of the above, there is no such presumption

ANSWERS

1	B	31	A	61	D	91	D
2	B	32	A	62	A	92	B
3	B	33	B	63	C	93	C
4	C	34	C	64	C	94	A
5	A	35	A	65	B	95	D
6	A	36	B	66	C	96	C
7	B	37	B	67	B	97	D
8	B	38	D	68	D	98	B
9	D	39	C	69	A	99	B
10	A	40	B	70	B	100	A
11	C	41	C	71	D		
12	C	42	C	72	B		
13	B	43	D	73	A		
14	D	44	D	74	B		
15	B	45	C	75	C		
16	A	46	D	76	B		
17	C	47	B	77	D		
18	B	48	D	78	B		
19	A	49	A	79	C		
20	B	50	A	80	B		
21	B	51	B	81	C		
22	C	52	D	82	C		
23	B	53	C	83	B		
24	C	54	B	84	A		

25	D	55	B	85	D
26	C	56	C	86	A
27	C	57	B	87	B
28	D	58	C	88	C
29	C	59	A	89	C
30	D	60	B	90	B

2017

1. Indian Constitution is ___.

(A) Unitary
(B) Federal
(C) Quasi-federal
(D) None of the above

2. The words 'socialist' and 'secular' were added in the Preamble of the Indian Constitution by the ___ Constitutional Amendment.

(A) 42nd
(B) 32nd
(C) 25th
(D) 9th

3. "Equality of opportunity in matters of public employment" is provided under Article ___.

(A) 14
(B) 15
(C) 16
(D) 17

4. The President can make laws, when the Parliament is not in session by issuing ___.

(A) Orders
(B) Bills
(C) Ordinance
(D) Notification

5. In which of the following cases, the Supreme Court held that the Union Government cannot dismiss a duly elected State Government on the sole ground that the ruling party in the state suffered an overwhelming defeat in the election of the Lok Sabha?

(A) S. R. Bommai v. Union of India
(B) Karljnanidhi v. Union of India
(C) Jayalalitha v. State
(D) None of the above

6. The power of the Supreme Court of India to decide disputes between the Centre and the States falls under its ___.

(A) Advisory jurisdiction
(B) Appellate jurisdiction
(C) Original jurisdiction
(D) Constitutional jurisdiction

7. In which of the following cases, the Supreme Court used its power of Judicial review?

(A) Golaknalh Case
(B) Bank Nationalization Case
(C) Minerva Mills Case
(D) All of the above

8. The Supreme Court considered the scope of Freedom of speech and expression under Article 19(1)(a) for the first time in ___.

(A) Cross Roads Case
(B) K.A. Abbas Case
(C) Bandit Queen Case
(D) None of the above

9. In which of the following Cases, Supreme Court held that right to legal aid is a Fundamental Right?

(A) Sunil Batra Case
(B) M. H. Hoskot Case
(C) Prem Shanker Shukla Case
(D) None of the above

10. Reservation of seats for the Scheduled Castes and Scheduled Tribes in every Panchayat is provided under Article ___ of Constitution of India.

(A) 2430
(B) 2740
(C) 2750
(D) 2720

11. In which of the following provisions mesne profit has been defined in the Code of Civil Procedure?

(A) Section 2(4)
(B) Section 2(B)
(C) Section 2(12)
(D) Section 2(14)

12. Pecuniary jurisdiction of the court is contained in ___ of Code of Civil Procedure.

(A) Section 6
(B) Section 7
(C) Section 8
(D) Section 9

13. Principle of res judicata applies to ___.

(A) Suits only
(B) Execution proceedings only
(C) Arbitration proceedings only
(D) Suits as well as execution proceedings

14. Which of the following Section of the Code of Civil Procedure, 1908 deals with

stay of suits?

(A) Section 9
(B) Section 10
(C) Section 11
(D) Section 12

15. A suit for the partition of immovable property, shall be instituted in the court within the local limits of whose jurisdiction the ___.

(A) Property is situated
(B) Plaintiff resided

(e) Defendant resided
(D) Any of the above

16. Which of the following provisions under the Code of Civil Procedure, 1908 deals with rejection of plaint?

(A) Order 7, Rule 7
(B) Order 7, Rule 8
(C) Order 7, Rule 10
(D) Order 7, Rule 11

17. Which of the following order dears with issue and service of summons?

(A) Order V
(B) Order VI

(e) Order VII
(D) Order IV

18. Defendant failed to file a written statement even after the stipulated time. The court pronounced the judgement. It is ___.

(A) Legal
(B) Illegal

(e) Justifiable
(D) Irregular

19. An application to set aside an ex parte decree shall be filed before ___.

(A) The High Court
(B) The court which passed the decree
(C) The court to which an appeal lies from the decree
(D) None of the above

20. In a suit by A against B, C and D, ex parte decree was passed. C and D were not served with summons while B was served. In such a situation ___.

(A) Decree against all of them can be set aside
(B) Decree against 8 cannot be set aside

(e) Decree against all of them cannot be set aside
(D) None of the above

21. An accused arrested can be kept in custody without producing him before the magistrate, after his arrest for a period of ___.

(A) 12 hours
(B) 24 hours
(C) 48 hours
(D) 90 days

22. Section 41A, 41B, 41C and 41D were incorporated in the Code of Criminal Procedure, 1973 by ___.

(A) The Code of Criminal Procedure (Amendment) Act, 2005
(B) The Code of Criminal Procedure (Amendment) Act, 2006
(C) The Code of Criminal Procedure (Amendment) Act, 2008
(D) None of the above

23. In which of the following cases, the Supreme Court held that 'no arrest can be made because it is lawful for the police officer to do so. The existence of the power to arrest is one thing and the justification for the exercise of it is quite another. The police officer must be able to justify the arrest apart from his power to do so'?

(A) State of Gujarat v. Lal Singh
(B) Joginder Kumar v. State of UP
(C) Nandini Satpathy v. P. L. Dani
(D) None of the above

24. When a police officer files a report under Section 195(1)(a) of CrPC, it is known as a ___.

(A) Complaint
(B) Refer Report
(C) Police Report
(D) None of the above

25. Offence for which, a police officer, has no authority to arrest without warrant is called a ___.

(A) Bailable offence
(B) Non-cognizable offence
(C) Non-compoundable offence
(D) None of the above

26. The accused filed an application before the magistrate to allow him to appear

through his power of attorney holder. The magistrate allowed the petition. The order is ___.

(A) Legal.
(B) Illegal
(C) Improper
(D) Irregular

27. Executive Magistrates are appointed under ___ of the Code of Criminal Procedure, 1973.

(A) Section 20
(B) Section 18
(C) Section 14
(D) Section 15

28. Which of the following Sections of the Code of Criminal Procedure, 1973 deals with conditional order for removal of nuisance?

(A) Section 133
(B) Section 134
(C) Section 135
(D) Section 136

29. Chapter XI of the Code of Criminal Procedure, 1973 deals with ___.

(A) Maintenance to wives, children and parents
(B) Maintenance of public order and tranquillity

(e) Preventive action of police
(D) None of the above

30. A new proviso was added to Section 157(1) of the Code of (Criminal Procedure 1973 by the Code of Criminal Procedure (Amendment) Act, 2008 in relation to an offence of ___.

(A) Murder
(B) Rape
(C) Terrorist Acts
(D) None of the above

31. Which of the following Sections of the Indian Evidence Act deals with the relevancy of admissions, and confessions?

(A) Sections 6 - 16
(B) Sections 17 - 31
(C) Sections 32 - 33
(D) Sections 34 - 39

32. Motive is insignificant when ___.

(A) Direct evidence is available
(B) Direct evidence is not available

(C) Only circumstantial evidence is available
(D) None of the above

33. An admission may be ___ in nature.

(A) Oral
(B) Documentary
(C) Oral and Documentary
(D) Oral or documentary or contained in electronic form

34. In order to make the confession admissible, the person ___.

(A) May not be an accused at the time of making confession
(B) Must be an accused at the time of making the confession
(C) Must be a suspect at the time of making the confession
(D) None of the above

35. In which of the following cases did the, Supreme Court held that a retracted confession can be used against the accused and it is not against Article 20(3) of the Constitution of India?

(A) Mubarak Ali v. State
(B) Palwinder Kaur v. State of Punjab
(C) Kalawati and another v. State of HP
(D) None of the above

36. A and B are jointly tried for the murder of C. It is proved that A said, B and I murdered C. The court may consider the effect of this confession as against ___.

(A) A only
(B) B only
(C) Both A and B
(D) None of the above

37. Section 114A was introduced by the Criminal Law Amendment Act, 1983, following the widespread protest against the judgement in the ___.

(A) Mathura Case
(B) Vishakha Case
(C) Naliavati Case
(D) None of the above

38. The examination of a witness by the party who calls him shall be called ___.

(A) Re-examination
(B) Cross examination
(C) Examination-in-chief
(D) None of the above

39. Previous judgments are relevant to support the plea of ___ in civil cases.

(A) Res judicata
(B) Res subjudice
(C) Limitation
(D) None of the above

40. The contents of a document can be proved by ___.

(A) Primary evidence only
(B) Direct evidence only
(C) Primary or secondary evidence
(D) None of the above

41. A, who knows swimming, failed to save the life of a drowning child and the child died as a result of A's omission.

(A) A is liable for not saving the drowning child
(B) A is not liable for not saving the drowning child
(C) Act is protected by general exceptions of the Indian Penal Code
(D) None of the above

42. A person who consents, suffer no injury is known as ___.

(A) De minimis non curat lex
(B) Actus non facit reum nisi mens sit rea
(C) Volenti non fit injuria
(D) None of the above

43. Which of the following Sections of the Indian Penal Code deals with right of private defence of the body and of the property?

(A) Section 98
(B) Section 96
(C) Section 97
(D) Section 99

44. A instigates B to murder D. B in pursuance of the instigation stabs D. D recovers from the wound.

(A) A is guilty of instigating B to commit murder
(B) A is guilty of attempt to murder
(C) A is not guilty since intended act did not happen
(D) None of the above

45. Obstructing public servant in discharge of public functions is an offence punishable under ___ of the Indian Penal Code.

(A) Section 186
(B) Section 187

(C) Section 188
(D) Section 189

46. A, knowing that B has murdered Z, assists B to hire the body with the intention of screening B from punishment. Under which of the following Sections of the Indian Penal Code can A be punished?

(A) Section 200
(B) Section 201
(C) Section 202
(D) Section 203

47. A doctor registered as a medical practitioner and entitled to practice in Homoeopathy only, prescribed an allopathic medicine to the patient. The patient died. The doctor is guilty of ___.

(A) Death by rash and negligent act
(B) Murder
(C) Culpable homicide not amounting to murder
(D) None of the above

48. Criminal Breach of Trust is defined under ___ of the Indian Penal Code.

(A) Section 403
(B) Section 404
(C) Section 405
(D) Section 406

49. In which of the following cases, the Supreme Court held that legal and valid marriage is not a necessary ingredient to attract Section 498A of the Indian Penal Code?

(A) Reema Agarwal v. Anupam and others
(B) Sushil Kumar Sharma v. Union of India and others
(C) Arun Vyas v. Anita Vyas
(D) None of the above

50. A makes an attempt to pick the pocket of Z by thrusting his hand into Z's pocket. A fails in the attempt in consequence of Z's having nothing in his pocket

(A) A is guilty under Section 511 of the Indian Penal Code
(B) A is not guilty under Section 511 of the Indian Penal Code
(C) A is guilty of no offence
(D) None of the above

51. Which of the following Sections of the Limitation Act, 1963 deals with expiry of

prescribed period when court is closed?

(A) 2
(B) 3
(C) 4
(D) 5

52. An order made on an application filed beyond the period of limitation is ___.

(A) Illegal
(B) Without jurisdiction
(C) Irregular
(D) None of the above

53. In a suit for recovery of possession of a house from a deemed trustee of wakf property ___.

(A) No limitation applies
(B) Limitation is applicable
(C) Depends
(D) None of the above

54. The period of limitation for filing an application for the execution of any decree (other than a decree granting a mandatory injunction) or order of any civil court is ___.

(A) 1 year
(B) 2 years
(C) 3 years
(D) 12 years

55. Exclusion of time under Section 14 is ___.

(A) Mandatory
(B) Discretionary
(C) Directory
(D) None of the above

56. Which of the following Sections of the Limitation Act, 1963 deals with the 'Effect of substituting or adding new plaintiff or defendant'?

(A) 21
(B) 22
(C) 23
(D) 24

57. In case of a suit for compensation for an act which does not give rise to a cause of action unless some specific injury actually results there from, the period of limitation shall be computed from the time ___.

(A) When the injury results
(B) When the act occurred
(C) Depends

(D) None of the above

58. The jurisdiction to great exemption under Section 14 of Limitation Act, 1963 is given exclusively to ___.

(A) Civil Court
(B) High Court
(C) Supreme Court
(D) None of the above

59. The period of limitation for a suit for compensation for infringing copyright or any other exclusive privilege is ___.

(A) 1 year
(B) 2 years
(C) 3 years
(D) 12 years

60. The period of limitation for filing an application to set aside a decree passed ex parte to rehear an appeal heard ex parte, is ___.

(A) 10 days
(B) 30 days
(C) 90 days
(D) 1 year

61. A vested interest created in favour of an unborn person comes under ___.

(A) Section 20
(B) Section 24
(C) Section 19
(D) None of the above

62. Actionable claim means claim to any ___.

(A) Debt or beneficial interest
(B) Debt alone
(C) Beneficial interest, other than debt
(D) All of the above

63. Doctrine of Election in the Transfer of Property Act, 1882 is provided under ___.

(A) Section 35
(B) Section 38
(C) Section 34
(D) None of the above

64. The term 'Transfer of Property' is defined in the Transfer of Property Act, 1882 in ___.

(A) Section 3
(B) Section 5
(C) Section 2(a)

(D) Not defined in the Act

65. The registration of mortgage is not required where the mortgage is ___.

(A) Simple mortgage
(B) Anomalous mortgage
(C) English mortgage
(D) Mortgage by deposit of title deeds

66. Any provisions made as a clog on redemption is ___.

(A) Void
(B) Voidable
(C) Valid
(D) Enforceable

67. The lease of immovable property is terminable by either party by a notice of ___.

(A) 15 days
(B) 3 months
(C) 1 month
(D) 6 months

68. Puisne mortgagee is the ___.

(A) Assignee of the equity of redemption
(B) Co-mortgagee
(C) Subsequent mortgagee
(D) All of the above

69. In a lease of immovable property what is transferred, is the ___.

(A) Interest in the property
(B) Right to enjoy the property
(C) Mesne profit
(D) Possession alone

70. Transfer of immovable property made with intent to defeat or delay the creditors of the transferor is known as ___.

(A) Feeding the grant
(B) Transfer lis pendens
(C) Fraudulent transfer
(D) Transfer by ostensible owner

71. The rule in Pinnel's Case relates to ___.

(A) Part performance
(B) Minor's contract
(C) Fraud
(D) Undue influence

72. When an offer is addressed to the public at large, the offer is called ___.

(A) Advertisement
(B) Specific offer
(C) General offer
(D) Auction

73. X makes a proposal to Y, which Y accepts. But before the acceptance comes to the knowledge of X, Y revokes his acceptance by telegram. When is the revocation complete?

(A) When the telegram is despatched
(B) When the telegram is received by X
(C) When the contents of the telegram come to the knowledge of X
(D) When X accepts the revocation

74. A threatened to commit suicide his wife and son if refused to execute a deed in his favour. They executed the deed. The deed is said to have been obtained by ___.

(A) Fraud
(B) Undue influence
(C) Coercion
(D) Misrepresentation

75. Wagering agreements are void but collateral transactions will be ___.

(A) Void
(B) Voidable
(C) Valid
(D) Valid, at the discretion of court

76. Owner of a cinema-hall contracts to exhibit a film in the month of October. In the month of September, the hall collapsed during an earthquake. The contract ___.

(A) Is valid and binds the owner of the cinema-hall to exhibit the film
(B) Is not frustrated
(C) Has become impossible to perform
(D) Has to be honoured and so the owner should reconstruct the hall to exhibit the film

77. If a person accepts a lesser sum of money than what was contracted for a discharge of the whole debt, it is known as ___.

(A) Remission
(B) Alteration
(C) Rescission
(D) Waiver

78. Under English law a contract of insurance other than life insurance is ___.

(A) Contract of agency
(B) Contingent contract
(C) Contract of guarantee

(D) Contract of indemnity

79 The leading case Carlill v. Carbolic Smoke Ball Co. relates to ___.

(A) Capacity of parties
(B) Minor's agreement
(C) General offer
(D) Tender

80. 'Consensus ad idem' means ___.

(A) Consent of the parties obtained illegally
(B) Parties identified the same thing in the same sense
(C) Contract between the same parties
(D) Contract without consent

81. Distribution of property among heirs in Class II of the Schedule under Section 11 shall be divided between them ___.

(A) One share
(B) Equally
(C) 1/3rd share
(D) 1/4th share

82. Who among the following is a Class - I heir?

(A) Brother's son
(B) Sister's son
(C) Brother's daughter
(D) None of the above

83. Coparcenary is ___.

(A) A creature of Hindu law
(B) Created by agreement between parties
(C) Created by act of parties
(D) None of the above

84. A person who dies without making testamentary disposition in respect of his property under Section 3(g) is ___.

(A) Coparcener
(B) Intestate
(C) Testator
(D) Legatee

85. General rules of succession in the case of the succession of the female Hindus are dealt with under ___.

(A) Section 16
(B) Section 20
(C) Section 21
(D) Section 15

86. A widow inherits property of her husband on his death. Whether a subsequent re-marriage would divest her of property in view of Section 24 and Section 14 of the Hindu Succession Act, 1956?

(A) Yes
(B) No
(C) Depends
(D) None of the above

87. One who shares (equally) with others in inheritance in the estate of a common ancestor is called a ___.

(A) Cognate
(B) Coparcener
(C) Agnate,
(D) None of the above

88. As per Section 14 of the Hindu Succession Act, 1956 any property possessed by a female Hindu, whether acquired before or after the commencement of the Act shall be held by her as ___.

(A) A full owner
(B) A limited owner
(C) Joint owner
(D) None of the above

89. Which Section of the Indian Succession Act, 1925 defines codicil?

(A) Section 2(f)
(B) Section 2(a)
(C) Section 2(b)
(D) Section 2(h)

90. A will or any part of a will, the making of which has been caused by fraud or coercion or by such importunity is ___.

(A) Valid
(B) Void
(C) Voidable
(D) None of the above

91. The specific performance of any contract specified in Section 10 of the Specific Relief Act may be enforced ___.

(A) As of right
(B) As per discretion of court
(C) Mandatorily
(D) None of the above

92. What is the period of limitation fixed for filing a suit for specific performance of a contract?

(A) 2 years
(B) 3 years

(C) 7 years
(D) 14 years

93. Which of the following Sections of the Specific Relief Act deals with specific performance of part of contract?

(A) Section 12
(B) Section 13
(C) Section 14
(D) Section 15
(B) Void
(C) Voidable
(D) None of the above

94. In which of the following cases has the Supreme Court held that when granting of damages is an adequate relief, the specific performance would be refused?

(A) Prakash Chandra v. Angadlal
(B) Maria v. Bilkees
(C) Chand Rani v. Kamal Rani
(D) None of the above

95. A party who has rescinded a contract ___.

(A) Can recover damages
(B) Cannot recover damages
(C) Depends
(D) None of the above

96. In a suit for specific performance of a contract, the plaintiff may also claim compensation for its breach ___.

(A) In addition to such performance
(B) In Substitution of such performance
(C) Either in addition to or in substitution of such performance
(D) None of the above

97. A declaration made under Section 34 is binding on ___.

(A) The parties of the suit
(B) Persons claiming through them respectively
(C) Where any of the parties are trustees, on the persons for whom, if in existence at the date of the declaration, such parties would be trustees
(D) All of the above

98. Perpetual injunction is defined in Section ____ of the Specific Relief Act.

(A) Section 36
(B) Section 37
(C) Section 38

(D) Section 39

99. A party can file a suit for rectification ____.

(A) At any time when fraud is discovered
(B) At any time a mistake has come to light
(C) Within three years of execution of instrument
(D) Either (A) or (B)

100. Which of the following contracts cannot be specifically enforced?

(A) A contract for the non-performance of which compensation in money is an adequate relief
(B) A contract which runs into such minute or numerous details
(C) A contract which is in its nature determinable
(D) All of the above

ANSWERS

1	C	31	B	61	A	91	B
2	A	32	A	62	A	92	B
3	C	33	D	63	A	93	A
4	C	34	B	64	B	94	A
5	A	35	C	65	D	95	B
6	C	36	C	66	A	96	C
7	D	37	A	67	A	97	D
8	A	38	C	68	C	98	B
9	B	39	A	69	B	99	D
10	A	40	C	70	C	100	D
11	C	41	B	71	A		
12	A	42	C	72	C		
13	D	43	C	73	B		
14	B	44	A	74	C		
15	A	45	A	75	C		
16	D	46	B	76	C		
17	A	47	A	77	A		
18	A	48	C	78	D		
19	B	49	A	79	C		
20	B	50	A	80	B		
21	B	51	C	81	B		
22	C	52	A	82	D		
23	B	53	A	83	A		
24	A	54	D	84	B		
25	B	55	A	85	D		
26	B	56	A	86	B		
27	A	57	A	87	B		
28	A	58	A	88	A		
29	C	59	C	89	C		
30	B	60	B	90	B		

2018

1. In which of the following cases, Supreme Court held that Preamble can be amended without altering its basic features?

(A) Golaknath Case
(B) Maneka Gandhi Case
(C) S.R. Bommai v. Union of India
(D) Kesavananda Bharati Case

2. When there is a conflict between an Act made by the Parliament and a State legislature on the same subject, which of the following doctrines shall be applicable?

(A) Doctrine of colourable legislation
(B) Doctrine of pith and substance
(C) Doctrine of repugnancy
(D) None of these

3. "Capital Punishment is not violative of Article 21 of the Constitution of India". It has been held in the case of___

(A) Muthu v. State
(B) Bachan Singh v. State of Punjab
(C) Bhikaji v. State of M.P.
(D) Smt. Gian Kaur v. State of Punjab

4. When there is a conflict between Fundamental Rights as declared by Part-II and the Directive Principles of State Policy (Part-IV), which will prevail___

(A) Directive Principles
(B) Fundamental Rights
(C) Both (A) and (B)
(D) Either (A) nor (B)

5. ___ of the Indian Constitution lays down that Union of India and the States are juristic persons and can sue and be sued.

(A) Article 225
(B) Article 285
(C) Article 300
(D) Article 348

6. In which of the following Cases the Supreme Court held that capitation fee is unconstitutional?

(A) St. Stephens College v. State
(B) Indra Sawhney v. Union of India
(C) Mohini Jain v. State
(D) None of these

7. In which of the following cases the Supreme Court held that right to shelter is a part of fundamental right guaranteed under Article 21 of the Constitution of India?

(A) Olga Tellis Case
(B) Sheela Barse Case
(C) Sarala Mudgal Case
(D) None of these

8. When a writ is issued to an inferior court or tribunal on ground of exceeding the jurisdiction or acting contrary to the rules of natural justice, it is called a writ of___

(A) Certiorari
(B) Mandamus
(C) Quo Warranto
(D) Habeas corpus

9. We borrowed the Concept of Fundamental Duties from the___

(A) American Constitution
(B) Irish Constitution
(C) Canadian Constitution
(D) USSR Constitution

10. Which of the following Articles of the Constitution of India guarantees Right of minorities to establish and administer educational institutions?

(A) Article 28
(B) Article 29
(C) Article 27
(D) Article 30

11. An ex parte decree can be set aside on the ground that___

(A) Summons were not duly served
(B) Non-appearance of defendant as copies of documents filed with plaint were not provided to defendant
(C) Defendant refused to receive the summons and thereafter no fresh summons were issued to him
(D) An ex parte decree cannot be set aside under any circumstance

12. In which of the following cases, the Code of Civil Procedure, 1908 provides for passing a preliminary decree?

(A) Suits for dissolution of partnership
(B) Suit for accounts between principal and agent
(C) Suits partition and separate possession
(D) All of these

13. In deciding the question of jurisdiction one must always have regard to the___

(A) Form of the suit
(B) Substance of the matter
(C) Status of parties
(D) None of these

14. In a suit where doctrine of res judicata is applicable, the suit is liable to be___

(A) Dismissed
(B) Rejected
(C) Stayed
(D) None of these

15. X residing in Delhi publishes statements defamatory of Y in Calcutta. Y can sue X at___

(A) Delhi
(B) Calcutta
(C) Either in Delhi or in Calcutta
(D) At any court at the option of the plaintiff

16. Which of the following Sections of the Code of Civil Procedure, 1908 deals with the place of suing regarding movable property?

(A) Section 17
(B) Section 18
(C) Section 19
(D) Section 20

17. In order to claim set off, which of the following conditions must be satisfied?

(A) Suit must be for recovery of money and the sum must be ascertained
(B) Sum must not exceed the pecuniary jurisdiction of the court
(C) Sum must be legally recoverable by defendant from plaintiff
(D) All of these

18. The court passes an ex parte decree against A. A files another suit alleging that the decree is obtained by the plaintiff by fraud. The suit is___

(A) Maintainable
(B) Not maintainable
(C) Depends
(D) None of these

19. A second appeal under Section 100 of the Code of Civil Procedure lies___

(A) On question of facts
(B) On substantial question in law
(C) On mixed questions of law and fact
(D) All of these

20. A suit for the partition of immovable property, shall be instituted in the court within the local limits of whose jurisdiction the___

(A) Property is situated
(B) Plaintiff resided
(C) Defendant resided
(D) Any of these

21. The procedure for serving the summons is provided in ___ of the Code of Criminal Procedure, 1973.

(A) Section 59
(B) Section 60
(C) Section 61
(D) Section 62

22. X a married man had illicit relations with Y and a child was born from that relationship. Later X deserted Y. Y filed an application for maintenance to her and her child from X. Decide___

(A) Y and her child are entitled to maintenance from X
(B) Y and her child are not entitled to maintenance from X
(C) Y is not entitled but her child is entitled to maintenance from X
(D) None of these

23. An order under Section 144 of the Code of Criminal Procedure, 1973___

(A) May be passed ex-parte
(9) Cannot be passed ex-parte
(C) Can be passed only after an inquiry
(D) None of these

24. The Supreme Court upheld the constitutional validity of Section 151 of the Code of Criminal Procedure, 1973 in___

(A) Joginder Kumar v. State of Uttar Pradesh
(B) M. C. Abraham v. State of Maharashtra
(C) D. K. Basu v. State of West Bengal
(D) Ahmed Noormohammed v. State

25. Which of the following powers is not available to a Police Officer who receives an order from the magistrate to investigate a non-cognizable offence?

(A) Power to search
(B) Power to seize
(C) Power to arrest
(D) None of these

26. Which of the following Sections of the Code of Criminal Procedure, 1973 deals with the 'examination of witnesses by police'?

(A) Section 159
(B) Section 160
(C) Section 161
(D) Section 165

27. Which of the following Sections of the Code of Criminal Procedure, 1973 deals with medical examination of the victim of rape?

(A) Section 163A
(B) Section 164A
(C) Section 165A
(D) Section 166A

28. Who among the following may file an application for plea bargaining?

(A) Accused
(B) Complainant
(C) Prosecutor
(D) None of these

29. Which of the following Sections of the Code of Criminal Procedure deals with 'set-off'?

(A) Section 428
(B) Section 429
(C) Section 430
(D) Section 431

30. In which of the following cases, the Supreme Court held that mere rejection of anticipatory bail applications cannot be a ground for arrest?

(A) M.C. Abrahan v. State
(B) State v. Ramakrishna
(C) Nirmal Jeet v. State
(D) None of these

31. Under Section 3 of the Indian Evidence Act, fact in issue means___

(A) Fact, existence or non-existence of which is not disputed by the parties
(B) Fact, existence or non-existence of which is disputed by the parties
(C) Fact, existence or non-existence of which is admitted by the parties
(D) All of these

32. A court can treat a presumption as tantamount to proof when the presumption is___

(A) Rebutted
(9) Dispelled
(C) Not rebutted
(D) None of these

33. In a trial for the murder of B, by A, which of these facts is not relevant?

(A) A was absconding immediately after the murder of B
(B) A and B were seen together before murder
(C) A had borrowed Rs. 50,000 from B
(D) A was in Bombay on that day, while the murder of B was committed in Chennai

34. When the court has to form an opinion as to the digital signature of any person, the opinion of the certifying authority which has issued a digital signature certificate is___

(A) Relevant
(B) Irrelevant
(C) Inadmissible
(D) None of these

35. Res gestae is an exception to the___

(A) Relevancy Rule
(B) Hearsay Rule
(C) Circumstantial evidence I
(D) None of these

36. A statement made by an accused to the police is___

(A) Not at all admissible whether it is a confession or an admission
(B) Admissible if it is not a confession and it is not during the course of investigation
(C) Admissible if it is a voluntary confession
(D) None of these

37. Presumption as to genuineness of certified copies is contained in ___ of the Indian Evidence Act.

(A) Section 78
(B) Section 79
(C) Section 80
(D) Section 81

38. A, accused of murder, alleges that, by reason of unsoundness of mind, he did not know the nature of the act. The burden of proof is on ___.

(A) The prosecution
(B) The accused
(C) The Police

(D) None of these

39. A preliminary examination before the chief examination is suggested in the case of ___.

(A) Defence witnesses
(B) Expert witnesses
(C) Child witnesses
(D) None of these

40. A leading question, without the permission of the court, may be asked during ___.

(A) Examination-in-chief
(B) At any time
(C) Cross examination
(D) None of these

41. The principle of criminal liability 'Actus non facit reum nisi mens sit rea' means___

(A) The act alone does not amount to guilt; it must be accompanied by a guilty mind
(B) Mens rea alone is punishable unless followed by actus reus
(C) Actus reus without mens rea is punishable
(D) None of these

42. A intending to kill B, shoots at B but only wounds him very slightly. On his being taken, to the hospital the ambulance collided with a bus and B was killed. Here___

(A) A is liable for murder since he intended so
(B) A is not liable for murder since the result is too remote and accidental in its occurrence
(C) This covers the general exceptions
(D) None of these

43. Which of the following offence is punishable with death?

(A) Section 305
(B) Section 364A
(C) Section 396
(D) All of these

44. For which of the following offence, common object is not an essential ingredient?

(A) Rioting
(B) Affray
(C) Unlawful Assembly
(D) None of these

45. Mr. A, a candidate for Andhra Pradesh Assembly Elections distributes mobile phones to some voters and requesting their vote in return. Mr. A has committed offence under which of the following Section?

(A) Section 171A
(B) Section 171B
(C) Section 172A
(D) Section 172B

46. A doctor registered as a medical practitioner and entitled to practice in Homoeopathy only, prescribed an allopathic medicine to the patient. The patient died. The doctor is guilty of___

(A) Death by rash and negligent act
(B) Murder
(C) Culpable homicide not amounting to murder
(D) None of these

47. Attempt to commit suicide is___

(A) Not an offence
(B) Punishable under Section 309 of Indian Penal Code
(C) Punishable under Section 306 of Indian Penal Code
(D) None of these

48. A, a police officer, tortures Z in order to induce Z to confess, that he committed a crime. A is guilty of an offence under the provisions of Section ___ of the Indian Penal Code.

(A) 331
(B) 332
(C) 330
(D) 333

49. Whoever does any act so rashly or negligently as to endanger human life or the personal safety of others, shall be punished under of the Indian Penal Code.

(A) Section 336
(B) Section 337
(C) Section 338
(D) Section 339

50. Under IPC exhibition of an object with intent to insult the modesty of the woman is an offence under Section___

(A) 353
(B) 294
(C) 509
(D) 293

51. Which of the following Sections of the Limitation Act, 1963 deals with the effect of

death on or before the accrual of the right to sue?

(A) Section 13
(B) Section 14
(C) Section 15
(D) Section 16

52. Which of the following Sections of the Limitation Act, 1963 deals with acquisition of easement by prescription?

(A) Section 25
(B) Section 26
(C) Section 27
(D) Section 28

53. Section 27 of the Limitation Act, 1963 provides that on the expiry of the period of limitation for filing a suit for possession___

(A) The right itself gets extinguished
(B) Remedy is barred
(C) Expiry of period
(D) None of these

54. The period of limitation for a suit for an account and a share of the profits of dissolved partnership is___

(A) One year
(B) Two years
(C) Three years
(D) Four years

55. The period of limitation for a suit by a mortgagor to redeem or recover, possession of immovable property mortgaged is___

(A) Thirty years
(B) Two years
(C) Three years
(D) Twelve years

56. The period of limitation for filing an application to the Supreme Court for special leave to appeal, in a case where leave to appeal was refused by the High Court is___

(A) 30 days
(B) 60 days
(C) 90 days
(D) One year

57. Which of the following Sections of the Limitation Act, 1963 mandates that every suit instituted, appeal preferred, and application made after the prescribed period shall be dismissed although limitation has not been set up as defense?

(A) Section 2
(B) Section 3
(C) Section 4
(D) Section 5

58. What is the period of limitation for a suit on a promissory note or bond payable by instalment?

(A) Three years
(B) Five years
(D) Ten years

(q) Six months

59. The notice of dishonour of cheque is served on the drawer on 29.05.1995. The period at 15 days expired on 14.06.1995. Complaint is filed on 15.11.1995.

(A) Complaint is within time
(B) Complaint is barred by limitation

(e) Notice of dishonour not valid
(D) None of these

60. Dismissal of a civil appeal a time barred is___

(A) A decree
(B) Not a decree
(C) Summons
(D) None of these

61. Accumulation of income can be directed under Section 17 for a period not longer than___

(A) The life time of transferor
(B) A period of 12 years

(q) A period of 20 years
(D) The life time of transferor or a period of 18 years from the date of transfer

62. Feeding the grant by estoppel comes into operation when the transfer is made ___.

(A) Fraudulently or erroneously
(B) Under the coercion
(C) Under the mistaken impression that the transferor is authorized
(D) After the transferee acted in good faith

63. The condition restraining absolute alienation is not void when it is___

(A) For the benefit of the lessor
(B) For the benefit of the legal heir
(C) For the benefit of the lessee
(D) None of these

64. Lis pendens is not applicable to suit or proceedings which is___

(A) Ex-parte
(B) Collusive
(C) Pending service of notice
(D) In execution

65. Where the mortgagor ostensibly sells the mortgaged property, the transaction is called___

(A) Anomalous mortgage
(B) Mortgage by deposit of the title deeds
(C) English mortgage
(D) None of these

66. The right of a mortgagee to institute a suit for foreclosure is not available when___

(A) The mortgaged property is under lease
(B) The mortgaged property is alienated
(C) A decree has been made for the redemption of the mortgaged property
(D) All of these

67. Mortgaged property can be sold without the intervention of court only in the case of___

(A) Simple mortgage
(B) Anomalous mortgage
(C) English mortgage
(D) Mortgage by deposit of title deeds

68. Where the tenant continues to remain in possession even after the expiry of notice to quit, he is treated as___

(A) A trespasser
(B) Tenant at will
(C) Tenant at sufferance
(D) None of these

69. The following among is not an actionable claim___

(A) Claim for arrears of rent
(B) Share in a partnership
(C) Claim for unpaid dower of a Muslim woman
(D) A decree of a Civil Court

70. 'Donatio mortis causa mean'___

(A) Gift made by a person on his death
(B) Gift to a dying person
(C) Gifts which are made in contemplation of death
(D) None of these

71. A person who is not a party to a contract but has some interest in the consideration of that contract___

(A) Can enforce that contract subject to certain exceptions
(B) Can enforce that contract
(C) Cannot enforce that contract
(D) None of these

72. Forbearance to sue the promisor in return for a promise made by the promisor___.

(A) Always serves as good consideration
(B) Does not serve as good consideration at all
(C) Serves as good consideration if it is induced by coercion
(D) Serve as good consideration only when it is induced by the request of the promisor

73. The communication of acceptance is complete as against the proposer___

(A) When it is put in the course of transmission so as to be out of the power of the acceptor
(B) When it comes to the knowledge of the proposer
(C) When the acceptance is communicated
(D) None of these

74. 'Threatening to commit certain acts forbidden by Indian Penal Code' is associated with which one of the following?

(A) Misrepresentation
(B) Fraud
(D) Coercion
(D) Mistake

75. When one party's consent has been caused as a result of mistake of law, the contract is___

(A) Voidable
(B) Valid
(C) Unenforceable
(D) Unlawful

76. A 'contingent contract' is a contract___

(A) To do something, if some event, collateral to such contract does happen
(B) To do something, if some event, does happen
(C) To do or not to do something, if some event collateral to such contract, does or does not, happen
(D) Not to do something, if some event, collateral to such contract does or does not happen

77. A, B and C jointly promise to pay Rs. 6,000 to X. X files a suit against A to recover the amount___

(A) X can sue A for the recovery of Rs. 2,000 only
(B) X must sue B for Rs. 2,000
(C) X can recover the amount from anyone of them
(D) None of these

78. A owes B Rs. 3,000, C pays to B Rs. 2.000 and B accepts it in satisfaction of his claim against A. This payment ___.

(A) Is not a discharge of the whole claim
(B) Is a discharge of the entire claim
(C) Can be a discharge only when the balance is paid
(D) Will be a discharge only if the amount is paid by A

79. For the acts of sub-agent, lawfully appointed___

(A) The sub-agent is not responsible to the principal
(B) The sub-agent is responsible to the principal directly
(C) The agent is responsible to the principal
(D) The agent is not responsible to the principal

80. B owes to C a debt guaranteed by A. The debt becomes payable. C does not sue 'B' for a year after the debt has become payable___

(A) A is discharged from suretyship
(B) A is not discharged from suretyship
(C) C cannot recover from B
(D) None of these

81. A male member of a joint family and his sons, grandsons and great grandsons constitute a___

(A) Cognate
(B) Coparcenary
(C) Agnate
(D) None of these

82. A male Hindu dies leaving behind his father, mother, one adopted son, three daughters and two natural born sons. He has left behind him a self acquired property. The distribution of the property along the heirs will be between the ___.

(A) Father, mother, adopted son, three daughters and two natural born sons

(B) Mother, adopted son, three daughters and two natural born sons
(C) Father, adopted son, three daughters and two natural born sons
(D) Mother, three daughters and two natural born sons

83. Who among the following is not a Class-1 heir?

(A) Brother
(B) Daughter of a pre-deceased daughter
(C) Daughter of a pre-deceased son
(D) Son of a pre-deceased son

84. Which of the following Sections of the Hindu Succession Act, 1956 mandates that property of a female Hindu is to be her absolute property?

(A) Section 14
(B) Section 15
(C) Section 16
(D) Section 17

85. Under the Hindu Succession Act, the property of a male Hindu dying intestate shall devolve according to the provisions of___

(A) Section 8
(B) Section 9
(C) Section 14
(D) Section 6

86. Which Section of the following of the Indian Succession Act, 1925 treats agnates and cognates and male and female heirs equally?

(A) Section 26
(B) Section 27
(C) Section 32
(D) Section 33A

87. A Holograph Will is a will written by the___

(A) Coparcener
(B) Advocate
(C) Testator
(D) Successor

88. A legacy is bequeathed to A and in case of his death to B. If A survives the testator, the legacy to B___

(A) Becomes vested
(B) Does not take effect
(C) Takes effect
(D) Representatives of A takes

89. A copy of the will certified under the seal of the court with a grant of administration to the estate of the testator is known as___

(A) Letter of Administration
(B) Executor
(C) Probate
(D) Privileged will

90. In which Section of the following of the Indian Succession Act, 1925 it is provided that where a bequest is made to a person by a particular description, and there is no person in existence at the testator's death who answers the description, the bequest is void under___

(A) Section 111
(B) Section 112
(C) Section 114
(D) Section 116

91. A suit for possession of an immovable property, under Section 6 of the Specific Relief Act can be filed within ___ of dispossession.

(A) 12 years
(B) 3 years
(C) 1 year
(D) 6 months

92. Which of the following Sections of the Specific Relief Act deals with recovery of specific movable property?

(A) Section 7
(B) Section 8
(C) Section 9
(D) Section 10

93. An authoritative pronouncement by the court in respect of a person's right to property or his status is called___

(A) Rescission
(B) Rectification
(C) Declaration
(D) None of these

94. Section 34 of the Specific Relief Act deals with___

(A) Mere declaration of rights of the parties
(B) Declaration of rights of the parties with or without an award of compensation
(C) Specific performance with declaration of rights of the parties
(D) None of these

95. An order of the court to a party to the proceedings to do or not to do a specified act is called___

(A) Declaration
(B) Rescission
(C) Injunction
(D) None of these

96. Which of the following injunctions is always without any time limits?

(A) Temporary injunction
(B) Mandatory injunction
(C) Perpetual injunction
(D) None of these

97. The principia of qua timet means___

(A) Some past injury to the rights or interests of a person
(B) Some future probable injury to rights or interests of a person
(C) Some past injury to the rights or interests of a person
(D) Some small injury capable of being estimated in money

98. Can the court award compensation in a case where specific performance is impossible?

(A) Yes
(B) No

(G) Impossible
(D) None of these

99. Which of the following can be rectified?

(A) A mistake in the transaction itself
(B) A mistake in the way in which that transaction has been expressed in writing
(C) When there is breach
(D) None of these

100. Under Section 12(2) of the Specific Relief Act, 1963, part performance of a contract can be enforced by___

(A) The promisee
(B) The promisor

(G) Either the promisee or the promisor
(D) Only the promisee and not the promisor

ANSWERS

1	D	31	B	61	D	91	D
2	C	32	C	62	A	92	A
3	B	33	C	63	A	93	C
4	B	34	A	64	B	94	A
5	C	35	B	65	D	95	C
6	C	36	B	66	C	96	C
7	A	37	B	67	C	97	B
8	A	38	B	68	C	98	A
9	D	39	C	69	D	99	B
10	D	40	C	70	C	100	B
11	A	41	A	71	C		
12	D	42	B	72	A		
13	B	43	D	73	A		
14	A	44	B	74	C		
15	C	45	B	75	B		
16	C	46	A	76	C		
17	D	47	B	77	C		
18	A	48	C	78	B		
19	B	49	A	79	C		
20	A	50	C	80	B		
21	D	51	D	81	B		
22	C	52	A	82	B		
23	A	53	A	83	A		
24	D	54	C	84	A		
25	C	55	A	85	A		
26	C	56	B	86	B		
27	B	57	B	87	C		
28	A	58	A	88	B		
29	A	59	A	89	C		
30	A	60	B	90	B		

2019-2020

1. Who among the following was the Special Public Prosecutor in the Disproportionate Assets Case in which Tamil Nadu Chief Minister Jayalalithaa was convicted for four years?

(A) Anand Grover
(B) Bhavani Singh
(C) Siddarth Luthra
(D) None of them

2. Government of India Act, 1935 was a lengthy document consists of 321 Sections and 10 Schedules. The statement is ___.

(A) True
(B) False
(C) Partly correct
(D) None of these

3. How many times has the Preamble to the Constitution of India amended?

(A) Once
(B) Twice
(C) Thrice
(D) None

4. The First Session of the Constituent Assembly was held at ___.

(A) Delhi
(B) Bombay
(C) Calcutta
(D) None of these

5. Which of the following Articles of the Constitution of India guarantees freedom to manage (*sic) religious affairs?

(A) Article 25
(B) Article 26
(C) Article 27
(D) Article 28

6. Which one of the following Articles about Fundamental Rights is directly related to the exploitation of Children?

(A) Article 18
(B) Article 19
(C) Article 22
(D) Article 24

7. Which of the following Articles was/were amended to rectify the effect of Golaknath's judgement?

(A) Article 13
(B) Article 368
(C) Article 31
(D) Both (A) and (B)

8. How many items are there in the Ninth Schedule when it was introduced?

(A) 8
(B) 9
(C) 10
(D) 12

9. Which of the following cases upheld the right against solitary confinement?

(A) Sunil Batra Case
(B) Ramesh Thapar Case
(C) Prem Shanker Shukla Case
(D) None of these

10. Is Judicial Review a part of basic structure of Indian Constitution?

(A) Yes
(B) No
(C) Depends
(D) None of these

11. "Decree" has been defined in Section ___ of the Code of Civil Procedure.

(A) Section 1(1)
(B) Section 1(2)
(C) Section 2(1)
(D) Section 2(2)

12. In the case of inconsistency between Sections and the Rules, ___ shall prevail.

(A) Sections
(B) Rules
(C) Orders
(D) None of these

13. The body of the Code of Civil Procedure containing Sections can be amended by___.

(A) The Supreme Court
(B) The High Courts
(C) The Parliament
(D) None of these

14. Civil Proceedings instituted by Presentation of Plaint is called ___.

(A) Suit
(B) Caveat
(C) Application
(D) None of these

15. Can a Civil Court pass more than one

orders in suit?

(A) Yes
(B) No
(C) Never
(D) None of these

16. The first uniform Code of Civil Procedure was enacted in the year___.

(A) 1908
(B) 1859
(C) 1882
(D) 1872

17. The substantive part of the Code of Civil Procedure is contained in___.

(A) Sections
(B) Rules
(C) Orders
(D) None of these

18. Is it necessary to state the amount of costs incurred in the suit?

(A) Yes
(B) No
(C) Depends
(D) None of these

19. Can the Court issue commissions for examination of a person in prison?

(A) Yes
(B) No
(C) Never
(D) Depends

20. Is it necessary for the Court to pronounce the judgement in all issues?

(A) Yes
(B) No
(C) Never
(D) None of these

21. Section 2(g) of the Code of Criminal Procedure 1973 defines___.

(A) Enquiry
(B) Inquiry
(C) Investigation
(D) None of these

22. In a Warrant case instituted on police report, the trial begins when the___.

(A) Accused appears
(B) Charge is framed
(C) Witnesses are examined
(D) None of these

23 An illegality in the investigation___.

(A) Vitiate the trial
(B) Does not vitiate the trial in any case
(C) Does not vitiate the trial unless miscarriage of justice has been caused
(D) None of these

24. Identification of arrested persons can be ordered by the Court on the request of the___.

(A) Complainant
(B) Arrested person or his nominee
(C) Officer-in-charge of a Police Station
(D) None of them

25. Every Summons shall be served by___.

(A) Public Servant
(B) Police Officer
(C) Officer of the Court
(D) Any one of them

26. A warrant may be directed to any person for the arrest of___.

(A) Any escaped convict
(B) A proclaimed offender
(C) Any person who is accused of a non-bailable offence and is evading arrest
(D) All of them

27. Can the evidence of witnesses be taken on oath by the Magistrate conducting an enquiry?

(A) Yes
(B) No
(C) Depends
(D) None of these

28. Any Court may alter or add to any charge at any time before the___.

(A) Evidence is closed
(B) Evidence is started
(C) Judgement is pronounced
(D) None of these

29. What is the maximum sentence of imprisonment which can be imposed for an offence tried as Summary Trial?

(A) Six months
(B) One year
(C) Two years
(D) Three months

30. Can a witness refuse to sign the deposition if it is not read over to him?

(A) Yes
(B) No
(C) Depends
(D) None of these

31. Which of the following types of evidence means "testimony"?

(A) Direct Evidence
(B) Circumstantial Evidence
(C) Both (A) and (B)
(D) None of these

32. Who drafted the Indian Evidence Act, 1872?

(A) Lord Denning
(B) A.V. Dicey
(C) Lord Macaulay
(D) J. F. Stephen

33. The Indian Evidence Act, 1872 does not mention___.

(A) Relevancy of Evidence
(B) Admissible Evidence
(C) Weight of Evidence
(D) All of these

34. The word 'relevant' is derived from the Latin term "relevare" which means___.

(A) Important
(B) Legally pertinent
(C) Significant
(D) None of these

35. Which of the following is not a Public document?

(A) Order of a competent authority fixing price of commodities
(B) An order issuing a search warrant
(C) A crop cutting report by a Collector
(D) Plaint on written statement in a suit

36. Relevancy is a ___.

(A) Question of fact
(B) Question of law
(C) Mixed question of fact and law
(D) None of these

37. Res gestae is an exception to the ___.

(A) Relevancy Rule
(B) Hearsay Rule
(C) Circumstantial Evidence
(D) None of these

38. Proof of a fact depends upon___.

(A) Accuracy of Statements
(B) Probability of it having existed
(C) Both (A) and (B)
(D) None of these

39. When one is unable to decide how the fact stands precisely, it can be termed as___.

(A) Proved
(B) Disproved
(C) Not proved
(D) None of these

40. The maxim falsus in uno, falsus in Omnibus is ___.

(A) A sound rule of law
(B) A sound rule of evidence
(C) Both (A) and (B)
(D) None of these

41. The principle of criminal liability "Actus non facit reum nisi means sit rea" is of origin of___.

(A) India
(B) Mohammedan Criminal law
(C) Common law
(D) None of these

42. Which of the following is not a sine qua non for making a person criminally liable?

(A) Mens rea
(B) Actus-rea
(C) Motive
(D) All of these

43. Which of the following is an inchoate offence?

(A) Attempt
(B) Abetment
(C) Criminal conspiracy.
(D) All of these

44. Which of the following Sections of the Indian Penal Code is added by the Information Technology Act, 2000?

(A) Section 28A
(B) Section 29A
(C) Section 27A
(D) Section 30A

45. Loss by unlawful means of property to which the person losing it is legally entitled___.

(A) Dishonest loss

(B) Wrongful loss
(C) Unlawful loss
(D) None of these

46. The word "electronic record" shall have the same meaning assigned to them is in the___.

(A) General Clauses Act
(B) Information Technology Act
(C) Right to Information Act
(D) Indian Evidence Act

47. No Court shall take cognizance of the offence punishable under Sec. 153A, except with the previous sanction of the___.

(A) Central Government
(B) State Government
(C) Either (A) or (B)
(D) District Magistrate

48. In a prosecution of an offence of criminal conspiracy the onus of proof is on___.

(A) Prosecution
(B) Accused
(C) Depends
(D) None of these

49. Which of the following is not a punishment provided under Indian Penal Code?

(A) Forfeiture of property
(B) Imprisonment with hard labour
(C) Transportation for life
(D) Death

50. Which of the following theory recognizes the principles of "eye for eye" and "tooth for tooth"?

(A) Deterrent theory
(B) Retribution theory
(C) Reformative theory
(D) None of these

51. Which of the following Sections of the Limitation Act, 1963 gives an inclusive definition of "easement"?
(A) 2(c)
(B) 2(f)
(C) 2(g)
(D) 2(h)

52. Which of the following Sections of Limitation Act, 1963 defines "Period of Limitation"?

(A) 2(i)
(B) 2(f)

(C) 2(k)
(D) 2(c)

53. Expiry of period of limitation___.

(A) Extinguishes the debt
(B) Renders the debts unenforceable
(C) Extinguishes the debt and renders it unenforceable
(D) None of these

54. As defined in Section 2(i) of the Limitation Act, 1963, 'suit' includes___.

(A) An appeal
(B) Application
(C) Both (A) and (B)
(D) Neither (A) nor (B)

55. An order made on an application filed beyond the period of limitation is___.

(A) Illegal
(B) Without jurisdiction
(C) Irregular
(D) None of these

56. In a suit for recovery of possession of a house from a deemed trustee of waqf property___.

(A) No limitation applies
(B) Limitation is applicable
(C) Depends
(D) None of these

57. Limitation runs from the___.

(A) Date the plaint is returned
(B) Date of order by which plaint is directed to be returned
(C) Depends
(D) None of these

58. Which of the following Sections of the Limitation Act, 1963 deals with acquisition of easement by prescription?

(A) 25
(B) 26
(C) 27
(D) 28

59. The period of limitation for a suit for an account and a share of the profits of dissolved partnership is ___.

(A) One year
(B) Two years
(C) Three years
(D) Five years

60. The period of Limitation for the suits relating to decrees and instruments is___.

(A) One year
(B) Two years
(C) Three years
(D) Five years

61. Inter Vivos means and includes___.

(A) Only living persons
(B) Living as well as dead person
(C) Living as well as juristic persons
(D) None of these

62. As per Section 13 of the Transfer o Property Act, 1882, a transfer of property is valid in the case of an unborn person if the interest therein is created for___.

(A) Enjoyment
(B) Possession
(C) The benefit
(D) All of these

63. "Subrogation" is a Roman word which means___.

(A) Surrender
(B) Exhaustion
(C) Substitution
(D) Alteration

64. Contribution to Mortgage debt in the Transfer of Property Act, 1882 comes under___.

(A) Section 82
(B) Section 83
(C) Section 82A
(D) None of these

65. The definition of actionable claims was substituted by the amendment in which year?

(A) 2002
(B) 1929
(C) 1900
(D) None of these

66. To make the assignment of actionable claims perfect notice to the debtor is___.

(A) Necessary by the transferor
(B) Necessary by the transferee
(C) Necessary by both the parties
(D) Not necessary

67. Right derived to a mortgagee to obtain a decree for foreclosure in the event when the mortgage money___.

(A) Is outstanding
(B) Is defaulted
(C) Becomes payable
(D) Becomes due

68. Pendency of suit for the purpose of Section 52 commences from the date on which___.

(A) Plaint presented
(B) Summons issued
(C) Suit admitted
(D) None of these

69. Doctrine of Holding out is related to___.

(A) Transfer by an ostensible owner
(B) Election
(C) Feeding the grant by Estoppels
(D) None of these

70. Doctrine of Election is explained in the Transfer of Property Act, 1882 in___.

(A) Section 35
(B) Section 36
(C) Section 34
(D) None of these

71. The Indian Contract Act, 1872 is not exhaustive. The statement is___.

(A) True
(B) False
(C) Partly correct
(D) None of these

72. The popular case Askari Mirza vs Jaikishori relates to___.

(A) Fraud
(B) Undue Influence
(C) Coercion
(D) Mistake

73. Which of the following right(s) is/ are not available to the agent?

(A) Right to sell
(B) Right to compensation
(C) Right to retain
(D) All of these

74. A guarantee obtained by means of keeping silence as to material circumstances is___.

(A) Valid
(B) Void
(C) Invalid

(D) Voidable

75. Which one is not a remedy for breach of contract?

(A) Damages
(B) Injunction
(C) Fine
(D) Specific performance

76. Quasi-contracts are dealt with in___.

(A) Section 62
(B) Sect on 63-68
(C) Section 68-72
(D) Section 72-75

77. Promissory estoppel is sometimes spoken of as a substitute for___.

(A) Novation
(B) Quasi-contract
(C) Consideration
(D) Coercion

78. The leading case Balfour vs Balfour relates to___.

(A) Capacity of parties
(B) Acceptance of offer
(C) Communication
(D) Intention to contract

79. An agency is terminated___.

(A) By the principal revoking the authority
(B) By the agent renouncing the business of agency
(C) By either the principal or agent dying for becoming of unsnap mind
(D) All of these

80. Which of the following Sections of Indian Contract Act, 1872 deals with bailee's particular lien?

(A) 167
(B) 168
(C) 169
(D) 170

81. Which of the following Sections of the Hindu Succession Act, 1956, deals with the properties to which the Act is not applicable?

(A) Section 5
(B) Section 6
(C) Section 7
(D) Section 8

82. Legacy means___.

(A) A gift of property by way of will
(B) A gift of property by way of gift deed
(C) A gift of movable property
(D) A gift of immovable property

83. By the Amendment Act of 2005, Section 6 of the Hindu Succession Act was___.

(A) Amended
(B) Substituted
(C) Repealed
(D) None of these

84. In order to attract Section 14 of the Hindu Succession Act, 1956, the possession of property may be___.

(A) Actual Possession
(B) Symbolic Possession
(C) Constructive Possession
(D) Any of these

85. According to Section 10 of the Hindu Succession Act, 1956, the intestate's widow shall take ___ share.

(A) 1
(B) 2
(C) 3
(D) 4

86. Coparcenary is a narrower body, then joint family. The statement is___.

(A) True
(B) False
(C) Partly correct
(D) None of these

87. General rules of Succession in the case Succession of Female Hindus are dealt with under ___.

(A) Section 16
(B) Section 20
(C) Section 21
(D) Section 15

88. "Life estate granted to a Hindu Woman by a will also becomes her absolute estate". The statement is___.

(A) True
(B) False
(C) Partly correct
(D) None of these

89. When two persons are related by blood or adoption, wholly through males, it is called ___.

(A) Cognate
(B) Agnate
(C) Both (A) and (B)
(D) Coparcener

90. The property mentioned in Section 14 of Hindu Succession Act, 1956, does not include the Stridhana property. The statement is___.

(A) True
(B) False
(C) Partly correct
(D) None of these

91. Specific Relief is a form of judicial redress. This statement is___.

(A) True
(B) False
(C) Partly correct
(D) None of these

92. The remedy of a person unsuccessful in a suit under Section 6 of the Specific Relief Act, 1963 is to file ___.

(A) Appeal
(B) Revision
(C) Review
(D) A regular suit establishing his title to the suit property

93. Section 36 of the Specific Relief Act, 1963 classifies injunction into ___ categories.

(A) Two
(B) Three
(C) Four
(D) Five

94. Which of the following Sections of the Specific Relief Act, 1963 deals with the effect of declaration?

(A) Section 36
(B) Section 37
(C) Section 38
(D) Section 35

95. Which of the following is termed as the Converse of Specific Performance?

(A) Rectification
(B) Rescission
(C) Both (A) and (B)
(D) None of these

96. Can the Court award compensation in a case where Specific Performance is impossible?

(A) Yes
(B) No
(C) Depends
(D) None of these

97. Which of the following Sections of the Specific Relief Act, 1963 deals with the power of the Court to award compensation?

(A) Section 19
(B) Section 20
(C) Section 21
(D) Section 22

98. The Specific Relief Act, 1963 grants ___.

(A) Specific Relief only
(B) Preventive Reliefs
(C) Both (A) and (B)
(D) None of these

99. Which of the following remedies is provided by the Specific Relief Act, 1963 regarding contracts?

(A) Damages
(B) Specific Performance
(C) Both (A) and (B)
(D) None of these

100. The Specific Relief Act was a result of the ___.

(A) 10th Law Commission
(B) 11th Law Commission
(C) 9th Law Commission
(D) 8th Law Commission

ANSWERS

1	B	31	A	61	C	91	A
2	A	32	D	62	C	92	D
3	A	33	C	63	C	93	A
4	A	34	B	64	A	94	D
5	X	35	D	65	C	95	B
6	D	36	B	66	D	96	A
7	D	37	B	67	D	97	C
8	X	38	B	68	A	98	C
9	A	39	C	69	A	99	B
10	A	40	D	70	A	100	C
11	D	41	C	71	A		
12	A	42	C	72	C		
13	C	43	D	73	A		
14	A	44	B	74	C		

15	A	45	B	75	C
16	B	46	B	76	C
17	A	47	C	77	C
18	A	48	A	78	D
19	A	49	C	79	D
20	A	50	B	80	D
21	B	51	B	81	A
22	X	52	X	82	A
23	C	53	B	83	B
24	C	54	X	84	D
25	D	55	A	85	A
26	D	56	A	86	A
27	A	57	A	87	D
28	C	58	A	88	A
29	D	59	C	89	B
30	A	60	C	90	B

- 76 -

2021-2022

1. Consider the following statements:

Article 20 of the Constitution of India provides that ___.

(i) No person accused of any offence shall be compelled to be a witness against himself

(ii) No person shall be prosecuted for the same offence more than once

Of the above statements:

(A) Only (i) is true
(B) Only (ii) is true
(C) Both (i) and (ii) are true
(D) Both (i) and (ii) are false

2. The President of India may be removed from his office on which of the following ground/s?

(A) Proved misbehaviour
(B) Incapacity
(C) Both (A) and (B)
(D) Violation of the Constitution

3. In which case it was laid down that the "amendment in the Constitution is exercise of legislative function of the Parliament"?

(A) Shankari Prasad v. Union of India
(B) Golakh Nath v. State of Punjab
(C) Sajjan Singh v. State of Punjab
(D) Keshavanand Bharti v. State of Kerala

4. The power of Judicial Review in India is prossessed by:

(A) Supreme Court of India only
(B) All the High Courts only
(C) All the Courts in India
(D) Supreme Court as well as High Courts

5. Council of States can withhold Money Bill for a period of:

(A) 14 days
(B) One month
(C) Three months
(D) None of these

6. Which one of the following is the correct statement?

In deciding the question as to the disqualification of a Member of Parliament, the President shall act:

(A) According to the opinion of Election Commission
(B) According to the opinion of the Supreme Court
(C) With the aid and advice of the Council of Ministers
(D) In his own discretion

7. Which one of the following is not an essential condition for appointment as a judge of Supreme Court?

(A) A citizen of India
(B) At least five years' experience as judge of a High Court or of two or more such courts in succession
(C) Must have completed the age of 35 years
(D) At least ten years' experience as an advocate of a High Court or of two or more such courts in succession

8. Article 21 of the Constitution of India incorporates the right to "Doctor's assistance". In which of the following cases, this was decided?

(A) Indian Medical Council v. V. P. Shantha
(B) Sunil Batra v. Delhi Administration
(C) Parmanand Katara v. Union of India
(D) "X" v. "Z" Hospital

9. Find out the mismatched pair:

(A) S. C. Advocate - on - Record Association v. U. O. I. = Constitutionality of N. J. A. Commission
(B) Shreya Singhal v. U. O. I. = Recognition of unwed mother
(C) Shatrughan Chauhan v. U. O. I. Clemency Power of President
(D) National Legal Services Authority v. U. O. I. = Recognition of Third Gender

10. Which one of the following cases is related to doctrine of pith substance?

(A) Dr. Yash Pal v. State of Chhattisgarh
(B) Prafulla Kumar v. Bank of Commerce
(C) D. C. Wadhwa v. Sate of Bihar
(D) State of Bombay v. F. N. Balsara

11. Pleadings must be signed by:

(A) The party only
(B) The pleader only
(C) The party as well as pleader
(D) None of these

12. Under Section 3 of CPC, courts of small causes, are subordinate to which of the following:

(A) District Court only
(B) High Court only
(C) Both (A) and (B)
(D) Neither (A) nor (B)

13. Who amongst the following is not "a public officer" within the meaning of Section 2(17) of CPC?

(A) A Judge
(B) A municipal councilor
(C) A person in the service of Government for the performance of public duty
(D) An inspector of police

14. Which of the following provision is related with set-off under CPC?

(A) Order VIII Rule 5
(B) Order VIII Rule 6
(C) Order VII Rule 5
(D) Order VII Rule 6

15. The foreign judgement, subject to certain exceptions, is given binding character under:

(A) Section 12 of CPC
(B) Section 13 of CPC
(C) Section 14 CPC
(D) Section 15 CPC

16. Under which provision of the Code of Civil Procedure, 1908 the collector may be appointed as receiver?

(A) Order XL Rule 5
(B) Order XLI Rule 1
(C) Order XL Rule 2
(D) Order XLI Rule 5

17. Which one of the following is not a suit of civil nature?

(A) Suit for dissolution of marriage
(B) Suit for rights to hereditary office
(C) Suit for upholding mere dignity or honor
(D) Suit for specific relief

18. Find out the mismatched pair:

(A) Res judicata = Section 11, CPC
(B) Power of Supreme Court to transfer suits etc. = Section 24, CPC
(C) Compensatory costs in respect of false or vexatious claims or defenses = Section 35A, CPC
(D) Costs for causing delay = Section 35B, CPC

19. Find out the mismatched pair:

(A) Exemption of certain women from personal appearance = Section 132, CPC
(B) Prohibition of arrest of women in execution of decree for money = Section 57, CPC
(C) Right to lodge Caveat = Section 148A, CPC
(D) Language of the subordinate courts = Section 137, CPC

20. Which of the following provides for filing of suits by indigent persons:

(A) Order XXXII
(B) Order XXXIII
(C) Order XXII A
(D) None of these

21. The provision relating to health and safety of arrested person have been prescribed under which one of the following Sections of the Cr. P. C.?

(A) Section 50 A
(B) Section 53 A
(C) Section 55 A
(D) Section 60 A

22. Under Section 167 of the Cr. P. C., the magistrate can authorize detention for a total period of 90 days during investigation in cases of offences punishable:

(A) With death
(B) With imprisonment for life
(C) With imprisonment for a term not less than 10 years
(D) All of these

23. What does the expression "transit remand" denote?

(A) It is a transfer of prisoner from one jail to another
(B) It is a transfer of criminal case from one court to another
(C) It is taking out an accused by police from one state to another state
(D) It is taking out of the accused from court to prison

24. A police officer is duty bound to register case on receiving information of cognizable offence. Reliability of information is not condition precedent for registration. The above rule is incorporated in:

(A) Section 153 of Cr.P.C.
(B) Section 154 of Cr.P.C.
(C) Section 155 of Cr.P.C.
(D) Section 156 of Cr.P.C.

25. "All evidence in an inquiry or trial shall be taken in the presence of the accused." Which Section of the Cr. P. C. lays down the above rule?

(A) Section 273
(B) Section 274
(C) Section 275
(D) Section 276

26. Which one of the following offences, a Chief Judicial Magistrate, cannot try in a summary way?

(A) Theft, where the value of property does not exceed two thousand rupees
(B) Theft, where the value of the property stolen exceeds three thousand rupees evidence
(C) A complaint made under the Cattle Trespass Act
(D) Offences under Section 454 and 456 of the IPC

27. The power to grant anticipatory under Section 438 Cr. P. C. vests with:

(A) The Court of Magistrate
(B) Only in the Court of Sessions
(C) Only in the High Court
(D) Both the Court of Sessions and High Court

28. Which one of the following Sections of Cr. P. C., deals with High Courts power of revision?

(A) Section 395
(B) Section 401
(C) Section 399
(D) Section 396

29. D. K. Basu v. State of West Bengal (1997) Cr. L. J. 743 is the case dealing with.

(A) Arrest of persons
(B) Mode of taking and receiving
(C) Transfer of criminal cases
(D) None of these

30. Read the following statements:

(i) Provisions for Plea Bargaining are contained in Chapter XXIA of the Cr. P. C.

(ii) Chapter XXIA of the Cr. P. C. was added on the recommendation of Justice Verma Committee Report.

Of the above statements:

(A) (i) is true but (ii) is false
(B) (i) is false but (ii) is true

(C) Both (i) and (ii) are true
(D) Both (i) and (ii) are false

31. The case of R. M. Malkani v. State of Maharashtra is related to which of the following:

(A) Leading Question
(B) Accomplice
(C) Res gestae
(D) None of these

32. "Witnesses are the eyes and ears of Justice", who said so?

(A) Kant
(B) Bentham
(C) Pollock
(D) Ihering

33. Reliability of date of birth for the purpose of Indian Evidence Act is contained in:

(A) Section 33
(B) Section 34
(C) Section 35
(D) Section 36

34. Under Section 14 of the Evidence Act, which of the following facts becomes relevant, namely?

(A) Facts showing state of mind
(B) Facts showing state of body
(C) Facts showing state of bodily feelings
(D) All of these

35. Read the following statements:

(i) The term 'confession' is nowhere defined in the Evidence Act

(ii) Lord Atkin had clarified 'confession' in Pakla Narain Swami v. Emperor

(iii) The SC of India has accepted the definition given by Lord Atkin in Pawnder Kaur v. State of Punjab

Of the above statements:

(A) Only (i) and (ii) are true
(B) Only (ii) and (iii) are true
(C) Only (i) and (iii) are true
(D) All (i), (ii) and (iii) are true

36. Read the following statements:

(i) The presumption of Legitimacy of child is governed by S. 112 of the Evidence Act

(ii) Narendra Nath Pahari v. Ram Govind Pahari is a leading case on the legitimacy of a child born during the subsistence of valid marriage

Of the above statements:

(A) (i) is true but (ii) is false
(B) (i) is false but (ii) is false
(C) Both (i) and (ii) are true
(D) Both (i) and (ii) are false

37. Find out the odd one case:

(A) Pickard v. Sears
(B) Sarat Chunder Dey v. Gopal Chunder Dey
(C) Queen Empress v. Abdullah
(D) Sri Krishna v. Kurukshetra University

38. Assertion (A): 'A' is accused before the court of sessions of attempting to murder a police officer whilst on the trial before 'B', a session judge. 'B' may be examined as to what occurred.

Reason (R): A judge or Magistrate is a competent witness.

(A) Both (A) and (R) are true
(B) Both (A) and (R) are false
(C) (A) is true but (R) is false
(D) (A) is false but (R) is true

39. Point out the mismatched pair:

(A) Communication during marriage = Section 112
(B) Evidence as to affairs of state = Section 123
(C) Confidential communication with legal advisers = Section 128
(D) Evidence of an accomplice = Section 133

40. Which Section of Indian Evidence Act defines Leading Question:

(A) Section 138
(B) Section 139
(C) Section 140
(D) Section 141

41. Taking property dishonestly from the dead body:

(A) Does not amount b any offence under IPC
(B) Amounts to the offence of theft
(C) Amounts to the offence of criminal misappropriation
(D) Amounts to the offence of criminal breach of trust

42. In which one of the following cases did the Supreme Court explain the concept of grave and sudden provocation as a mitigating circumstance reducing the gravity of the offence from murder to culpable homicide not amounting to murder ?

(A) State v. Dasrath
(B) Jagroop Singh v. State of Haryana
(C) K. M. Nanavati v. State of Maharashtra
(D) Ujagar Singh v. Emperor

43. 'X' on receiving grave and sudden provocation from 'Z' intentionally causes the death of 'Y, who is brother of 'Z'. 'X' has committed the offence of:

(A) Murder
(B) Grievous hurt
(C) Culpable homicide not amounting to murder
(D) Attempt to murder

44. 'X' with a view to murdering 'Y' enters Y's bedroom at night when 'Y' is out of station. 'X' is guilty of:

(A) Murder
(B) House trespass
(C) Attempt to murder
(D) Not guilty

45. In which one of the following cases the SC of India has struck down S. 303 IPC as unconstitutional?

(A) Machhi Singh v. State of Punjab
(B) Gyan Kaurv. State of Punjab
(C) Mithu v. State of Punjab
(D) Santa Singh v. State of Punjab

46. The case of R. V. Dudley and Stephens is popular for its use as criminal defence of:

(A) Necessity of the treasure
(B) Self-defense
(C) Good-faith
(D) Mistake of fact

47. Which one of the following statements is correct?

In Sedition:

(A) The consequence is immaterial
(B) The consequence is material
(C) The consequence acts as a mitigating factor
(D) The consequence becomes material only if it is foreseen

48. A bullock-cart carrying a box of treasure

is intercepted by 'A'. The offence of theft is committed by 'A' if and as soon as:

(A) He seizes the bullock
(B) The bullock is made to move by him in his direction
(C) He takes the box of treasure
(D) He takes the valuable contents

49. 'A' obtained a sum of Rs. 10,000 from 'B' by putting 'B' in fear of death. Which one of the following offences was committed by 'A'?

(A) Cheating
(B) Robbery
(C) Mischief
(D) Extortion

50. Use of violence by a member of an assembly of five or more persons in furtherance of common object will constitute:

(A) Affray
(B) Assault
(C) Rioting
(D) Unlawful assembly

51. Find out the false statement:

(A) The law of limitation is part of lex fori
(B) The Limitation Act, 1963 does not make any racial or class distinction
(C) For filling a writ petition under Article 32 of the Constitution, limitation of 120 days is prescribed in the Act
(D) Provisions of the Act are not applicable for an application under the Religious Endowment Act

52. Under Section 3 of the Limitation Act, the competent court is required to consider the question of limitation:

(A) Only when opposed by the opposite patty
(B) Only when the defendant denies the liability
(C) Only when the opposite party fails to reply
(D) Suo motu even when the defendant has not taken any such objection regarding limitation

53. Consider the following:

(i) The Supreme Court in N. Balakrishnan v. M. Krishnamurthy (1998) 7 SCC 123 refused to condone the delay on the ground of sufficient cause.

(ii) In the case of R. B. Ramalingam v. R. B. Bhavneshwari (2009) 2 SCC 689, the SC observed that the test of sufficient cause is purely an individualistic test.

Of the above statements:

(A) (i) is true but (ii) is false
(B) (i) is false but (ii) is true
(C) Both (i) and (ii) are true
(D) Both (i) and (ii) are false

54. Consider the following:

(i) Under Section 13 of the Limitation Act, the time is excluded if the application for leave to sue or appeal as indigent person is allowed.

(ii) The establishment of 'good faith' is a prerequisite condition before granting benefit of Section 13 to the party.

Of the above statements:

(A) Only (i) is true and (ii) is false
(B) Only (ii) is true and (i) is false
(C) Both (i) and (ii) are true
(D) Both (i) and (ii) are false

55. Find out the incorrect statement:

(A) Section 24 of the Limitation Act is unconditional
(B) If a question of limitation arises, the instrument must be deemed to have been made with reference to the Gregorian Calendar
(C) In computing the period of limitation, the day from the period is to be reckoned has to be included
(D) Where a mortgage provided for payment of principal within 3 years from 06.10.2012, the period expires on the midnight of 06.10.2015

56. Section 15 of the Limitation Act, 1963 does not apply to:

(A) Suits
(B) Appeals
(C) Application for the execution of a decree
(D) None of these

57. In which of the following cases, Section 10 of the Limitation Act, 1963 applies?

(A) Express trust only
(B) Implied trust only
(C) Both (A) and (B)
(D) None of these

58. Consider the following:

(i) Where once time has begun to run, no subsequent disability or inability to institute a suit or make an application stops it.

(ii) In the case of a continuing breach of contract or in the case of a continuing tort, a fresh period of limitation begins to run at every moment of the time during which the breach or the tort, as the case may be, continues.

Of the above statements:

(A) (i) is true but (ii) is false
(B) (i) is false but (ii) is true
(C) Both (i) and (ii) are true
(D) Both (i) and (ii) are false

59. Which Section of the Limitation Act, 1963 provides provisions regarding acquisition of easement by prescription?

(A) Section 21
(B) Section 23
(C) section 25
(D) None of these

60. Under the Transfer of Property Act, 1882 the condition restraining alienation is provided in:

(A) Section 10
(B) Section 9
(C) Section 8
(D) Section 7

61. Which one of the following is not an actionable claim?

(A) Claim for arrears of rent
(B) A share in partnership
(C) A claim to mesne profit
(D) Ordinary as well as endowment life insurance policies

62. The term 'sale' in the TPA, 1882 is defined in Section:

(A) 53
(B) 54
(C) 55
(D) 56

63. Which of the following is not correctly matched with respect to TPA,1882?

(A) Oral Transfer : Section 9
(B) Rule against perpetuity : Section 14
(C) Doctrine of Election : Section 35
(D) Transfer by Ostensible Owner : Section 40

64. Which one of the following provisions of TPA relate to 'usufructuary mortgage'?

(A) Section 58(a)
(B) Section 58(b)

(C) Section 58(d)
(D) Section 58(e)

65. As per the provisions contained in TPA, in case of gif, if the donee dies before acceptance, then:

(A) The gif is voidable
(B) The gift is valid
(C) The gif is void
(D) None of these

66. "A" transfers Rs. 5000 to "B" on condition that he shall execute a certain lease within three months after A's death and if he should neglect to do so, to "C". "B" dies in the life time of "A". Which Section of TPA shall apply in deciding legal right of "C"?

(A) Section 27
(B) Section 28
(C) Section 29
(D) Section 30

67. A marriage settlement made to defeat and defraud creditor is voidable under Section 53 TPA. This was held in the case of:

(A) Sultan Ahmad v. Rashid Ahmad AIR 1990 All. 47
(B) Vinayak v. Mureshwar, AIR 1956 Punj 46
(C) Alamelu v. Meenakshi AIR 1960 Mad. 536
(D) None of these

68. Under the provisions of TPA, the unborn person acquires vested right on transfer for his benefit:

(A) Immediately upon his birth
(B) Upon his attaining majority
(C) After death of his father / guardian
(D) None of these

69. Novation of a contract means:

(A) The renewal of original contract
(B) Substitution of a new contact in place of original contract
(C) Cancellation of contract
(D) Alteration of contract

70. "X" enters into a contract with "Y" for which "Y' is guilty of fraud. "X" can:

(A) Set aside the contract and recover damages
(B) Set aside the contract but cannot recover damages
(C) Recover damages but cannot set aside the contract
(D) Recover damages for actual loss suffered

71. When a person making a false statement believes the statement to be true and does not intend to mislead to the other party to the contract, it is known as:

(A) Mistake
(B) Fraud
(C) Misrepresentation
(D) Undue influence

72. Which one of the following statements is correct?

Generally quasi-contractual obligations are based on the theory of:

(A) Implied term
(B) Unjust enrichment
(C) Just and reasonable solution
(D) None of these

73. A contract of life insurance, the performance of which depends upon a future event, falls under the category of:

(A) Contract of indemnity
(B) Contract of guarantee
(C) Contingent contract
(D) Uncertain contract

74. Lending money to a borrower, at high rate of interest, when the money market is tight, renders the agreement of loan:

(A) Void
(B) Valid
(C) Voidable
(D) Illegal

75. A and B are friends. A told to B to show him a new movie in a posh multiplex, upon which A promised to offer him lunch in a five-star hotel. B showed him a movie in a multiplex, but A gave lunch to B in a road side dhaba. Decide A's liability:

(A) A is liable because there was intention to create legal relationship between A and B
(B) A is not liable because there was no intension to create legal relationship between A and B
(C) A was mistaken
(D) B was mistaken

76. Which one of the following cases is related to damages for breach of contract?

(A) Lalman Shukla v. Gauri Dutt
(B) Carlil v. Carbolic Smoke Ball
(C) Hadley v. Vaxendale
(D) Taylor v. Caldwell

77. If no time is specified in the contract for its performance:

(A) The contract is void for uncertainty
(B) The contract is voidable at the option of either party
(C) The contract is not void for uncertainty and it may be performed within a reasonable time
(D) The contract is void as time is the essence of contract

78. Who among the following is not a Class I heir as per the HS Act, 1956?

(A) Widow of a predeceased
(B) Son of a predeceased son
(C) Brother's son
(D) Son of a predeceased

79. Consider the following:

(i) A child, who was in the womb at the time of the death of an intestate, shall not inherit to the intestate even if he / she is born alive under the provisions of the HS Act, 1956.

(ii) If a Hindu has ceased to be a Hindu by conversion to another religion, children born to him / her after such conversion and their descendants shall be disqualified from inheriting the property of any of their Hindu relatives.

Of the above statements:

(A) (i) is true but (ii) is false
(B) (i) is false but (ii) is true
(C) Both (i) and (ii) are true
(D) Both (i) and (ii) are false

80. Consider the following:

(i) A person shall be disqualified from succeeding to any property under the HS Act, 1956 if he is blind or impotent.

(ii) If an intestate has left no heir qualified to succeed to his / her property, such property shall devolve on the Government, as per provision contained in HS Act.

Of the above statements

(A) (i) is true but (ii) is false
(B) (i) is false but (ii) is true
(C) Both (i) and (ii) are true
(D) Both (i) and (ii) are false

81. Who among the following is not a Class II heir as per the HS Act,1956?

(A) Father
(B) Son's daughter's son

(C) Widow of a predeceased son
(D) Father's mother

82. Which one of the following Section of the HS Act, 1956 provides that property of a female Hindu to be her absolute property?

(A) Section II
(B) Section 12
(C) Section 13
(D) Section 14

83. The provision of the HS Act do not apply on which of the followings:

(A) To Arya Samajis
(B) To illegitimate child, both of whose parent are Hindus
(C) To any person who is a covert to Hindu religion
(D) To a member of scheduled tribe within the meaning of Clause 25 of Article 366 of the Constitution of India

84. Find out the incorrect statement regarding will making:

(A) A person of sound mind, as long as he is not a minor, can make a will
(B) As per Section 74 of the Indian Succession Act, a format is prescribed for drafting a will
(C) A person can make a will any time and any number of times
(D) The will is signed by the maker and two witnesses

85. Read the following in context of the Indian Succession Act:

(i) The domicile of origin of every person of legitimate birth is in the country in which at the time of his birth, his father was domiciled.

(ii) The domicile of origin of an illegitimate child is in the country in which at the time of his birth, his mother was domiciled.

Of the above statements:

(A) (i) is true but (ii) is false
(B) (i) is false but (ii) is true
(C) Both (i) and (ii) are true
(D) Both (i) and (ii) are false

86. Part VI of the Indian Succession Act deals with:

(A) Testamentary succession
(B) Intestate succession
(C) Protection of property of deceased

(D) Probates, letter of administration and administration of assets of deceased

87. An order of decree under Section 6 of the Specific Relief Act is:

(A) Appealable only
(B) Reviewable only
(C) Appealable as well as reviewable
(D) Neither appealable nor reviewable

88. The general principles on which the perpetual injunction could be granted under the SR Act are contained in:

(A) Section 37
(B) Section 38
(C) Section 39
(D) Section 40

89. Part III of the SR Act, 1963 deals with:

(A) Specific relief
(B) Declaratory decrees
(C) Preventive relief
(D) None of these

90. Under Section 10, which of the following can be specifically enforced?

(A) Contingent contracts
(B) Contract to form partnership
(C) Contract to get back objects of historic value
(D) Marriage contract

91. Section 26 of the SR Act fixes the time limit for discovery of mistake or fraud to be:

(A) Six months
(B) Three months
(C) One year
(D) No time limit is fixed

92. Relief of rescission is granted in cases:

(A) Where the contract is void
(B) Where the contract is voidable
(C) Where the contract is both void and voidable
(D) Where the contract is neither void nor voidable

93. Which section of the SR Act provides for grant of temporary and permanent injunctions?

(A) Section 35
(B) Section 36
(C) Section 37
(D) None of these

94. Section 31 of the SR Act is related to:

(A) Cancellation of instruments
(B) Partial cancellation of instruments
(C) Rescission of contract
(D) None of these

95. Power to award compensation in certain case is contained in which of the following Sections:

(A) Section 20
(B) Section 21
(C) Section 22
(D) None of these

96. The term 'domestic violence' in the Protection of Women from Domestic Violence Act, 2005 is based on:

(A) UN Framework for Model Legislation on Domestic Violence and UN Declaration on Elimination of Violence against Women
(B) ICCPR and ICESCR
(C) UDHR
(D) Constitution of India

97. "Magistrate" under Protection of Women from Domestic Violence means:

(A) Judicial Magistrate of First Class
(B) Metropolitan Magistrate exercising Jurisdiction under Cr.P.C.
(C) Judicial Magistrate of Second Class
(D) Both (A) and (B)

98. Which of the following order may be passed by a Magistrate in relation to domestic violence?

(A) Protection order
(B) Residence order
(C) Monetary reliefs
(D) All of these

99. A Protection officer under the Protection of Women from Domestic Violence Act, 2005 is a:

(A) Civil servant
(B) Public servant
(C) Government servant
(D) None of these

100. Under the Protection of Women from Domestic Violence Act, on what basis, the concerned magistrate may pass an ex parte or interim order?

(A) Affidavit
(B) Statement made by parties before the magistrate
(C) Both (A) and (B)
(D) None of these

ANSWERS

1	C	11	C	21	C		
2	D	12	C	22	D		
3	A	13	B	23	C		
4	D	14	B	24	B		
5	A	15	B	25	A		
6	A	16	A	26	B		
7	C	17	C	27	D		
8	C	18	B	28	B		
9	B	19	B	29	A		
10	D	20	B	30	A		
31	C	61	C	91	D		
32	B	62	B	92	B		
33	C	63	D	93	C		
34	D	64	C	94	A		
35	C	65	C	95	B		
36	C	66	A	96	A		
37	A	67	C	97	D		
38	A	68	A	98	D		
39	C	69	B	99	B		
40	D	70	B	100	A		
41	C	71	C				
42	C	72	B				
43	A	73	C				
44	B	74	B				
45	C	75	B				
46	A	76	C				
47	A	77	C				
48	B	78	C				
49	D	79	B				
50	D	80	B				
51	C	81	C				
52	D	82	D				
53	B	83	D				
54	C	84	B				
55	C	85	C				
56	B	86	A				
57	C	87	D				
58	C	88	A				
59	C	89	C				
60	A	90	C				

2022-2023

1. Match List-I with List-II and select the correct answer using the code given below the Lists:

List- I	List- II
(a) A.D.M. Jabalpur	(i) Bearer Bonds v. Shukla case
(b) M.S.M. Sharma v. S.K. Sinha	(ii) Habeas Corpus Case
(c) R.C. Cooper v. Union of India	(iii) Bank Nationalisation case
(d) R.K Garg v. Union of India	(iv) Search light case

	(a)	(b)	(c)	(d)
(A)	(ii)	(i)	(iv)	(iii)
(B)	(iv)	(ii)	(i)	(iii)
(C)	(ii)	(iv)	(i)	(iii)
(D)	(ii)	(iv)	(iii)	(i)

2. Article 141 of the Constitution lays down that the law declared by the Supreme Court shall be binding on all Courts within the territory of India. Therefore, the Supreme Court:

(A) Is bound by its earlier decisions as the expression 'all Courts' includes Supreme Court also
(B) Is not bound by its own decisions and may reverse a previous decision
(C) Can reverse a previous decision only when a new legislation is enacted having the effect of abrogating decision
(D) Can reverse a previous decision only when that previous decision was given as a result of overlooking another previous decision

3. The State of J&K enjoys a special status under Article 370 of the Constitution, but under Article 370(3), the President may declare that Article 370 shall cease to be operative. Consider the following statements in this regard. This power of the President is subject to:

(i) Public Notification

(ii) Recommendation of Parliament

(iii) Advice of the Union Council of Ministers

(iv) Recommendation of the Constituent

Assembly of J&K

Of these statements

(A) (i) and (iii) are correct
(B) (i) and (ii) are correct
(C) (i) and (iv) are correct
(D) (i) and (iv) are correct

4. Right to Life emanates from:

(A) Article 21 and includes Right to Die
(B) Article 19 and does not include Right to Die
(C) Article 19 and 20 does not include Right to Die
(D) Article 21 and does not include Right to Die

5. That no person accused of an offence shall be compelled to be a witness against himself is a/an:

(A) Directive principle which the Stale should apply while enacting criminal law
(B) Human right under Universal Declaration of Human Rights to which India is a party
(C) Fundamental right
(D) Ordinary constitutional right

6. Bijoe Emmanual v. State of Kerala case is also known as:

(A) National Anthem Case
(B) Reasonable Classification Case
(C) Backward Classes Case
(D) Right to Life Case

7. The law declared by the Supreme Court is binding on all the Courts within the territory of India, but Supreme Court is not bound by its own decisions, was declared by the Supreme Court itself in:

(A) Indira Nehru Gandhi v. Rajnarian
(B) Madhav Rao Schindia v. Union of India
(C) Bengal Immunity Co. Ltd v. State of Bihar
(D) Both (A) and (B)

8. In which case it was held that taking specimen fingerprints and hand writing from accused is not hit by Article 20(3) as being witness against himself:

(A) State through SPE and CBI, AP vs M. Krishna Mohan
(B) Jaya Sinha vs State of Karnataka
(C) Oriental Insurance Co. Ltd. vs Raj Kumari
(D) None of these

9. The Directive Principles of State Policy are fundamental for the:

(A) Upliftment of backward classes
(B) Protection of individual rights
(C) Administration of justice
(D) Governance of state

10. Consider the following judgements delivered by the Supreme Court of India:

(i) Keshvananda Bharati v. State of Kerala

(ii) Re Berubari Case

(iii) Excel Wear v. Union of India

The chronological sequence of the above judgements is:

(A) (i), (iii), (ii)
(B) (i), (ii), (iii)
(C) (iii), (i), (ii)
(D) (ii), (i), (iii)

11. In which of the following cases the Supreme Court held that FIR was not substantive evidence and could only be used to corroborate its maker?

(A) Union of India v. A. Kumar, AIR 010 SC 2735
(B) C. Magesh v. State of Karnataka, AIR 2010 SC 2768
(C) Anil Kumar v. B. S. Neelakanta, AIR 2010 SC 2715
(D) Viietn Gazrm v. State, AIR 2010 SC 2712

12. Under which of the following Sections of the Indian Evidence Act, the evidence of the dumb witness is taken into consideration?

(A) Section 116
(B) Section 117
(C) Section 118
(D) Section 119

13. A Court cannot compel the parties to undergo blood test, to establish the legitimacy of the child because it would amount to declaring the mother as unchaste and child as Illegitimate. This view was laid down in which of the following cases?

(A) Pawan Kumar v. Mukesh Kumara
(B) Subash v. Lata Shah
(C) Ningamma v. Chikkaiah
(D) Gautam Kundu v. State of West

14. "Facts not otherwise relevant are relevant if they are inconsistent with any fact in issue of relevant fact". Which of the following Sections of the Indian Evidence Act

contains the aforesaid principle of law?

(A) Section 9
(B) Section 10
(C) Section 11
(D) Section 12

15. Mode of proof of a custom is contained in:

(A) Section 32(4) of Indian Evidence Act
(B) Section 32(7) of Indian Evidence Act
(C) Section 48 of Indian Evidence Act
(D) All of these

16. Hearsay evidence becomes relevant:

(A) When it is ratified by admission or confession
(B) When it comes under the ambit of Section 6 of the Indian Evidence Act, 1872
(C) When it is mentioned in any public document or is presumed by the Court
(D) In all of the categories mentioned

17. Under Indian Evidence Act, 1872 a copy compared with a copy of a letter made by a copying machine is:

(A) Primary evidence
(B) Oral evidence
(C) Secondary evidence
(D) Any of the evidence

18. Under which one of the following Sections of the Indian Evidence Act, 1872, the previous conviction of a person is relevant:

(A) Explanation I to Section 14
(B) Explanation II to Section 14
(C) Explanation III to Section 14
(D) Explanation IV to Section 14

19. Maxim *'omnia praesumuntur rite esse aeta'* means:

(A) All facts are presumed to be rightly done
(B) All facts are presumed to be not rightly done
(C) All facts are presumed to be wrongly done
(D) All facts are presumed to be not wrongly done

20. The right to private defence is available with respect to:

(A) Harm to body
(B) Harm to movable property
(C) Harm to immovable property
(D) All of these

21. In which provision of Indian Penal Code the definition of 'valuable security' is explained?

(A) Section 29
(B) Section 30
(C) Section 31
(D) Section 13

22. For the application of Section 149 of IPC:

(A) Active participation of each of person is required
(B) A person should be a member of unlawful assembly
(C) Both (A) and (B) are correct
(D) None of these

23. 'X', a doctor informs his patient 'Y' that he has cancer which is in its last stage. 'X' requests 'Y' to arrange his family affairs as he cannot survive for more than a couple of weeks. 'Y' dies because of shock on hearing this. 'X' is:

(A) Guilty of murder as he knew that such a disclosure will cause death
(B) Not guilty since communication was made in good faith for the benefit of 'Y'
(C) Guilty of causing death by negligence
(D) Guilty of culpable homicide not amounting to murder as he knew that such a disclosure is likely to cause of death

24. Match List-I with List-II and select the correct answer using the code given below the Lists:

List-I	List-II
(a) Death is caused to safeguard property	(i) Exception 2 to Section 300
(b) Death caused by a child of six years	(ii) Murder
(c) Death by an act with the intention of causing bodily injury which is sufficient ordinarily to cause death	(iii) No offence
(d) Death of trespasser of the house who was escaping	(iv) Right of Private defence

	(a)	(b)	(c)	(d)
(A)	(ii)	(i)	(iv)	(iii)
(B)	(i)	(iii)	(ii)	(iv)
(C)	(iv)	(ii)	(iii)	(i)
(D)	(iv)	(iii)	(ii)	(i)

25. Which one of the following is associated with common intention?

(A) Similar intention
(B) Pre-meditated concert
(C) Same intention
(D) Unanimous decision in a meeting to do a particular act

26. 'X' and 'Y' agree to commit theft in 'Z's house but no theft is actually committed. They are guilty of:

(A) No offence
(B) Criminal conspiracy
(C) Abetment by conspiracy
(D) Abetment by instigation

27. The distinction between Section 299 and Section 300 was first elaborately discussed in the case:

(A) Vasudev v. State of U.P.
(B) Om Prakash v. State of Punjab
(C) Deo Narain v. State of U.P.
(D) Reg v. Govinda

28. Which Section of the IPC provides for an 'attempt to dacoity'?

(A) Section 393
(B) Section 394
(C) Section 395
(D) Section 396

29. Every State Government in co-ordination with the Central Government shall formulate Victim Compensation Scheme (VCS) for providing fund for compensation to victims falls under Section 357-A of Cr.P.C. with effect from 31-12-2009. This Section was inserted by:

(A) Code of Criminal Procedure (Amendment) Act, 2008 (5 of 2009)
(B) Code of Criminal Procedure (Amendment) Act, 2005 (25 of 2005)
(C) Criminal Procedure Law (Amendment) Act, 2005 (2 of 2006)
(D) Code of Criminal Procedure (Amendment) Act, 2001 (50 of 2001)

30. The person seeking suspension of conviction should specifically draw the

attention of the Appellate Court to the consequences that may arise if the conviction is not stayed as held by the Supreme Court in:

(A) Sheo Prasad Bhor v. State of Assam, AIR 2007 SC 918
(B) P.V. George v. State of Kerala, AIR 2007 SC 1034
(C) Navjot Singh Sidhu v. State of Punjab, AIR 2007 SC 1003
(D) Kuldip Nayar v. Union of India, (2006) 7 SCC 1

31. When there is a dispute between two Courts relating to exercise of jurisdiction in a criminal matter and said Courts are under subordination of different High Courts, the matter shall be decided under Section 186 of CrPC by the:

(A) Supreme Court
(B) High Court of the larger State
(C) High Court having more judges
(D) High Court within Whose local limits of appellate jurisdiction the proceeding first commenced

32. Warrant case has been defined under Section 2(x) of CrPC as a case relating to an offence punishable with death, imprisonment for life or imprisonment for a term:

(A) Exceeding three years
(B) Exceeding two years
(C) Exceeding one year
(D) Exceeding one year but less than two years

33. An arrested person has a Right to Consult a legal practitioner of his choice. The consultation with the lawyer:

(A) May not be in the presence of the police officer
(B) Maybe in the presence of the police officer but not within his hearing
(C) Maybe in the presence of the police officer and within his hearing
(D) Both (A) and (B)

34. In cases of consecutive sentence on conviction of several offences at one trial by a Metropolitan Magistrate, the aggregate punishment:

(A) Shall not exceed twice the amount of punishment which the Magistrate is competent to inflict for a single offence
(B) Shall not exceed the amount of punishment which the Magistrate is competent to inflict for a single offence as prescribed under Section 29 of CrPC
(C) Shall not exceed three times the amount of punishment which the Magistrate is competent to inflict for a single offence
(D) Shall not exceed 14 years

35. Period of limitation of filing claims and objections to the attachment of any property attached under Section 83 of CrPC, by any person other than the proclaimed person, as provided under Section 84 of CrPC:

(A) Within three months of attachment
(B) Within six months of attachment
(C) Within one year of attachment
(D) Within two months of attachment

36. Under Section 91 of CrPC, a person who is summoned to produce a document(s) on appearance before the Court:

(A) Becomes a witness and can be subjected to cross-examination
(B) Does not become a witness and cannot be subjected to cross-examination
(C) Becomes a witness but cannot be subjected to cross-examination
(D) Does not become a witness but can be subjected to cross-examination

37. Objection to the attachment of a property in execution can be raised:

(A) By the parties to the suit
(B) By the stranger/third party
(C) Both (A) and (B)
(D) None of these

38. After dismissal of a suit under Order IX, Rule 8 of CPC, a fresh suit on the same cause of action, under Order IX, Rule 9 of CPC:

(A) Is barred
(B) Is not barred under any circumstance
(C) Is not barred subject to law of limitation
(D) None of these

39. For the application of the principle res subjudice, which of the following is essential?

(A) Suits between the same parties or litigating under the same title
(B) The two suits must be pending disposal in a Court
(C) The matter in issue in the two suits must be directly and substantially the same
(D) All of these

40. On default in filing of written statement under Order VIII, pronouncement of judgement is:

(A) Mandatory
(B) Discretionary
(C) Directory
(D) None of these

41. Under Section 114 of CPC, review is maintainable:

(A) When an appeal is provided, but no appeal preferred
(B) When no appeal is provided
(C) Both (A) and (B)
(D) Neither (A) nor (B)

42. In which of the following cases it was held that "the second appeal is permissible only if finding is perverse"?

(A) Dinesh Kumar v. Yusuf Ali, AIR 2010 SC 2679
(B) State v. M. L. Keshari, AIR 2010 SC 2587
(C) Bimlesh v. New India Assurance Co. Ltd., AIR 2010 SC 2591
(D) Dasmth v. State of Madhya Pradesh, AIR 2010 SC 2592

43. Under which Provision of CPC, the court has jurisdiction to reject the plaint, which does not disclose a cause of action or where there is suppression of material fact?

(A) Order 7 Rule 11
(B) Order 8 Rule 11
(C) Order 7 Rule 1
(D) Order 5 Rule 1

44. The Supreme Court in which among the following cases observed that CPC Amendment Acts of 1999 and 2002 are Constitutionally valid?

(A) Salem Advocate Bar Association, Tamil Nada v. Union of India
(B) Delhi High Court Bar Association v. Union of India
(C) Allahabad High Court Bar Association v. Union of India
(D) Punjab and Haryana High Court Bar Association v. Union of India

45. In which case the Supreme Court held that Section 100-A of CPC which is substituted by CPC Amendment Act, 2002 will not have retrospective effect even though it brings within its fold those appeals preferred prior to coming into force of the said Amendment Act?

(A) M. George v. State of Kerala, AIR 2007 SC 1034
(B) Jagjit Singh v. State of Haryana, AIR 2007 SC 59
(C) Meetu v. State of Punjab, AIR 2007 SC 758
(D) Kamla Devi v. Khushal Kanwar, AIR 2007 SC 663

46. Which of the following Section provides the definition of shared household under the Protection of Women from Domestic Violence Act, 2005?
(A) Section 2(d)
(B) Section 2(f)
(C) Section 2(s)
(D) Section 3

47. The Supreme Court in Satish Chander Ahuja vs Sheha Ahuja (2020) held that the following needs to be established for the determination of whether a suit property was shared household or not:

(A) The aggrieved person under the said Act resided or was residing in the premise during the period when the domestic relationship existed
(B) The property was required to belong to the joint family of which the aggrieved person is apart
(C) Only (A)
(D) Both (A) and (B)

48. In the Protection of Women from Domestic Violence Act, 2005 'violence' includes:

(A) Economic violence
(B) Sexual violence
(C) Both(A) and (B)
(D) None of these

49. Where a Protection Officer fails to discharge his duties as directed by Magistrate without any sufficient cause, there he shall be liable:

(A) For dismissal
(B) To pay compensation
(C) To be punished with imprisonment or with fine or with both
(D) To be punished with fine only

50. Match the following as per the Sections of Domestic Violence Act, 2005:

(a) Section 6   (i)   Duties and

	(a)	(b)	(c)	(d)
(A)	(iii)	(iv)	(i)	(ii)
(B)	(i)	(ii)	(iii)	(iv)
(C)	(iv)	(ii)	(i)	(iii)
(D)	(iii)	(ii)	(i)	(iv)

(b) Section 7 — (ii) Duties of Government

(c) Section 9 — (iii) Duties of shelter homes

(d) Section 11 — (iv) Duties of medical facilities

functions of Protection Officers

51. When did the Domestic Violence Act 2005, come into force?

(A) 1 April, 2005
(B) 11 March, 2006
(C) 21 May, 2005
(D) 26 October, 2006

52. A notice of date of hearing fixed under Section 12 of the Domestic Violence Act, 2005 shall be given by the Magistrate to the:

(A) Respondent
(B) Protection Officer
(C) Service Provider
(D) In charge of Police Station

53. 'Child' under the Protection of Women from the Domestic Violence Act, 2005 includes:

(A) Adopted Child
(B) Step Child
(C) Foster Child
(D) All of these

54. Breach of Protection Order under Section 31 and 32 of the Domestic Violence Act, 2005 shall be an offence which is:

(A) Cognizable and bailable
(B) Cognizable and non-bailable
(C) Non-cognizable and bailable
(D) Non-cognizable and non-bailable

55. Protection of Women from Domestic Violence Act, 2005 derives its support from ___ of the Constitution of India.

(A) Article 14
(B) Article 14, 15 and 21
(C) Article 15 and 21
(D) Article 14 and 21

56. Section 6 of the Limitation Act, 1963 does not apply in case of:

(A) Suits
(B) Execution of a decree
(C) Appeal
(D) Suits and execution of a decree

57. Section 5 of the Limitation Act, 1963 applies for condonation of delay. To apply this provision

(A) Length of the delay is the only criterion
(B) Length of the delay does not matter, acceptability of the explanation is the only criterion
(C) Length of the delay certainly matters apart from the acceptability of the explanation
(D) Both (A) and (B)

58. For term loan, the period of limitation is three years from:

(A) Date of payment
(B) Date of default
(C) Due date of payment of each instalment
(D) Date of default in payment in each instalment

59. The fraud is contemplated by Section 17 of the Limitation Act, 1963 is that of:

(A) The plaintiff
(B) The defendant
(C) Stranger to the contract
(D) Either(A), (B) or (C)

60. Under the law of limitation, suits can be filed within three years in cases relating to:

(A) Accounts
(B) Contracts
(C) Declarations
(D) All of these

61. Section 11 of the Limitation Act, 1908 deals with suits:

(A) On foreign contracts
(B) On local contracts
(C) Banking contracts
(D) None of these

62. Second Appeal to Central Public Information Officer before Central Information Commission can be filed within:

(A) 90 days
(B) 30 days
(C) 45 days
(D) 60 days

63. Time limit for filing application to become legal representative due to death of defendant or respondent is:

(A) 30 days
(B) 90 days
(C) 45 days
(D) 60 days

64. Temporary injunction may be granted:

(A) To restrain any election
(B) To restrain dispossession from property
(C) To restrain any intended disciplinary action against public servant
(D) To restrain the result of any adverse entry against the public servant

65. Which of the following can be transferred under the provision of the Transfer of Property Act, 1882?

(A) The right to mesne profit
(B) A decree for mesne profit
(C) A transfer of property to a prostitute for future co-habitation
(D) A sub-lease of a farm for the retail sale of opium

66. Which of the following can be considered implied surrender of the lease?

(A) Non-acceptance of a new lease taking effect during the continuance of the existing lease
(B) Abandonment of possession by the lessee
(C) A surrender by one of the two joint lessee's implied surrender on the part second lessee
(D) None of these

67. Under the Provisions of the TP Act, 1882, the seller is duty bound to disclose:

(A) Patent defects in the property
(B) Latent defects in the property
(C) Both (A) and (B)
(D) Neither (A) nor (B)

68. Under the Provisions of the TP Act, 1882, the benefits of a contract can be assigned as an actionable claim and transferred unless:

(A) The contract is one which had been induced by personal qualifications or considerations as to the parties to it

(B) The benefit is coupled with an obligation which the assignor is bound to discharge
(C) Either (A) or (B)
(D) Neither (A) nor (B)

69. Under the Transfer of Property Act, 1882 vested interest is:

(A) Defeated by the death of the transferor
(B) Defeated by the death of the transferee
(C) Either or both (A) and (B)
(D) Neither (A) nor (B)

70. What is the default interest payable under Section 63 and 63A of the Transfer of Property Act, 1882?

(A) 8% per annum
(B) 9% per annum
(C) 10% per annum
(D) Interest rate is not mentioned in the Section

71. Where the mortgage is illegal for want of registration but the mortgage continues in possession of the mortgaged property, a valid mortgage comes in existence after the expiry of:

(A) 5 years
(B) 10 years
(C) 12 years
(D) 20 years

72. Which of the following are valid illustrations of an anamolous mortgage?

(A) A possessory mortgage without a conditional sate
(B) A possessory mortgage with a right to cause the mortgaged property to sale in the event of default in payment
(C) Both (A) and (B)
(D) Neither (A) nor (B)

73. Which of the following instruments have been excluded by the application of Section 137 of the Transfer of Property Act, 1882?

(A) Share
(B) Bill of Exchange
(C) Both (A) and (B)
(D) Neither (A) nor (B)

74. In which of the following cases, the Doctrine of Supervening Impossibility will apply?

(A) Difficulty in performance
(B) Commercial Impossibility
(C) Impossibility known to the parties at the

time of making of the contract
(D) Strikes, Lock-outs and civil disturbances

75. Under which of the following conditions can a proposal be revoked according to the Indian Contract Act, 1872?

(i) By the Communication of notice of revocation by the proposer to the other party

(ii) By the failure of the acceptor to fulfil a condition of proposal

(iii) By the death or insanity of the proposer

(iv) By the lapse of the time prescribed

(v) By notice of revocation after the acceptance is communicated

(A) (i), (ii) and (iv) only
(B) (ii), (iii), (iv) and (v) only
(C) (i), (ii), (iii) and (iv) only
(D) All (i), (ii), (iii), (iv) and (v)

76. In the Contract of Agency, implied agency may arise by:

(i) Agency by Estoppel

(ii) Agency of Necessity

(iii) Agency by Ratification

(iv) Agency by Holding out

(A) Both (i) and (ii)
(B) (i), (ii) and (iii)
(C) Both (ii) and (iv)
(D) Both (i) and (iii)

77. Which one of the following is a void contract?

(A) Unilateral contract
(B) A contract which ceases to be enforceable by law
(C) Implied contract
(D) Express contract

78. Which one is the correct sequence implied in the Indian Contract Act, 1872?

(i) Offer of proposal

(ii) Contract

(iii) Promise

(iv) Agreement

(v) Acceptance

Choose the correct answer from the options given below:

(A) (iii), (v), (i), (iv), (ii)
(B) (iv), (ii), (iii), (i), (v)
(C) (ii), (iv), (iii), (v), (i)
(D) (i), (v), (iii), (iv), (ii)

79. Statement (I): Agreement without consideration is always valid.

Statement (II): All contracts are agreements but all valid agreements are not contracts.

In the context of the above two statements, which one of the following codes is correct?

(A) Statement (I) and (II) both are correct
(B) Both statements (I) and (II) are incorrect
(C) statement (I) is incorrect and Statement (II) is correct
(D) Statement (I) is correct and Statement (II) is incorrect

80. Given below are two statements:

Statement I: Display of goods by a shopkeeper with prices marked by another person other than on them, is not an offer' but an offer to buy the goods.

Statement II: Price quotations, catalogues, and advertisements in newspaper for sale of an article do constitute a valid offer.

In the light of the above two statements, choose the most appropriate answer from the options given below:

(A) Both Statements (I) and (II) are correct
(B) Both Statements (I) and (II) are incorrect
(C) Statement (I) is correct but Statement (II) is incorrect
(D) Statement (I) is incorrect but Statement (II) is correct

81. What is consent under the Indian Contract Act, 1872?

(A) When acceptance of proposal is made by the party to whom the proposal is made
(B) When the acceptance is made the person to whom the invitation to the public to make an proposal is made
(C) When they agree upon the same thing in the same sense
(D) When both the parties agree upon a thing in the way it is understood by them

82. The Indian Contract Act, 1872 extends to:

(A) The State of Jammu and Kashmir
(B) The Union Territories of India
(C) The whole of India except the State of Jammu and Kashmir
(D) The whole of India

83. When did Hindu Succession Act come into force?

(A) 17 June, 1956
(B) 1 March, 1957
(C) 1 May, 1956
(D) 23 April, 1957

84. Which Section of the Hindu Succession Act, 1956 deals with the Order of Succession among heirs in the Schedule?

(A) Section 12 of Hindu Succession Act, 1956
(B) Section 9 of Hindu Succession Act, 1956
(C) Section 14 of Hindu Succession Act, 1956
(D) Section 20 of Hindu Succession Act, 1956

85. Section 19 of the Hindu Succession Act, 1956 provides:

(A) Mode of a succession of two or more heirs
(B) Converts descendants disqualified
(C) Order of succession among heirs in the Schedule
(D) Computation of degrees

86. Section 12 of Hindu Succession Act, 1956 deals with:

(A) Order of succession among agnates and cognates
(B) Devolution of interest in coparcenary property
(C) Full blood preferred to half-blood
(D) Overriding effect of Act

87. Section 25 of the Hindu Succession Act, 1956 deals with:

(A) Right of a child in the womb
(B) Murderer disqualified
(C) Disease, defect, etc., not to disqualify
(D) Testamentary succession

88. Will means deposition of property which takes effect:

(A) After the birth of testator
(B) After the death of testator
(C) During the life of testator
(D) None of these

89. A will is liable to be revoked or altered by the:

(A) Maker of it
(B) Legatee of it
(C) Executor of it
(D) None of these

90. Who can apply for revocation of succession certificate?

(A) Interested person
(B) Uninterested person
(C) Minor
(D) None of these

91. Appeal shall lie in ___ against the order of District Judge under Indian Succession Act, 1925.

(A) Supreme Court
(B) High Court
(C) Both (A) and (B)
(D) None of these

92. The Specific Relief Act, 1963 extends to:

(A) The whole of India except the State of Jammu and Kashmir
(B) The whole of India
(C) Only to capital cities of the States
(D) The whole of India except the Union Territories

93. Specific Relief can be granted only for the purpose of:

(A) Enforcing individual civil rights and not for mere purpose of enforcing a penal law
(B) Enforcing individual fundamental rights
(C) Enforcing individual criminal rights only
(D) Enforcing individual civil rights as well as criminal rights

94. When an injunction cannot be granted?

(A) To restrain any person from instituting or prosecuting any criminal matter
(B) To prevent the breach of a Contract the performance of which would not be specifically enforced
(C) To restrain any person from applying to any legislative body
(D) All the options are correct

95. How the preventive relief is granted under the Specific Relief Act, 1963 by the Court?

(A) At the discretion of the Court by perpetual
(B) At the discretion of the Court by injunction temporary
(C) Both (A) and (B) are correct
(D) None of these

96. The specific performance of a contract shall be enforced by the Court:

(A) Subject to the provisions of the Indian Contact Act, 1872
(B) Subject to the provisions of the IxB Code, 2016
(C) Subject to the provisions contained in Section 11(2), Section 14 and Section 16 of the Specific Relief Act, 1963
(D) None of these

97. Any person interested in a contract may sue to have it rescinded, and such rescission may be adjudged by the Court in which case(s):

(A) Where the contract is unlawful for causes not apparent on its face and the defendant is more to blame than the plaintiff
(B) Where the contract is voidable or terminable by the plaintiff
(C) Both (A) and (B) are correct
(D) None of these

98. ___ injunctions are such as are to continue until a specific time or, until the further order of the Court, and they may be granted at any stage of a suit, and are regulated by the Code of Civil Procedure, 1908.

(A) Perpetual
(B) Temporary
(C) Both (A) and (B) are correct
(D) None of these

99. Whether any appeal is allowed against the order or decree passed in any suit instituted under Section 6 of the Specific Relief Act, 1963?

(A) Yes, appeal can be allowed
(B) No, appeal shall lie from any order or decree passed in suit instituted under this Section, nor shall any review of any such order or decree be allowed
(C) Appeal can be allowed, if permitted by the court, who has given the order or decree
(D) None of these

100. A plaintiff instituting a suit for the specific performance of a contract in writing may pray in the alternative that, if the contract cannot be specifically enforced:

(A) It may be declared as unforceable
(B) It may be rescinded and delivered up to the cancelled; and the Court, if it refuses to enforce the contract specifically, may direct it to be rescinded and delivered up accordingly
(C) It may be declared as void
(D) None of these

ANSWERS

1	D	36	B	71	C
2	B	37	C	72	B
3	D	38	A	73	C
4	A	39	D	74	C
5	C	40	B	75	C
6	A	41	C	76	B
7	C	42	A	77	B
8	A	43	A	78	D
9	D	44	A	79	C
10	D	45	D	80	C
11	B	46	C	81	C
12	D	47	A/C	82	D
13	C	48	C	83	A
14	C	49	C	84	B
15	D	50	A	85	A
16	D	51	D	86	A
17	C	52	B	87	B
18	B	53	D	88	B
19	A	54	B	89	A
20	D	55	B	90	A
21	B	56	C	91	B
22	B	57	B	92	B
23	B	58	C	93	A
24	D	59	B	94	D
25	B	60	D	95	C
26	B	61	A	96	C
27	D	62	A	97	C
28	NV	63	B	98	B
29	A	64	B	99	B
30	C	65	B	100	B
31	D	66	B		
32	B	67	B		
33	D	68	C		
34	A	69	D		
35	B	70	B		

2023-2024

1. Through 42nd Constitutional Amendment, which of the following expressions were added to the Preamble?

a. Sovereign

b. Socialist

c. Secular

d. Integrity

Codes:

(A) Only a, b and c
(B) Only b, c and d
(C) Only a, c and d
(D) a, b, c and d

2. The constitution of Election Commission is provided in the Constitution under ___.

(A) Article 323
(B) Article 324
(C) Article 327
(D) Article 329

3. Which of the following Judges of the Supreme Court is famously known as the "Green Judge"?

(A) Justice V.R. Krishna Iyer
(B) Justice P.N. Bhagwati
(C) Justice Kuldip Singh
(D) Justice B.N. Kirpal

4. Can fundamental rights under Indian Constitution, be waived by a person?

(A) Yes, by every person
(B) Yes, but only by a certain group of persons
(C) Only right conferring a benefit on the individual can be waived
(D) Fundamental rights cannot be waived

5. Sixth Schedule of the Indian Constitution contains provisions with regard to administration of tribal areas of some States. Which of the following State is not included in it?

(A) Meghalaya
(B) Mizoram
(C) Tripura
(D) Manipur

6. President's Rule under Article 356 of Constitution remains valid in the State for the maximum period of ___.

(A) One year
(B) Two years
(C) Six months
(D) Three years

7. Which writ can be issued when appointment is contrary to the statutory provisions?

(A) Mandamus
(B) Certiorari
(C) Quo warranto
(D) Prohibition

8. Which Schedule of the Constitution of India contains the list of recognized languages?

(A) Sixth Schedule
(B) Seventh Schedule
(C) Eighth Schedule
(D) Fourth Schedule

9. Under Indian Constitution, what is not included in freedom to manage religious affairs?

(A) To establish and maintain institutions for charitable and religious purposes
(B) To own and acquire immovable property
(C) To manage its own affairs in matters of religion
(D) To construct a religious place on government land

10. The decision of Union of India v. H.S. Dhillon, AIR 1972 SC 1061 concerns ___.

(A) The power of the Parliament to make law with respect to a matter not enumerated in Concurrent List or State List.
(B) The exclusive powers of State Legislature to make law with respect to a matter enumerated in the State List.
(C) The scope of Parliament or Legislature of State to make law in respect of a matter enumerated in Concurrent List.
(D) The relation of Fundamental Rights and Directive Principles of State Policy.

11. Which of the following remedies is available against a court's order under Section 10?

(A) Appeal
(B) Revision
(C) Both (A) and (B)
(D) None of the above

12. Which of the following Sections of the

Code expressly prohibits a suit under certain circumstances?

(A) Section 10
(B) Section 11
(C) Section 47
(D) All of the above

13. Which Order of the Civil Procedure Code provides for a "Representative Suit"?

(A) Order I, Rule 8
(B) Order I, Rule 1
(C) Order II, Rule 1
(D) Order IV, Rule 4

14. Order XXXIX, Rule 2 of the Civil Procedure Code deals with ___.

(A) Attachment before judgement
(B) Temporary Injunction
(C) Execution of Decree
(D) Appointment of Receiver

15. Under which Section/Order of the Civil Procedure Code, a Provision is made to provide "free legal services to indigent persons"?

(A) Section 151
(B) Section 115
(C) Order XXXIII, Rule 18
(D) Order XXXIII, Rule 2

16. Mark the incorrect statement.

(A) Res judicata estops the parties from proving the previous decision to be incorrect.
(B) Res judicata corresponds to that part of the doctrine of estoppel which is known in English law as 'estoppel by record'.
(C) Res judicata is similar to estoppel.
(D) Res judicata ousts the jurisdiction of the court to try the case, while estoppel shouts the mouth of a party, being a rule of evidence.

17. The place of suing in a suit for restitution of conjugal rights is the place ___.

(A) Where the husband resides
(B) Where the wife resides
(C) If the wife has never lived at the husband's place the suit must be brought in the court of the place where the wife resides
(D) All of the above

18. A party may approach the court for an amendment of his opponent's pleading. Also known as 'compulsory amendment', it is provided for under ___.

(A) Order 6, Rule 14
(B) Order 6, Rule 15
(C) Order 6, Rule 17
(D) Order 6, Rule 18

19. If a party who has obtained an order for leave to amend pleading does not amend the same within how many days, he shall not be permitted to do without leave of the court?

(A) Fifteen days
(B) Fourteen days
(C) Twenty days
(D) Thirty days

20. Abatement of proceedings is provided for under ___.

(A) Order 22
(B) Order 23
(C) Order 24
(D) Order 25

21. The Bharatiya Nagrik Suraksha Sanhita 2023 received the assent of the President on ___.

(A) 24th December, 2023
(B) 25th December, 2023
(C) 26th December, 2023
(D) 27th December, 2023

22. Offences against other laws (except I.P.C.) if punishable with imprisonment for 3 years and upward but not more than 7 years, then ___.

(A) It will be cognizable and non-cognizable
(B) Non-cognizable and bailable
(C) Cognizable and bailable
(D) Non-cognizable and non-bailable

23. Consider the following statements:

1. A court has no power to release a woman on bail if the offence is punishable with death or imprisonment for life.

2. An accused shall not be released on bail by a court if he had been convicted previously on two or more occasions of a cognizable offence punishable with imprisonment for three years or more.

3. Necessity for identification by witnesses during investigation shall not be sufficient ground for rejection of bail.

Which of the statements given above are correct?

(A) 2 only
(B) 1 and 2 only
(C) 2 and 3 only
(D) 3 only

24. The Magistrate's power to order imprisonment in default under Section 30 ___.

(A) Cannot be in excess of the Magistrate's power to order sentence under Section 29
(B) Cannot exceed one-fourth of the period of imprisonment which the Magistrate is competent to sentence
(C) Both (A) and (B)
(D) Only (A)

25. Under Section 428, the period of detention undergone by a convict cannot be set off during ___.

(A) Investigation of the case
(B) Trial of the case
(C) Enquiry of the case
(D) Any other case

26. Compounding of offence under the provisions of the Code in criminal case when charge was framed, results in ___.

(A) Acquittal of accused
(B) Discharge of accused
(C) Release only
(D) Case filed only

27. A charge-sheet is filed under Section 302 of the I.P.C, against five accused 'A', 'B', 'C', 'D' and 'E'. 'A' and 'B' are absconding, 'C' is exempted from personal appearance by the order of the Court, 'D' and 'E' are present in the Court. The case can be committed to Sessions Court against ___.

(A) 'A' and 'B'
(B) 'D' and 'F"
(C) 'D' and 'E'
(D) All the accused

28. The Court can record demeanor of a witness under which Section of Cr.P.C.?

(A) Section 280
(B) Section 279
(C) Section 278
(D) Section 281

29. It is obligatory upon the Court to grant bail to the person convicted pending presentation of an appeal under ___.

(A) Section 389(1)
(B) Section 389(2)

(C) Section 389(3)
(D) Section 389(4)

30. Which of the following has been specifically excluded from the definition of complaint under Section 2(d) of the Code of Criminal Procedure, 1973?

(A) Protest petition
(B) Joint complaint
(C) Police report
(D) None of these

31. As per the Indian Evidence Act, 1872, how old should the electronic record be in order to attract Section 90 A?

(A) Five years
(B) Twelve years
(C) Twenty years
(D) Thirty years

32. According to the Indian Evidence Act, which one among the following statements is not correct?

(A) When it is shown that a person was alive within thirty years, the burden of proving that he is dead is on the person who affirms it.
(B) When it is shown that a person was not heard of for seven years by those who would naturally have heard of him if he had been alive, the burden of proving that he is alive is on the person who affirms it.
(C) When it is shown that a person is in possession of anything, the burden of proving that he is not the owner is on the person who affirms that he is not the owner.
(D) When it is shown that one person stands to the other in a position of active confidence, the burden of proving the good faith of a transaction between them is on the party that reposed confidence in the other.

33. What does Section 3 of the Indian Evidence Act deal with?

(A) Relevancy of facts
(B) Facts which need not be proved
(C) Facts in issue
(D) None of the above

34. Under which Section of the Indian Evidence Act can a witness be cross-examined on previous statements made by them in writing or reduced into writing?

(A) Section 145
(B) Section 146
(C) Section 147
(D) Section 148

35. What is the rule regarding the admissibility of evidence of character in civil cases under the Indian Evidence Act?

(A) Character evidence is always admissible
(B) Character evidence is never admissible
(C) Character evidence is admissible in certain circumstances
(D) None of the above

36. Which Section of the Indian Evidence Act deals with the relevancy of statements made in the course of business?

(A) Section 32
(B) Section 33
(C) Section 34
(D) Section 35

37. Which of the following document is not a Public Document'?

(A) Judgement of a court
(B) Police charge-sheet
(C) Mercantile Contract
(D) Will

38. Section 92 of Indian Evidence Act is applicable to disputes between ___.

(A) the parties to the instrument only
(B) two strangers where the document is in question
(C) a party to the instrument and a stranger
(D) all of the above

39. Relevancy and admissibility under Evidence Act are ___.

(A) Synonymous
(B) Coextensive
(C) Neither synonymous nor extensive
(D) None of the above

40. The Indian Evidence Act, 1872 was drafted by ___.

(A) Lord Macaulay
(B) Sir James F. Stephen
(C) Lord Huxley
(D) Sir Henry Summermaine

41. Wrongful confinement in secret is dealt under ___.

(A) Section 344 of IPC
(B) Section 345 of IPC
(C) Section 346 of IPC
(D) Section 347 of IPC

42. 'A' is tried for voluntarily causing grievous hurt and convicted. The victim subsequently dies. The State wants to try 'A' for the offence of culpable homicide amounting to murder under IPC. Which one among the following is the correct legal position?

(A) 'A' cannot be tried for the second time as per Section 300 of Code of Criminal Procedure.
(B) 'A' was already convicted and punished and hence cannot be tried second time under the law.
(C) 'A' can be tried for the second time for culpable homicide amounting to murder.
(D) 'A' can be tried once again for the same offence that caused his death.

43. Extortion by threat of accusation of an offence punishable with death, imprisonment for life or imprisonment for ten years is dealt under ___.

(A) Section 385 of IPC
(B) Section 386 of IPC
(C) Section 387 of IPC
(D) Section 388 of IPC

44. 'A' holds 'B' down and fraudulently takes 'B's cell phone from B's trouser without his consent. Under IPC, 'A' commits the offence of ___.

(A) Robbery
(B) Extortion
(C) Dacoity
(D) Criminal misappropriation

45. 'A' obtain a decree against 'B' for a sum not due. It may be an offence under IPC, if 'A' has done so ___.

(A) Negligently
(B) Fraudulently
(C) In good faith
(D) All of the above

46. Giving or fabricating false evidence with intent to procure conviction of capital offence is provided under ___.

(A) Section 193 of IPC
(B) Section 194 of IPC
(C) Section 195 of IPC
(D) Section 196 of IPC

47. What punishment is provided under Section 298 of IPC for giving or fabricating false evidence with intent to procure conviction of capital offence?

(A) One year
(B) Two years
(C) Three years
(D) Six months

48. 'A' finds a gold ring on the road, knowing it to be the property of 'Z, he having unknowingly lost it there. 'A' picks up the ring and pledges it with a money lender to raise a loan, 'A' has committed ___.

(A) Dishonest misappropriation of property
(B) Criminal breach of trust
(C) Theft
(D) No offence

49. 'A' is carried off by the tiger. 'Z' fires at the tiger in good faith intending to rescue 'A', knowing it to be likely that the shot My kill 'A'. The shot fired by 'Z' gives 'A' a mortal wound. 'Z' has committed ___.

(A) No offence
(B) Culpable homicide not amounting to murder
(C) Offence of causing death by negligence
(D) Murder

50. 'A', a police officer tortures 'Z' in order to induce 'Z' to confess that he has committed a crime, here 'A' is guilty of offence of ___.

(A) Criminal force
(B) Assault
(C) Hurt
(D) Extortion

51. Which statements cover the definition of "domestic violence" under the PWDV Act, 2005?

1. Any physical, emotional, or economic harm inflicted by a family member.

2. Any act of violence committed against a woman in her home.

3. Any form of abuse that occurs within a domestic setting.

(A) 1 and 2 only
(B) 2 and 3 only
(C) 1, 2 and 3
(D) 1 only

52. Which of the following is not a form of domestic violence recognized under the PWDV Act, 2005?

(A) Physical abuse
(B) Verbal abuse
(C) None is true
(D) Both are true

53. Section 22 of the PWDV Act, 2005 provides for ___.

(A) Protection orders
(B) Residence orders
(C) Custody orders
(D) Compensation orders

54. What is the punishment provided under Section 31 of the PWDV Act, 2005?

(A) 3 years imprisonment
(B) 1 year imprisonment
(C) 5 years imprisonment
(D) 6 months

55. Statement 1: The PWDV Act, 2005 provides for the establishment of Protection Officers to assist victims of domestic violence.

Statement 2: The PWDV Act, 2005 provides for rehabilitation of children of victim of domestic violence.

(A) Only 1 is true
(B) Only 2 is true
(C) Both are true
(D) None of the above is true

56. Where the prescribed period of limitation for any application is expiring on a holiday, the application ___.

(A) should be made a day prior to holiday
(B) may be made on the day when the court reopens
(C) may be made within thirty days of reopening of the court
(D) may be made on any day after the court reopens

57. Section 5 of the Limitation Act applies to ___.

(A) Suits
(B) Appeals/Applications
(C) Both (A) and (B)
(D) None of these

58. Section 5 of the Limitation Act does not apply to ___.

(A) Suit
(B) Appeal
(C) Application
(D) All of these

59. Which of the following proposition is incorrect?

(A) Where the disability continues up to the death of that person, his legal representative may institute the suit within the same period after the death, as would otherwise have been allowed from the time so specified
(B) Where once time has begun to run, no subsequent disability or inability to institute a suit or make an application stops it
(C) In computing the period of limitation for any suit, the day from which such period is to be reckoned, shall not be excluded
(D) In computing the period of limitation for an application to set aside an award, the time requisite for obtaining a copy of award shall be excluded

60. In which of the following circumstance, the plaintiff shall not get the benefit as provided under Section 14 of the Limitation Act?

(A) Where another civil proceeding is disposed of after adjudication on merits by the competent court
(B) Where another civil proceeding is disposed of for want of jurisdiction to the said court
(C) Where another civil proceeding was diligently prosecuted by the plaintiff in good faith in a court having no jurisdiction to try the said matter
(D) None of the above

61. The important case of the Supreme Court N. Balakrishnan v. M. Krishnamurthy, (1998) 7 SCC 123 is related to ___.

(A) Length of delay is no matter; acceptability of the explanation is the only criterion
(B) The condonation of delay is a matter of discretion of the court
(C) Widened the scope and ambit of law of limitation
(D) All of the above

62. A suit for possession of immovable property based on title can be brought within 12 years from ___.

(A) the date of dispossession
(B) the date of demand of possession
(C) the date on which the defendant refuses to deliver possession
(D) the date on which possession of defendant becomes adverse

63. If the defendant is abroad during the period of limitation ___.

(A) such period is excluded from the period of limitation
(B) such period is included in the period of limitation
(C) such period is excluded from the period of limitation only if the period to stay abroad is more than thirty days
(D) none of these

64. Which of the following amount to presenting civil proceedings with 'due diligence and in good faith' within the meaning of Section 14 of the Limitation Act?

(A) Failure to pay the requisite court fee found deficient
(B) Error of judgement in valuing a suit
(C) Both (A) and (B)
(D) Neither (A) nor (B)

65. Indemnity-holder, acting within the scope of his authority, is entitled to recover from the promisor ___.

(A) All damages which he may be compelled to pay in any suit
(B) All costs which he may be compelled to pay in any suit
(C) All sums which he may have paid under the terms of any compromise of any suit
(D) All of the above

66. Continuing Guarantee has been defined under ___.

(A) Section 124 of the Indian Contract Act
(B) Section 129 of the Indian Contract Act
(C) Section 146 of the Indian Contract Act
(D) Section 148 of the Indian Contract Act

67. Who said that "An offer need not be made to an ascertained person, but no contract can arise until it has been accepted by an ascertained person"?

(A) Lord Atkin
(B) Lord Goddard
(C) Chashre and Fifoot
(D) Anson

68. Quasi-contract emerged from ___.

(A) Assumpsit
(B) Indebitatus assumpsit
(C) Non-feasance
(D) Misfeasance

69. Which of the following is not a quasi-contract?

(A) Obligation of person enjoying benefit of non-gratuitous act
(B) Responsibility of finder of goods
(C) Quantum meruit
(D) Novation

70. 'X' contracted with a tent house for erecting a shamiana for performing the marriage of his daughter. On the day of marriage, a curfew was clamped in the area preventing the celebration of the marriage. The shamiana owner claims the charges agreed to be paid by 'X'. In the light of the above, which one of the following is correct?

(A) 'X' has to pay the contracted charges
(B) 'X' need not pay the agreed charges but only reasonable charges
(C) 'X' can require the state to bear the claim for damages
(D) 'X' need not pay anything as the celebration of the marriage was impossible on account of the curfew

71. 'X' and 'Y' jointly take a loan from "Z with promise to repay the loan amount with interest within two years. Soon after taking the loan, 'X' is declared as an insolvent and remains insolvent till the date of repayment of loan. 'Y' also fails to repay the loan. 'X' on account of his status as insolvent enjoys immunity from legal proceedings. In these circumstances ___.

(A) 'Z' can in law institute a suit for recovery of, only 50% of the outstanding from Y
(B) 'Z' is entitled in law to sue Y alone for recovery of the entire outstanding amount
(C) 'Z' is not entitled to sue 'Y' also for recovery of loan amount till the order of insolvency of 'X' ceases to operate
(D) 'Z' is entitled in law to sue 'Y' for 50% of the principal amount due and the entire interest outstanding

72. Where two parties have made a contract which one of them has broken, the damages which the other party ought to receive in respect of such breach should be such as may fairly and reasonable be considered either arising naturally or reasonable be supposed to have been in contemplation of both the parties at the time of entering the contract. This statement was laid down in the case of ___.

(A) Frost v. Knight

(B) Hadley v. Baxendale
(C) Dunlop Pneumatic Tyre Ltd. v. New Garage and Motor Co. Ltd.
(D) General v. Barker

73. Section 73 of the Indian Contract Act, 1872 is based on the law of ___.

(A) Lumley v. Wagner case
(B) Paradine v. Jane case
(C) Taylor v. Caldwell case
(D) Hadley v. Baxendale case

74. For the purposes of the Specific Relief Act, 1963 the word "settlement" means ___.

(A) An instrument whereby the destination or devolution of successive interests in movable property is disposed of
(B) An instrument including codicil or will whereby the destination or devolution of successive interests in immovable property is disposed of or is agreed to be disposed of
(C) An instrument including codicil or will whereby the devolution of successive interests in movable or immovable property is disposed of
(D) An instrument including codicil or will whereby the destination or devolution of successive interests in movable or immovable property is disposed of or is agreed to be disposed of

75. The Specific Relief Act, 1963 is the product of ___.

(A) 8th Report of the Law Commission of India on Specific Relief on 1958
(B) 9th Report of the Law Commission of India on Specific Relief on 1958
(C) 10th Report of the Law Commission of India on Specific Relief on 1958
(D) None of the above

76. An order or decree passed in a suit presented under Section 6 of the Specific Relief Act is ___.

(A) Appealable
(B) Reviewable
(C) Neither appealable nor reviewable
(D) Appealable and reviewable both

77. A defendant in a suit for recovery of possession of immovable property ___.

(A) Can take the plea of lawful title and in the alternative the plea of adverse possession
(B) Cannot take the plea of lawful title and in the alternative the plea of adverse possession

as the two are antithetical to each other
(C) Can take a plea of lawful title and in the alternative the plea of adverse possession and succeed on both
(D) Can take a plea of lawful title and in the alternative the plea of adverse possession and succeed on either

78. If any person is dispossessed of immovable property without his consent otherwise than in due course of law, he may, by a suit, recover possession thereof, notwithstanding any other title that may be set up in such suit, within a period of ___.

(A) Six months from the date of dispossession
(B) Three months from the date of dispossession
(C) One year from the date of dispossession
(D) Three years from the date of dispossession

79. Which of the following proposition is correct?

(A) Where a party to the contract has not obtained substituted performance of contract in accordance with the provisions of Section 20 of the Specific Relief Act, 1963
(B) A contract, the performance of which involves the performance of a continuous duty which the court cannot supervise
(C) A contract, which is in its nature not determinable
(D) All of the above

80. Mr. 'A' makes an allegation that Mr. 'B' assaulted him and physically injured him. Mr. 'B' states that the allegation is mischievous and false. He seeks to file a suit to restrain Mr. 'A' from instituting or prosecuting any proceedings in a criminal matter. In view of Section 41 of the Specific Relief Act, 1963, which one of the following is true?

(A) The court can restrain Mr. 'A' from instituting or prosecuting any proceedings in a criminal matter
(B) The court can pass a restrain order provided it is proved that Mr. 'A' is making a false allegation
(C) The court can pass a restrain order in favour of Mr. 'B' provided he deposits appropriate security in court
(D) No such injunction can be granted

81. In which of the following case, Supreme Court ruled that a suit seeking merely declaration to title of ownership about a property without seeking possession, when the

plaintiff is not in possession of the property is not maintainable?

(A) Union of India v. Ibrahim, (2012) 8 SCC 148
(B) Rukhmabal v. Lala Laxminarayan, AIR (1960) SC 335
(C) Mayawanti v. Kaushalya Devi, (1990) 3 SCC 1
(D) Ramzan v. Hussaini, (1990) 1 SCC 104

82. In which of the following cases, injunction cannot be granted?

i. If it would impede or delay the progress or completion of any infrastructure project or interfere with the continued provision of relevant facility related thereto or services being the subject matter of such project

ii. When the plaintiff has personal interest in the matter

iii. To prevent the breach of a contract, the performance of which would not be specifically enforce iv. To restrain any person from instituting or prosecuting any proceeding in a civil matter

Codes:

(A) i and iv
(B) ii, iii and iv
(C) i and iii
(D) i, ii and iv

83. Doctrine of 'lis pendens' embodied in Section 52, Transfer of Property Act ___.

(A) Invalidate the transfer of immovable property during pending of the suit
(B) It only enacts that the purchaser pendente lite suit is bound by the result of the litigation
(C) It bars the transfer of property during pending of the suit
(D) It protects the right of collusive transferee

84. 'A' makes a gift of land to 'B'. 'C' sues 'A' for possession of the land. While the suit is pending, 'B' transfers the land to 'D'. 'A' dies and 'C' obtain a decree for possession against 'B' as legal representative of 'A'. Is 'D's title affected by the rule of lis pendens so as to be subject of 'C's decree?

(A) Yes, because transfer is without consideration
(B) No, because 'B' was not a party to the suit at the time of transfer by 'B' to 'D'
(C) 'B' is not legal representative of 'A' for 'C's decree
(D) After gift made to 'B', 'C' cannot sue 'A' for

possession of the land

85. Match List-I with List - II and select the correct answer using the codes given below the lists.

	List - I		List - II
a.	Sale	1.	Section 21
b.	Marshalling	2.	Section 122
c.	Gift	3.	Section 54
d.	Contingent interest	4.	Section 81

Codes:

(A) a-4, b-3, c-2, d-1
(B) a-3, b-4, c-2, d-1
(C) a-1, b-2, c-3, d-4
(D) a-1, b-4, c-3, d-2

86. 'A' takes a loan of Rs. 5,000 from 'B' and mortgages his house as security. In the mortgage deed, it was also mentioned that if he could not pay the amount within 5 years, then 'B' will have right to sell the house and recover his amount. If the money could not be recovered from sale of house, then 'A' will be personally liable. It is ___.

(A) Mortgage by conditional sale
(B) English mortgage
(C) Usufructuary mortgage
(D) Simple mortgage

87. The mortgagor's right to redeem the mortgage property accrues ___.

(A) at any time after the mortgage
(B) at any time after the mortgage money has become due
(C) at any time when the mortgagor wants
(D) at any time, mortgagee demands the money

88. The mortgagee has a right to sue for the mortgage money in the following cases namely ___.
(A) Section 68 (1) (c) where the mortgage is deprived of the whole or part of his security by or in consequence of the wrongful act or default of the mortgagor
(B) Section 68 (1) (d) where, the mortgagee being entitled to possession of the mortgaged property, the mortgagor fails to deliver the same to him or to secure the possession thereof to him without disturbance by the mortgagor or any person claiming under a title superior to that of the mortgagor
(C) Both (A) and (B)

(D) None of the above

89. Match List-I with List-II and select the correct answer using the codes given below the lists.

	List - I		List - II
a.	Doctrine of Subrogation	1.	Section 17, TPA
b.	Doctrine of Consideration	2.	Section 52, TPA
c.	Doctrine of Accumulation	3.	Section 61, TPA
d.	Doctrine of lis pendens	4.	Section 92, TPA

Codes:

(A) a-1, b-2, c-3, d-4
(B) a-3, b-2, c-1, d-4
(C) a-4, b-3, c-2, d-1
(D) a-4, b-3, c-1, d-2

90. 'A' owes money to 'B', who transfers the debt to 'C'. 'B', then demands the debt from 'A', who not having received notice of the transfer, as prescribed in Section 131 of T.P. Act, pays 'B'. The payment is ___.

(A) Void
(B) Voidable
(C) Valid and 'C' can sue 'A' for debt
(D) Valid and 'C' cannot sue 'A' for the debt

91. Which of the following gifts is valid?

(A) 'A' gives Rs. 5,000 to 'B' on condition that he shall murder 'C'
(B) 'A' makes a gift of his field to 'B' with a proviso that if 'B' becomes insolvent, 'B's interest in the field shall cease
(C) 'A' makes a gift of his field to 'B' with a condition that if 'B' does not within a year set fire to 'C's house, his interest shall cease
(D) 'A' makes a gift of a house to 'B' on the condition that the gift will be forfeited if 'B' does not reside in it

92. Under the provisions of Hindu Succession Act, 1956, any property inherited by a female Hindu from her father or mother shall devolve, in absence of any son or daughter of the deceased (including the children of any pre-deceased son of daughter) ___.

(A) Upon the heirs referred to in Section 15(1) of the Act
(B) Upon the heirs of deceased female Hindu's father

(C) Upon the heirs of deceased female Hindu's husband
(D) None of the above

93. Proceedings to be in camera and may not be printed or published, is provided in Section of the Hindu Marriage Act, 1955?

(A) Section 24
(B) Section 22
(C) Section 21
(D) Section 23

94. Escheat under Hindu Succession Act means ___.

(A) Individual dies intestate and doesn't leave behind an heir
(B) Individual dies intestate and doesn't leave behind an heir, who is qualified to succeed to the property
(C) Individual dies intestate and doesn't leave behind an heir, who is qualified to succeed to the property, the property devolves on the Government
(D) Individual dies intestate and doesn't leave behind an heir, who is qualified to succeed to the property, the property doesn't devolve on the Government

95. What is codicil?

i. It is a schedule to any kind of will.

ii. It must be created by the original creator of will.

iii. It is an addendum of any kind to a will.

iv. It doesn't alter provisions of the will.

Codes:

(A) i and ii
(B) ii and iv
(C) ii and iii
(D) iii and iv

96. In coparcenary property, each coparcener can acquire interest by ___.

(A) Partition
(B) Birth
(C) Attaining majority
(D) All of the above

97. Under the Hindu Succession Act, 1956, daughter's son and father of a male Hindu are legal heirs and they are placed as the following ___.

(A) Both are placed as class I heir of the Schedule
(B) Father is placed in class I and daughter's son is placed in class II of the Schedule
(C) Daughter's son is placed as class I and father as class II heir of the Schedule
(D) Both are class II heirs of the Schedule

98. The convert's descendants under the Hindu Succession Act, 1956 will be ___.

(A) qualified to inherit the property
(B) partially qualified to inherit the property
(C) partially qualified and partially disqualified to inherit the property
(D) disqualified to inherit the property

99. In the case of Prakash vs Phulwati, 2016 2 SCC 36, the court dealt with ___.

(A) Section 5 of Hindu Succession Amendment Act, 2005
(B) Interpretation of Section 6 of Hindu Succession Act, 1956 as amended by Hindu Succession Amendment Act, 2005
(C) Question of retrospective application of Hindu Succession Amendment Act, 2005
(D) None of the above

100. The system of a joint family with its incident of succession by survivorship is a peculiarity of the Hindu law. The beneficial interest of each coparcener in Mitakshara law is liable to fluctuation, increasing by the death of another coparcener and decreasing by the birth of a new coparcener.

(A) G. Rajendra v. Smt. G. Nalini, 2020
(B) Vineeta Sharma v. Rakesh Sharma, 2020
(C) Prakash v. Phulwati, 2020
(D) None of the above

Answers

1	B	41	C	81	A
2	B	42	C	82	C
3	C	43	D	83	B
4	D	44	A	84	B
5	D	45	B	85	B
6	D	46	B	86	D
7	C	47	XX	87	B
8	C	48	A	88	C
9	D	49	A	89	D
10	A	50	C	90	D
11	B	51	C	91	D
12	B	52	C	92	B
13	A	53	D	93	B

14	B	54	B	94	C
15	C	55	A	95	C
16	C	56	B	96	D
17	D	57	B	97	B
18	C	58	A	98	D
19	B	59	C	99	B
20	A	60	A	100	B
21	B	61	D		
22	X	62	D		
23	C	63	A		
24	C	64	D		
25	D	65	D		
26	A	66	B		
27	D	67	D		
28	A	68	B		
29	C	69	D		
30	C	70	D		
31	A	71	B		
32	D	72	B		
33	C	73	D		
34	A	74	D		
35	C	75	B		
36	A	76	C		
37	D	77	B		
38	A	78	A		
39	C	79	B		
40	B	80	D		

EXPLANATIONS

2011

1. (D) All of the above: Abetment involves instigating, conspiring, or aiding a crime, making the person responsible for the offense.

2. (C) Melvill, J. in R. V. Govinda: The case clarified the distinction between Sections 299 and 300, which define culpable homicide and its categories.

3. (D) 304-B of the IPC: Section 304-B covers dowry death, where the woman dies within seven years of marriage due to cruelty or dowry harassment.

4. (D) All of the above: Grievous hurt includes severe bodily harm such as emasculation, disfigurement, or injuries endangering life.

5. (C) Wrongful restraint: Preventing someone from moving in a direction they have the right to go without using force constitutes wrongful restraint.

6. (A) Abduction: Forcibly or deceitfully taking someone from one place to another constitutes abduction.

7. (D) People of India: The Preamble of the Constitution is a declaration made in the name of the people of India.

8. (A) Habeas Corpus: A legal writ used to challenge unlawful detention or imprisonment.

9. (B) An Important Constitutional Right: The right to contest elections, unless disqualified, is an important constitutional right.

10. (A) Free Legal Aid: Article 39A promotes equal access to justice by providing free legal aid for those unable to afford it.

11. (D) The President of India: The President appoints the members of the Union Public Service Commission (UPSC).

12. (D) 42nd Amendment: The 42nd Amendment prioritized Directive Principles over Fundamental Rights.

13. (D) Chief Justice of India: The President of India's oath is administered by the Chief Justice of India.

14. (D) Article 117: Deals with special provisions related to Finance Bills in the Indian Constitution.

15. (C) Article 358: Suspends provisions of Article 19 during an Emergency, limiting fundamental rights.

16. (C) Fifth Schedule: Governs the administration and control of Scheduled Areas and Scheduled Tribes in India.

17. (C) 1999: Section 89 of the CPC was inserted in 1999 to provide alternative dispute resolution options.

18. (A) Two months: A two-month notice is required before filing a suit against the government, as per Section 80 CPC.

19. (D) None of the above: A limitation question does not operate as res judicata since it involves procedural time constraints.

20. (D) Applies to the whole of India except Jammu and Kashmir, Nagaland, and Tribal Areas: The CPC applies throughout India with exceptions in specific regions.

21. (B) Can be arrested: A judgment debtor may be arrested if they fail to comply with a court's payment order.

22. (C) Can be attached by an order: Movable property not in possession of the debtor can be attached by prohibiting its transfer.

23. (D) All of the above: Precept is an authoritative order or writ issued by a competent authority.

24. (C) Judgment Debtor's Debtor: A garnishee order directs a third party owing money to the judgment debtor to pay the creditor.

25. (C) Of its own motion: Suo motu refers to an action taken by a court on its own initiative.

26. (A) "Actus curiae neminem gravabit": A court's actions should not harm anyone involved in the legal process.

27. (B) Section 75 of the Indian Evidence Act, 1872: It deals with the rules for private documents as evidence.

28. (A) Admission: Defined in Section 17 of the Indian Evidence Act, an admission is a statement that suggests an inference about a relevant fact.

29. (A) Section 23 of the Indian Evidence Act: Admissions in civil cases are relevant and may be used as evidence.

30. (D) Section 141 of the Indian Evidence Act: A leading question is one suggesting the answer the questioner expects.

31. (A) Examination-in-Chief: Section 137 of the Indian Evidence Act defines the initial questioning of a witness by the calling party.

32. (B) Cross-Examination: The questioning of a witness by the opposing party after the examination-in-chief.

33. (A) Section 115 of the Indian Evidence Act: Deals with the principle of estoppel, preventing contradictory statements.

34. (B) Dumb Witness: A witness unable to speak may communicate through gestures, writing, or sign language.

35. (B) "Actus me invito factus non est mens actus": An act done against one's will is not considered their act.

36. (C) Robbery: A crime that combines theft and extortion, with the use of force or threats.

37. (A) Unsound Mind: Includes individuals like "idiots," who lack mental capacity to understand or manage their affairs.

38. (A) Affray: A public disturbance caused by fighting in a public place.

39. (A) Three years: A Magistrate of the first class can pass a sentence of imprisonment for up to three years.

40. (D) Section 41 Cr. P. C.: Allows police officers to arrest without a warrant for cognizable offenses.

41. (C): The power to search a place is provided under Section 47 of the Criminal Procedure Code (Cr. P. C.). This section grants a police officer the authority to conduct searches of locations such as homes, vehicles, or vessels, under certain circumstances, often requiring a warrant or prior approval.

42. (D): The process to compel individuals to appear before the Criminal Courts includes tools like summons, warrants, and attachment or sale of property. These mechanisms ensure that individuals involved in a case are present for the proceedings, and failure to comply can lead to further legal action.

43. (C): Section 82 of the Cr. P. C. allows for the proclamation of an absconder or proclaimed offender when a person against whom a warrant has been issued avoids execution. It marks the individual as avoiding justice, often leading to arrest and further legal penalties.

44. (B): Disputes regarding possession of immovable property are typically addressed by an Executive Magistrate. This individual has jurisdiction over property possession cases and can issue appropriate orders to resolve conflicts related to property ownership or occupancy.

45. (C): Section 161(3) of the Cr. P. C. outlines the procedure for recording statements of witnesses by a police officer during an investigation. This section is vital for ensuring the reliability of witness statements and securing evidence that can be used in criminal proceedings.

46. (D): Under Section 167 of the Cr. P. C., a Magistrate has the discretion to determine the type of custody an accused individual should be held in during the investigation process. This provision grants flexibility in managing the accused's detention.

47. (D): Section 225 of the Cr. P. C. does not deal with the joinder of charges. Instead, it addresses the trial of multiple offenses committed by an individual in separate transactions, emphasizing the need for separate trials for each offense.

48. (A): Section 300 of the Cr. P. C. incorporates the principle "Nemo debet bis vexari pro eadem causa," which means no one should be tried or punished twice for the same offense. This section provides a safeguard against double jeopardy.

49. (B): Chapter V of the Indian Evidence Act, 1872 deals with documentary evidence. It governs how documents are presented, examined, and authenticated as evidence in court proceedings, ensuring that documents are used fairly and legally in the judicial process.

50. (A): Section 62 of the Indian Evidence Act defines primary evidence as the document itself, presented to the court for inspection. Primary evidence is typically given more weight in court due to its direct and original nature compared to secondary evidence.

51. (A): An actionable claim is a transferable property, representing a right to enforce an obligation, such as a debt or damages. It can be legally transferred or assigned to another person and can be pursued in court for enforcement.

52. (C): A usufructuary mortgage allows the mortgagee to enjoy the benefits (such as income or produce) from the mortgaged property in lieu of interest on the debt. This form of mortgage grants the lender temporary possession of the property for a specific purpose.

53. (D): The responsibility to pay outgoings like taxes and utility bills typically lies with the buyer after the property transfer. The seller generally ensures that all dues are cleared before the transfer but is not obligated to pay ongoing outgoings after the property changes hands.

54. (D): The consideration for a lease often includes a premium, which is a one-time payment made by the lessee to the lessor in exchange for granting the lease. This premium is distinct from the periodic rent payment.

55. (D): An ostensible owner is someone who presents themselves as the owner of a property but does not have legal ownership. This may be done to facilitate transactions or deceive others into believing they have rights over the property.

56. (C): Section 14 of the Transfer of Property Act addresses the Rule Against Perpetuity, which restricts the creation of future interests in property that may vest too remotely. This rule ensures that property interests are not tied up indefinitely, preventing unreasonable restrictions on ownership.

57. (C): The limitation period for filing a suit

based on a promissory note is three years from the date of execution. This is outlined in the Limitation Act and sets a time frame within which a legal claim can be made regarding a promissory note.

58. (B): The limitation period for a suit by a surety against a co-surety for an excess payment is three years. This period begins once the surety has made the payment beyond their share and wishes to recover the overpayment from the co-surety.

59. (D): The limitation period for a landlord to recover possession of a property from a tenant after the tenancy has been terminated is twelve years. This provides the landlord ample time to initiate legal proceedings to regain possession.

60. The limitation period for filing a Review Petition for a judgment review by a court (other than the Supreme Court) is 30 days, as provided in Article 124 of the Limitation Act. This short period ensures that reviews are filed in a timely manner after the judgment or order.

61. (B): Section 12(2) of the Limitation Act excludes the time taken to obtain a copy of the decree or order being appealed against from the limitation period for appeals, reviews, or revisions. This ensures that parties are not penalized for delays outside their control.

62. (A): 'Time requisite' under Section 12(2) of the Limitation Act refers to the absolutely necessary time that is required to obtain a copy of the decree or order. This period is excluded from the calculation of the limitation period for filing appeals, reviews, or revisions.

63. (D): Section 17 of the Limitation Act allows an extended limitation period in cases of concealment, fraud, or mistakes by the defendant. This provision ensures that the plaintiff can still pursue a claim if the defendant's actions prevented the plaintiff from discovering their legal right.

64. (B): Section 17 of the Limitation Act does not apply to execution applications. It specifically relates to cases where the limitation period for filing a suit or appeal is extended due to fraud, concealment, or mistake, but does not extend to execution applications.

65. (B): The limitation period for challenging a sale executed under a decree is 60 days. This time frame allows parties to contest the validity of the sale and seek its cancellation if there are grounds for doing so.

66. (C): Section 14 of the Limitation Act allows for the exclusion of time spent due to factors like deficiency in court fees or errors in the judgment on the valuation of a suit. These

situations are considered reasonable delays, and the time spent is not counted against the party's claim.

67. (A): In Vallikannu vs. R. Sengaperumal, the court disqualified the daughter-in-law from claiming her father-in-law's property due to her husband's involvement in murdering his father. The court emphasized the principle of disqualifying heirs involved in heinous crimes.

68. (C): The presumption under Section 21 of the Hindu Succession Act, 1956 that the younger person survives the elder is rebuttable. This means it can be challenged with contrary evidence to establish otherwise.

69. (A): Section 27(a) of the Indian Succession Act, 1925 ensures equal inheritance rights for male and female heirs among agnates and cognates. This provision promotes gender equality in matters of succession.

70. (D): An instrument intended to be a will executed by someone who lacks the mental capacity to understand its nature or contents is considered invalid. Legal capacity and understanding are essential for a valid will.

71. (B): Section 112 of the Indian Succession Act, 1925 states that if a bequest is made to a person described by a particular description, but no person fitting that description exists at the testator's death, the bequest is void.

72. (A): When a testator repeats a bequest within the same will using identical wording, the legatee is entitled to only one legacy, regardless of the repetition. This prevents multiple claims for the same bequest.

73. (B): Schedule V of the Indian Succession Act, 1925 outlines the "Form of Caveat." This schedule provides the format for filing a caveat in cases related to wills or intestate succession matters.

74. (C): Section 14 of the Hindu Succession Act, 1956 applies to both movable and immovable property, ensuring equal inheritance rights for both male and female heirs over any type of property.

75. (D): Section 5 of the Specific Relief Act provides that a suit for possession can be filed within 12 years. This is the time limit within which an individual can claim possession of a property to which they are legally entitled.

76. (C): The Specific Relief Act allows for the recovery of possession of both movable and immovable property, providing legal remedies based on the specific circumstances of the case.

77. (D): Section 26 of the Specific Relief Act does not prescribe a specific time limit for the

discovery of mistakes or fraud in a case. The section mainly deals with the issue of suits for specific performance and injunctions.

78. (C): Section 40 of the Specific Relief Act allows a party who has been wrongfully restrained or enjoined to claim damages. This section provides a remedy for individuals suffering harm due to wrongful legal actions taken against them.

79. (C): Section 11 of the Specific Relief Act, 1963 enables specific performance of contracts related to trusts. It allows courts to enforce such contracts, ensuring that the terms related to trust management and administration are upheld.

80. (B): Under the Specific Relief Act, the obligation is a personal right (right in personam), not a right in rem. This means the right is enforceable against specific individuals, not the public at large.

81. A: The court can refuse a declaratory decree under the Specific Relief Act if it deems it unnecessary or inappropriate based on the case's facts and circumstances.

82. C: Part performance of a contract can be enforced by both the promisor and promisee under Section 12(2) of the Specific Relief Act if certain conditions are met.

83. A: Section 8 of the Specific Relief Act provides remedies for the recovery of movable property from someone in possession or control who wrongfully refuses to deliver it.

84. D: Section 6 of the Specific Relief Act does not grant the court the power to adjudicate on title or remove structures in suits involving land disputes.

85. A: "Donatio mortis causa" refers to a gift made in anticipation of imminent death, contingent upon the donor's death.

86. B: The right of redemption allows the mortgagor to reclaim mortgaged property by paying off the full mortgage debt.

87. C: The doctrine of lis pendens prevents property transactions during pending litigation, as the outcome affects the property.

88. D: Section 35 of the Specific Relief Act deals with the doctrine of election, concerning accepting or rejecting conflicting rights.

89. B: To convert a proposal into a promise, the acceptance must be absolute and unqualified, conforming to the proposal's terms.

90. D: Contracts of Adhesion are pre-drafted, standardized contracts offered on a take-it-or-leave-it basis.

91. A: An agreement to discover treasure by magic is void, as it involves an impossible act.

92. C: In a hire-based bailment, the bailor is liable for any faults in the goods, even if unaware.

93. C: A contract of guarantee can be oral or written, depending on the agreement between the guarantor and creditor.

94. D: An anticipatory breach occurs if the promisor repudiates the contract before the performance date, allowing the promisee to treat it as breached.

95. A: A sub-agent is employed by an agent and acts under the agent's control in agency-related business.

96. C: A contingent contract, like one to pay Rs. 20,000 if B's house burns, depends on a specific event.

97. B: Consideration is not required to create an agency; the relationship is based on the principal-agent dynamic.

98. A: An agreement with unlawful object or consideration is void and unenforceable.

99. C: An "heir" under Section 3(f) of the Hindu Succession Act refers to anyone entitled to inherit an intestate person's property, including women.

100. D: The Hindu Succession Amendment Act, 2005, effective from September 9, 2005, grants daughters equal inheritance rights in ancestral property.

2012

1. (c) R. C. Cooper v. Union of India challenged the nationalization of Indian banks, upholding the Bank Nationalization Act, 1969, in a landmark 1970 ruling with significant implications for the banking sector.

2. (a) Five fundamental rights are guaranteed exclusively to Indian citizens under Articles 19-22, including the right to freedom of speech, peaceful assembly, and residence within India.

3. (d) Schedule XII of the Indian Constitution defines the division of powers between Municipalities and the State Government, addressing the structure, powers, and functions of Municipalities for local self-government.

4. (b) Presidential satisfaction under Article 356 for imposing President's Rule is subject to judicial review, allowing courts to examine it for malafide or constitutional violations.

5. (c) The Lokpal Bill was introduced under Article 253 to implement international treaties, establishing Lokpal and Lokayuktas to combat public sector corruption.

6. (c) Under Article 304, state legislatures can impose reasonable restrictions on trade and commerce within the state or with other states to protect public interests.

7. (a) Article 245 relates to the Doctrine of Territorial Nexus, which limits the jurisdiction of laws made by Parliament and state legislatures based on territorial jurisdiction.

8. (b) The 42nd Amendment of 1976 added "socialist" and "secular" to the Preamble, changing India's description to a "sovereign, socialist, secular, and democratic republic."

9. (b) Karnataka has a bicameral legislature, consisting of the Legislative Assembly (Vidhana Sabha) and the Legislative Council (Vidhana Parishad).

10. (d) Amendments to Supreme Court provisions require a special majority, requiring approval from both Houses of Parliament with a two-thirds majority of members present and voting.

11. (b) A suit is dismissed for non-joinder of a necessary party under Order 1, Rule 9 of the CPC, meaning a necessary party's absence renders the suit incomplete.

12. (d) A legal representative, under Section 2(11) of the CPC, steps into the shoes of a deceased party, representing their estate in ongoing legal proceedings.

13. (a) Under Order X, Rule 1A, a court can direct parties to choose an alternative dispute resolution (ADR) method like mediation or arbitration to resolve their dispute.

14. (b) Discovery by interrogatories and inspection is governed by Order XI of the CPC, enabling parties to seek written responses and inspect relevant documents.

15. (a) Section 152 of the CPC allows correction of clerical or arithmetical mistakes in judgments or orders to ensure accuracy and avoid injustice.

16. (c) Compensatory costs for false or vexatious claims are imposed under Section 35A of the CPC, discouraging frivolous litigation and compensating the opposing party.

17. (b) Abetment of proceedings under Order XXII of the CPC governs suits and appeals following changes in a party's legal status, requiring substitution of representatives.

18. (d) A temporary injunction is granted when there is a prima facie case, irreparable injury, and the balance of convenience favors the applicant.

19. (c) Section 96 of the CPC grants the right to appeal an original decree, allowing an aggrieved party to challenge the trial court's decision in a higher court.

20. (d) Adjournment is governed by Order XVII, Rule 1 of the CPC, allowing the court to postpone hearings for reasons like unavailability of parties or need for further evidence.

21. (b) A non-cognizable offense does not allow arrest without a warrant, requiring police to follow procedures, including court permission, before making an arrest.

22. (d) Assistant Public Prosecutors, appointed under Section 25 of the Cr.P.C., assist the Public Prosecutor in conducting criminal cases on behalf of the state.

23. (d) A police officer, magistrate, or private person may arrest someone depending on the situation, with specific legal conditions guiding each type of arrest.

24. (d) Under Section 50 of the Cr.P.C., the arrested person is not entitled to be informed of their right to bail for non-bailable offenses during arrest without a warrant.

25. (c) A summons must be issued in writing and in duplicate under the Cr.P.C., ensuring formal notification and providing a record for the court.

26. (B) Under Section 167 of the Cr.P.C., an Executive Magistrate can grant remand for a maximum period of 7 days, allowing detention during investigation.

27. (D) Section 223 of the Cr.P.C. allows the joint trial of several persons accused of related offenses, ensuring an expeditious and fair trial.

28. (B) Section 259 of the Cr.P.C. allows a court to convert a summons case into a warrant case if the circumstances require arresting the accused.

29. (B) Section 313 of the Cr.P.C. provides the court the power to examine the accused, allowing them to explain the circumstances and evidence against them.

30. (C) Section 357 of the Cr.P.C. allows both trial and appellate courts to order compensation for victims, including dependents, in criminal cases.

31. (B) The Indian Evidence Act, 1872 aims to consolidate, define, and amend the law regarding the admissibility and evaluation of evidence in legal proceedings.

32. (B) The Law of Evidence is an adjective law, as it dictates the procedural rules for presenting and evaluating evidence in legal proceedings.

33. (A) For a fact to be relevant under the Indian Evidence Act, it must be legally relevant, having a logical connection to the issue in question.

34. (D) A confession of one accused is admissible against all co-accused if tried jointly for the same offense, under the principle of joint trial.

35. (D) A dying declaration is admissible in

both civil and criminal cases, as it is considered truthful due to the belief that the declarant is near death.

36. (A) An expert can provide an opinion on foreign law, assisting the court in understanding the applicable legal principles from other jurisdictions.

37. (C) Secondary evidence is admissible when the primary evidence cannot be produced, provided the party accounts for the absence of the original.

38. (D) The burden of proving possession of a ticket lies with the accused in a case of traveling without a ticket, as per the presumption of fact.

39. (B) A presumption of fact arises when a document creating an obligation is in the obligor's possession, assuming the obligation has been discharged.

40. (C) In both civil and criminal cases, spouses can be competent witnesses for or against each other, subject to rules of relevancy and admissibility.

41. (B) Section 25: Fraudulent intent is defined under IPC Section 25, which refers to actions done with intent to defraud in criminal offenses.

42. (B) Section 34: Section 34 establishes joint liability, meaning all participants in a criminal act with common intent are equally liable.

43. (A) Ignorance of Law is no excuse: "Ignorantia juris non excusat" means ignorance of the law does not justify failure to comply with it.

44. (B) Legal insanity: Section 84 allows for legal insanity as a defense, exempting those unable to understand their actions due to unsoundness of mind.

45. (A) Self-preservation: Private defense allows individuals to protect themselves or others from unlawful harm.

46. (A) Offenses related to marriage: Chapter XX of IPC addresses offenses like adultery, cruelty, and abduction of a married woman.

47. (D) Knowledge, intention, and action: A crime requires a guilty mind (mens rea) and a wrongful act (actus reus).

48. (B) Mubarak Hussain vrs State of Rajasthan: The Supreme Court ruled that intoxication is a defense only if it prevents the accused from forming the intent.

49. (D) Rape: Fraudulent consent makes the act rape, as deception invalidates consent.

50. (A) True: "Every murder is culpable homicide" means murder is a form of culpable homicide but not all culpable homicides are murder.

51. (A) Pari Materia: Statutes on similar matters, like the Limitation Act and the Code of Civil Procedure, should be read together.

52. (A) 3 years: The Limitation Act provides a 3-year period for suits regarding balance due on a current account.

53. (A) 3 years: The Limitation Act allows 3 years to file a suit for possession of immovable property after forfeiture or breach.

54. (B) In time: Section 4 excludes time when the court is closed, allowing the suit to be filed after the closure period.

55. (B) According to advocate's wishes: The Limitation Act allows a suit to be filed after court closure, based on the advocate's instructions.

56. (D) 12 months: Appeals from acquittal orders under Section 417 must be filed within 12 months.

57. (B) 20 years: Easementary rights are acquired through 20 years of uninterrupted use.

58. (B) 30 days: The limitation period for setting aside a sale in execution of a decree is 30 days.

59. (A) Plea of change of law: A change in law can be raised as a defense even after the limitation period expires.

60. (A) 9 years: If no specific period is provided, the general limitation period is 9 years.

61. (D) All of the above: "Attached to the earth" includes things rooted, embedded, or attached to what is embedded.

62. (B) Condition Precedent: A transfer is contingent on fulfilling the condition of residing with another person.

63. (C) Both: Restrictive covenants are contractual terms that limit property use or enjoyment, imposed by the transferor.

64. (B) Section 43: Section 43 describes "feeding the estoppel by grant," preventing a transferor from denying a subsequent interest in the property.

65. (D) Part Performance: The doctrine of Part Performance allows specific performance if the agreement is partially executed.

66. (D) All of the above: English mortgage involves binding the mortgagor to repay, transferring property, and reconveying it after payment.

67. (C) Exchange: When ownership of one thing is mutually exchanged for another, it's called an exchange.

68. (D) By all of the above: A lease can end through merger, forfeiture, or surrender.

69. (B) Mortgagee: "Redeem up, foreclose down" refers to the rights of a mortgagee to redeem prior mortgages and foreclose subsequent ones.

70. (B) Rules against tacking: The rule against

tacking prevents a mortgagee from gaining priority by combining their original security with a new one.

71. (C) Law of agreements creating obligations: The Law of Contracts governs agreements that create legal obligations.

72. (A) Invitation to offer: An auction sale without reserve is an invitation to offer, not a binding offer.

73. (A) Present, past, or future: Consideration in contracts can involve past, present, or future actions or promises.

74. (C) Quasi-contracts: Quasi-contracts impose obligations to prevent unjust enrichment in the absence of a formal contract.

75. (C) Surety: A surety has the right of subrogation, stepping into the creditor's position to recover a debt.

76. (D) Banker: Bankers can claim a general lien on assets until the customer's debts are settled.

77. (A) Contract of Guarantee: A promise to ensure another's payment is a contract of guarantee.

78. (A) Voidable at the option of the aggrieved party: Fraud or misrepresentation makes a contract voidable by the deceived party.

79. (C) Addis vrs Gramaphone Co.: Damages for breach of contract are meant to compensate loss but exclude mental distress.

80. (A) Discharges the debt: Acceptance of a lesser sum in full satisfaction discharges the original debt.

81. (A) Section 8: Under the Hindu Succession Act, when a male Hindu dies intestate, his property devolves according to Section 8, which outlines the succession rules for class I heirs like sons, daughters, widows, and mother.

82. (C) Survivorship: When A dies leaving sons B, C, and D, the property passes by survivorship. This principle means the surviving co-owners inherit the deceased's share.

83. (D) Full owner: Under the Hindu Succession Act, a female Hindu holds property as a full owner, whether acquired before or after the Act's commencement, giving her complete ownership rights.

84. (B) Cognate: A cognate is someone related to the deceased through a female relative, such as a sister or granddaughter, under Hindu law.

85. (B) Class II heirs: Class II heirs, like the father and son's daughter's son, are defined under the Hindu Succession Act, including more distant relatives like siblings and nephews.

86. (D) Intestate and testamentary succession: The Indian Succession Act covers both intestate (without a will) and testamentary (with a will) succession, providing rules for property administration and distribution.

87. (C) Court: An Administrator is appointed by the court to manage a deceased person's estate when no executor is named or the named executor is unable to act.

88. (D) Testator: A Holograph Will is written by the testator, the person making the will, typically in their own handwriting without needing witnesses.

89. (A) Does not take effect: If A survives the testator, a legacy to A, with a contingency to B if A dies, does not take effect as A survived.

90. (B) Probate: Probate is a certified copy of the will, sealed by the court, granting the executor the authority to administer the testator's estate according to the will.

91. (C) Section 18: Section 18 of the Specific Relief Act allows courts to enforce contracts with variations, provided the essential terms remain the same and the variations don't substantially alter the agreement.

92. (C) Both (a) and (b): Section 12 of the Specific Relief Act focuses on substantial compliance with contract conditions, prioritizing the contract's substance over strict adherence to literal terms.

93. (D) All of the above: Specific performance is based on factors like whether damages are an adequate remedy, court discretion, and mutuality of the contract. It's not granted if any of these conditions are missing.

94. (A) No suit can be brought against the owner: Section 15 of the Specific Relief Act prohibits suits against the property owner, except by those with special rights, like tenants or mortgagees.

95. (D) A reminder man for tenant, not for life: Under Section 15 of the Specific Relief Act, a reminder man (someone with a future interest) cannot enforce specific performance unless they meet certain requirements.

96. (D) All of the above: Section 14 of the Specific Relief Act excludes specific performance for contracts where damages are sufficient, personal skills are involved, or the contract is determinable in nature.

97. (C) Where property is sold in distinct lots, with separate contracts for each lot: When property is sold in separate lots with individual contracts, each contract is considered distinct, unlike a single contract for the whole property.

98. (D) None of the above: In a specific

performance suit, the defendant cannot defend based on uncertainty, excess power, hardship, or unfair advantage but may challenge the contract's enforceability or seek equitable remedies.

99. (A) Section 26 (1): Section 26(1) of the Specific Relief Act allows rectification of an instrument if there is fraud or mutual mistake by the parties during its creation or execution.

100. (B) Section 27 (2): Section 27(2) gives courts discretion to refuse rescinding a contract and instead award compensation if it considers that to be more equitable in the circumstances.

2013

1. (B) The Doctrine of colourable legislation is not tied to Article 13, which deals with judicial review and the power to declare laws void if they violate fundamental rights. Colourable legislation occurs when a law appears to be constitutional but has an unconstitutional purpose, focusing on legislative intent.

2. (A) The Berhampur University Student Union is not a state under Article 12. Article 12 defines "state" for the purpose of fundamental rights, which includes the government and local authorities, but university student unions are not included.

3. (C) Freedom of speech and expression is not limited to citizens. It is a fundamental right under Article 19(1)(a), applying to all individuals within India, regardless of citizenship status.

4. (B) Protection of life and personal liberty under Article 21 extends to all persons, both citizens and non-citizens, ensuring they are not deprived of these rights except by law.

5. (C) Article 20(3) protects against self-incrimination, ensuring that no person accused of a crime can be compelled to testify against themselves, reinforcing the principle against testimonial compulsion.

6. (D) Organizing Village Panchayats is a Directive Principle of State Policy, aiming to promote local self-government and empower rural communities, fostering democratic participation.

7. (C) The Right to Education, under Article 21A, is a fundamental right, not a Directive Principle of State Policy, providing free education to children between 6 and 14 years.

8. (D) Promoting Indian culture is not listed as a fundamental duty in the Constitution. Fundamental duties focus on moral responsibilities such as respecting the Constitution and upholding public harmony.

9. (B) In I.C. Golak Nath vs. State of Punjab (1967), the Supreme Court evolved the doctrine of prospective overruling, stating constitutional amendments could not alter fundamental rights and applying rulings only from the judgment date.

10. (B) In Gian Kaur vs. State of Punjab, the Supreme Court held the 'right to die' is not a fundamental right under Article 21, affirming that the right to life does not include the right to end life.

11. (D) A preliminary decree is issued in cases of partition, partnership, possession, and mesne profits, determining rights and liabilities but requiring further proceedings to finalize the details.

12. (B) Section 6 of CPC addresses pecuniary jurisdiction, determining the court's authority based on the value of the subject matter in the suit, ensuring proper filing.

13. (C) Set-off can be legal or equitable. Legal set-off applies to claims arising from the same transaction, while equitable set-off allows for claims not related by transaction but relevant to fairness in litigation.

14. (C) An application to set aside an ex-parte decree is a remedy for a party who believes they were unfairly represented in a court decision made in their absence.

15. (C) "Nemo debet bis vexari pro una et eadem causa" protects individuals from being prosecuted or harassed multiple times for the same offense, ensuring fairness and finality.

16. (B) In maintenance decree execution, up to one-third of a person's salary can be attached to ensure compliance while still maintaining their ability to support themselves.

17. (B) Under Section 100 of the CPC, a second appeal lies to the High Court if a party is aggrieved by a decision on a question of law from the lower appellate court.

18. (D) Section 89 of the CPC encourages alternative dispute resolution methods such as mediation or arbitration, offering more efficient, cost-effective ways to resolve disputes outside court.

19. (C) Section 115 of the CPC allows the High Court to correct jurisdictional errors by revising decisions of subordinate courts that have exceeded or failed to exercise their jurisdiction.

20. (A) If an indigent person's suit abates due to their death, the court fee is recoverable from the deceased's estate, ensuring the burden is not placed on other parties.

21. (D) A warrant case refers to offenses punishable by death, life imprisonment, or more than two years of imprisonment, authorizing

arrest warrants from the outset.

22. (C) In summary trials by a Magistrate First Class, sentences can be up to two years of imprisonment, simplifying proceedings for minor offenses.

23. (B) Section 125 of the CrPC allows for maintenance orders for wives, children, and parents who are unable to maintain themselves due to neglect or refusal from the person responsible.

24. (C) Section 304 of the CrPC provides legal aid at state expense to an accused person unable to afford legal representation, ensuring a fair trial.

25. (B) Section 300 of the CrPC upholds double jeopardy, preventing a person from being tried twice for the same offense after conviction or acquittal.

26. (D) Section 39 of the CrPC mandates reporting certain serious offenses, including those related to national security and murder, to the authorities.

27. (A) Section 45 of the CrPC protects Armed Forces personnel from arrest during the performance of their duties, ensuring they are not hindered by unnecessary arrests.

28. (C) Section 416 of the CrPC allows for the postponement of a capital sentence for a pregnant woman, acknowledging the impact of her condition.

29. (A) Section 366 of the CrPC requires a Court of Session's death sentence to be confirmed by the High Court before execution.

30. (D) Section 354 of the CrPC outlines the essential components of a judgment, including the decision and reasons, ensuring clarity and fairness in judicial rulings.

31. (D) A "leading question," as defined in Section 141 of the Indian Evidence Act, is one that suggests the desired answer, potentially influencing the response.

32. (A) Section 115 of the Indian Evidence Act governs estoppel, preventing individuals from contradicting statements they have made if others have relied on them to their detriment.

33. (A) Section 125 of the Indian Evidence Act allows for the admissibility of statements regarding the commission of offenses, providing evidence in criminal cases.

34. (A) A "dumb witness" refers to someone unable to speak but still capable of testifying using alternative means like writing or sign language.

35. (D) Section 75 of the Indian Evidence Act deals with the proof of private documents, setting requirements for establishing authenticity and contents in court.

36. (D) A "retracted extra-judicial confession" occurs when an accused retracts a confession made outside of court proceedings, challenging its credibility.

37. (D) Under Section 45 of the Indian Evidence Act, expert opinions serve as corroborative evidence, helping clarify complex matters in court.

38. (D) Section 8 of the Indian Evidence Act allows the introduction of evidence regarding conduct, motive, or preparation, relevant to establishing facts in a case.

39. (A) Section 47A of the Indian Evidence Act governs the relevance of opinions about electronic signatures, ensuring their admissibility and authenticity in court.

40. (D) Section 17 of the Indian Evidence Act defines "admission," referring to statements suggesting inferences adverse to the speaker's interest.

41. (A) William Blackstone defines a crime as a violation of public rights, affecting the entire community, not just individuals.

42. (A) Strict liability offenses do not require intent or recklessness; individuals are responsible for the consequences of their actions regardless of mental state.

43. (C) Section 304B of the IPC penalizes dowry death, holding individuals accountable for causing a woman's death due to dowry-related abuse.

44. (D) In Mubarak Ali vs. State of Bombay, the Supreme Court ruled that criminal jurisdiction is determined by the locality of the offense, not the offender's nationality.

45. (D) The Supreme Court affirmed that if an offense mandates imprisonment, both the company and its directors can be criminally liable and subject to imprisonment.

46. (B) The phrase "They also serve who only stand and wait" was used in Ramnath vs. State of Madhya Pradesh, emphasizing the importance of silent support in the justice system.

47. (D) Section 377 of the IPC criminalizes unnatural offenses, referring to sexual acts considered against the natural order.

48. (B) "Qui facit per alium per se" is the principle of vicarious liability in criminal law, meaning a person can be held liable for another's actions under their direction.

49. (D) The Supreme Court struck down the mandatory death penalty under Section 303 IPC in Mithu v. State of Punjab, declaring it unconstitutional, as it violated the right to life under Article 21 of the Constitution.

50. (A) The Supreme Court in Shersingh v. State of Punjab ruled that delays in disposing of mercy petitions by the President or Governor do not invalidate the death penalty, as mercy lies with the executive.

51. (C) The Law of Limitation serves two purposes: it prevents outdated claims from being asserted and bars legal action to enforce a right once the limitation period expires.

52. (B) The limitation period for an account and share of profits in a dissolved partnership is three years from the dissolution date.

53. (C) The doctrine of sufficient cause allows for delay in filing suits or appeals if the delay is due to valid reasons, providing flexibility in the application of limitation.

54. (D) Limitation is addressed under Entry 13 of List III (Concurrent List) of the Indian Constitution, allowing both central and state governments to legislate on it.

55. (B) The right to use various easements on government property becomes absolute after 30 years of uninterrupted enjoyment, as per Section 25 of the Limitation Act.

56. (A) The Law of Limitation bars court action after the limitation period expires but does not extinguish the underlying right, which can still be satisfied voluntarily.

57. (C) The period for appealing a decree or order to the High Court under the Code of Civil Procedure is 90 days from the date of the decree or order.

58. (A) The Limitation Act, 1963, came into force on 1st January 1964, replacing the 1908 Act, and governs limitation periods in India.

59. (B) A suit for specific performance must be filed within three years from the date fixed for performance or when performance is refused.

60. (A) Once the limitation period begins, no disability or inability to initiate a suit suspends the running of time for the action.

61. (D) "Nemo dat quod non habet" means one cannot transfer what they do not possess, ensuring that only legal owners can transfer property rights.

62. (A) A condition restricting B from selling property to anyone other than C is void, as it impedes the free alienation of property.

63. (A) Lis Pendens, under Section 52 of the Transfer of Property Act, renders any transfer of property during the pendency of a suit affecting its title void.

64. (C) Foreclosure is a legal remedy where a court decree bars a mortgagor from redeeming mortgaged property, effectively transferring ownership to the mortgagee.

65. (B) A gift of immovable property must be made by a registered instrument, signed by the donor and attested by at least two witnesses, to be valid.

66. (C) An equitable mortgage is created by depositing title deeds as security, without transferring legal ownership, unlike a registered mortgage.

67. (D) A lease of immovable property for more than a year or with yearly rent must be created through a registered instrument as per the Transfer of Property Act.

68. (D) A person can transfer property to themselves and others, as co-ownership arrangements are valid under property law.

69. (A) A claim to mesne profits, which compensates for wrongful possession, is not an actionable claim under law but a consequence of unlawful possession.

70. (D) A gift under Mohammedan law does not require a registered instrument; it is valid with declaration, acceptance, and delivery of possession, though registration is advisable.

71. (C) A general offer is made to the public or a specific group, and can be accepted by anyone meeting the specified terms, forming a binding contract.

72. (B) Under English law, past consideration is not valid, as consideration must be contemporaneous with the promise to form an enforceable contract.

73. (C) Displaying articles with prices in a showroom is an invitation to offer, not an offer itself, inviting customers to propose the purchase.

74. (A) A minor's agreement is void ab initio, meaning it is automatically void from the start, as minors lack the legal capacity to contract.

75. (C) Hadley v. Baxendale established that damages for breach of contract should cover only losses that were foreseeable by both parties at the time of contracting.

76. (B) M.C. Chako v. State Bank of Travancore involves the privity of contract principle, determining the rights and obligations of the parties involved in a contract.

77. (D) Section 124 of the Indian Contract Act defines indemnity contracts, where one party agrees to compensate another for losses or damages.

78. (D) A contract for saving someone from drowning is enforceable despite the absence of consideration, due to moral obligations and exceptions under contract law.

79. (D) The case of The Commissioner of Wealth Tax, Mysore v. Vijayaba Dowger

Maharani Saheb pertains to contingent contracts, where performance depends on specific events.

80. (C) A continuing guarantee may be revoked by notice to the creditor or upon the death of the surety, ending liability for future transactions.

81. (B) The Hindu Succession Act, 1956 came into force on 17th June 1956, governing Hindu succession and inheritance laws in India.

82. (B) In case A dies intestate, the property will pass entirely to S, the surviving son, as per the rules of intestate succession.

83. (A) The Hindu Succession Act, 1956 applies to Hindus in India, excluding the region of Jammu and Kashmir, which had separate succession laws prior to 2019.

84. (A) In the case of W's intestate death, the property will be divided into four equal parts among the husband, son, and unmarried daughters.

85. (D) Diseases are not grounds for disqualification under the Hindu Succession Act, which does not restrict inheritance based on health conditions.

86. (C) A codicil, under the Indian Succession Act, modifies or revokes provisions of an existing will without completely revoking the will itself.

87. (B) The degree of kindred for succession purposes is determined according to the table provided in Schedule 1 of the Indian Succession Act.

88. (B) The legacy is not valid because A failed to fulfill the condition of marrying with the consent of the specified parties before the marriage.

89. (D) Section 184 of the Indian Succession Act states that a person receiving indirect benefits under a will is not required to make an election between the benefit and any conflicting interests.

90. (A) The sale of property subject to a specific bequest is valid, even without the executor's assent, as long as the sale is done in good faith.

91. (D) The cancellation of an instrument under Section 31 of the Specific Relief Act requires the instrument to be void or voidable, with reasonable apprehension of injury to the plaintiff.

92. (B) Section 19 of the Specific Relief Act allows for the enforcement of specific performance of a contract, including necessary variations agreed upon by the parties.

93. (D) A non-party to a sale agreement is not essential for a specific performance suit, unless exceptions like novation or prior contracts apply.

94. (A) Section 6 of the Specific Relief Act protects a person in settled possession of immovable property against dispossession, even without a legal title.

95. (C) Section 5 of the Specific Relief Act allows a person entitled to possession of immovable property to recover it through a suit under the Civil Procedure Code.

96. (C) A person in possession of movable property, but not the owner, may be compelled to deliver it to the rightful owner if they have control over the property.

97. (C) All of the above. Injunctions can be granted under the Specific Relief Act to protect intellectual property, prevent a wife's husband from marrying again, and address passing-off actions.

98. (A) Section 18. Section 18 allows courts to enforce specific performance of a contract with agreed modifications or variations.

99. (A) Legal obligation. A mandatory injunction under Section 39 requires the plaintiff to show a breach of legal obligation for the court to order specific performance.

100. (B) Section 32. Section 32 allows the court to cancel part of an instrument while keeping valid portions intact in case of different rights or obligations.

2014

1. (b) 26th November, 1949. The Indian Constitution was adopted on 26th November, 1949, and became effective on 26th January, 1950.

2. (d) Co-operative Societies. The 9th Amendment (2011) added "Co-operative Societies" to Article 19(1)(c), broadening the right to form associations.

3. (a) Aruna Ramachandra Shanbaugh v. Union of India. The Supreme Court allowed passive euthanasia with guidelines in this case, recognizing the right to die with dignity.

4. (c) Office of Profit. In Jaya Bachchan v Union of India, the Supreme Court addressed whether holding a government position constitutes an office of profit.

5. (a) A Law of the Parliament. Article 3 grants Parliament the power to create new states or alter boundaries through legislation.

6. (c) Power of the President to promulgate ordinances. Under Article 123, the President can issue ordinances during Parliament recess, with the same effect as laws.

7. (a) Interpretation of statutes. The Pith and Substance doctrine helps resolve conflicts

between overlapping legislative fields.

8. (d) Art. 356. Article 356 empowers the President to impose President's Rule during a constitutional machinery breakdown in states.

9. (b) Art. 317. Article 317 provides the procedure for removing or suspending members of the Public Service Commission.

10. (b) Governor and High Court consultation. District judges are appointed by the Governor of the state, in consultation with the High Court.

11. (a) Section 11. Section 11 of the CPC establishes the principle of res judicata, barring subsequent suits on previously decided matters.

12. (b) Set-off. Set-off allows a defendant to offset debts in a civil suit, reducing or eliminating the plaintiff's claim.

13. (c) Power to alienate property. An attachment before judgment restricts a party's ability to transfer or dispose of property until the case concludes.

14. (c) Prima facie case, irreparable injury, and balance of convenience. These factors guide courts in granting injunctions.

15. (b) Reference. A reference enables subordinate courts to seek the High Court's opinion on legal questions in non-appealable cases.

16. (b) Only (i) and (iii) are correct. Legal set-off requires court fees and may involve time-barred claims, while equitable set-off does not.

17. (c) Interrogatories. Interrogatories are written questions used during the discovery phase to gather evidence from the opposing party.

18. (b) Representative suit. A representative suit is filed on behalf of a group with a shared interest in the case.

19. (d) Receiver. A receiver manages property during litigation to ensure its preservation and proper handling until resolution.

20. (b) Interpleader suit. A railway company can file an interpleader suit to resolve competing claims over disputed goods.

21. (a) To collect evidence. Investigations collect facts and evidence to assist the court in determining the truth.

22. (d) All of the above. Police can arrest without a warrant for cognizable offenses, proclaimed offenders, or deserters.

23. (c) In all the above cases. Section 37 requires everyone to assist a Magistrate or Police Officer in making arrests to prevent breaches of peace or harm.

24. (a) State Government. The State Government is responsible for establishing a Court of Session for each Sessions division.

25. (a) Shambhu Dass v. State of Assam. An FIR under Section 154 is not substantive evidence, only used for contradiction or corroboration.

26. (b) Section 164A of Cr.P.C. Section 164A mandates medical examination of rape victims with specific procedures and guidelines.

27. (b) Charge alteration or addition. If charges change, both parties may recall or re-examine witnesses unless the court deems otherwise.

28. (c) Joint charges. Persons may be charged jointly for related offenses or those committed during the same transaction.

29. (c) Compounding miscarriage. A woman can compound the offense of miscarriage with court permission before prosecution.

30. (b) Section 407 of Cr.P.C. Section 407 allows the High Court to transfer cases between subordinate courts within its jurisdiction.

31. (d) Confession of co-accused. A co-accused's confession can support evidence but cannot solely convict the accused.

32. (a) Best evidence rule exceptions. The Indian Evidence Act allows secondary evidence under specific circumstances when the original document is unavailable.

33. (d) Multiple dying declarations. No case specifically discussed the reliability of multiple dying declarations.

34. (a) Rational doubt. The accused benefits from a rational, honest doubt, not just skepticism, according to Cockburn's explanation.

35. (a) Shaik Fakruddin v. Shaik Mohammed Hasan. DNA tests can be disputed with proof of non-access, as held in this case.

36. (a) Accomplice testimony. An accomplice's testimony needs corroboration in material particulars to be considered credible.

37. (c) Handwriting proof. Handwriting authenticity can be proven through expert testimony or an acquaintance with the writer's handwriting.

38. (a) Acquittal of guilty preferred. The principle in Rang Bahadur Singh v. State of U.P. stresses acquitting the guilty over convicting the innocent.

39. (b) Section 85B, Evidence Act. It establishes that electronically secured records are valid for the time specified unless later disputed.

40. (a) Dr. Kumar Saha v. Dr. Sukumar Mukherjee. This case cited the Praful Desai judgment in addressing medical negligence and care standards.

41. (a) Section 166 of IPC. A public servant who knowingly disobeys execution orders is guilty under Section 166.

42. (d) Actus Reus components. Actus Reus includes conduct, result of conduct, and circumstances defined by law.

43. (a) Excluding mens rea. Strict liability offenses, like public nuisance, do not require proof of mens rea.

44. (a) House trespass. A's act of entering D's bedroom with intent to murder constitutes house trespass under IPC.

45. (c) Criminal conspiracy. Section 120-A defines conspiracy as an agreement to commit illegal acts or legal acts by illegal means.

46. (D) - X's act of showing a knife and demanding money and gold from Z on the highway is robbery. Robbery involves violence or intimidation in the course of theft.

47. (C) - Dacoity involves a group planning and committing robbery, whether by extortion or theft, with the intention of sharing the stolen property.

48. (A) - Rioting occurs when a member of an unlawful assembly uses violence to further a common objective, disturbing public peace and order.

49. (C) - Consent is not a valid defense for causing grievous hurt or death, as these offenses involve harm that cannot be justified by the victim's agreement.

50. (B) - Sedition requires both intent to disturb the government and the result of inciting unrest or violence among the public.

51. (A) - All legal instruments are made with reference to the internationally accepted Gregorian calendar.

52. (D) - Section 3 of the Limitation Act applies generally and sets limitation periods for filing suits, applications, and executions, without specific categories.

53. (C) - Set off and counterclaim are treated as separate suits under Section 3. Set off adjusts mutual claims, while a counterclaim is a defendant's claim against the plaintiff.

54. (C) - Section 3 applies to limitation periods under both local and special laws, which are state-specific or for particular purposes.

55. (D) - A time-barred debt cannot be claimed through set off, counterclaim, or a new suit. Legal remedies are lost once a debt becomes time-barred.

56. (B) - Section 4 excludes time during which courts are closed from the limitation period calculation, applicable if the court is closed during normal hours.

57. (D) - Legal disabilities under the Limitation Act include minority, insanity, and idiocy, which can extend the time for filing suits or actions.

58. (B) - An agent's acknowledgment of a debt on behalf of the liable person extends the limitation period for that debt.

59. (C) - A part payment, in writing by the person making it, resets the limitation period under Section 19 of the Limitation Act.

60. (C) - An ex parte decree can be set aside within 30 days from the decree date or knowledge, if summons or notice was not served properly.

61. (A) - Under the Transfer of Property Act, an instrument refers to a non-testamentary document affecting rights in immovable property.

62. (D) - "Attached to the earth" includes property rooted in, embedded in, or attached to the earth for beneficial enjoyment.

63. (C) - Section 35 requires acceptance of all parts of an instrument for a person to benefit from it, prohibiting selective adoption of favorable parts.

64. (D) - An actionable claim includes debts or claims recognized by civil courts and can be enforced through legal action.

65. (B) - A prior interest is necessary to create an interest for an unborn person, with the property passing to them upon birth.

66. (D) - A vested interest involves conditions that prevent it from being defeated by the transferee's death before possession and must be transferable.

67. (C) - A property transfer during ongoing proceedings is not void but may be affected by the proceeding's outcome.

68. (A) - A condition that X must live in a property sold to Z is void, as it restricts property rights and enjoyment.

69. (D) - Partition involves dividing property among co-owners and does not constitute a transfer of property.

70. (C) - Property transfers can be oral or in writing, with some requiring registration depending on the legal nature of the transfer.

71. (B) - In a contract accepting a proposal via post, acceptance occurs when the letter is posted, according to the "postal rule."

72. (A) - A proposal revocation by telegram before acceptance is effective when dispatched, making it effective immediately against the sender.

73. (A) - In unconscionable contracts, the burden of proving no undue influence rests with the person who dominates the other party's will.

74. (D) - Coercion, fraud, or misrepresentation renders a contract voidable. The aggrieved party can void it if these factors are present.

75. (A) - An agreement to conceal income is void due to its involvement in illegal activities and is unenforceable.

76. (A) - Restricting someone from a lawful profession, trade, or business in a specified area is a restraint of trade and void under Section 27.

77. (D) - A contingent contract depends on the occurrence of an uncertain future event, like a political event, as per Section 32 of the Indian Contract Act.

78. (A) - Reciprocal promises in a contract are performed in the order required by the nature of the transaction, as stated in Section 51.

79. (C) - A bailor is liable for damages to the bailee if faults in the goods, unknown to the bailee, are not disclosed, as per Section 152.

80. (D) - An agent is liable to compensate the principal for losses caused by misconduct under Section 237 of the Indian Contract Act.

81. (A) - An agnate is related to another by blood or entirely through a male, particularly in Hindu joint families.

82. (B) - Section 8 of the Hindu Succession Act governs the rules for succession of a Hindu male's property if he dies intestate.

83. (A) - A husband, as per Entry (a) of Section 15(1), is the legally wedded husband of a deceased woman at the time of her death.

84. (A) - Co-heirs in an intestate's property take it as tenants in common, each having a distinct share, as per Section 19 of the Hindu Succession Act.

85. (B) - Section 20 of the Hindu Succession Act grants inheritance rights to a child in the womb if born alive within a specified period.

86. (D) - An Indian Christian under the Indian Succession Act, 1925, is someone of Asiatic descent who professes any form of Christianity.

87. (D) - A wife's domicile under the Indian Succession Act follows her husband's domicile, which changes with marriage.

88. (B) - A husband does not automatically acquire an interest in the wife's property upon marriage, as per Section 20 of the Indian Succession Act.

89. (A) - The intestate's property, with no lineal descendants, is distributed under the Indian Succession Act, after deducting the widow's share.

90. (C) - Privileged wills under Section 65 of the Indian Succession Act allow soldiers, airmen, and mariners to make a will even under 18 years of age due to the nature of their professions.

91. (A) - A suit for possession under Section 6 of the Specific Relief Act must be filed within six months from the date of dispossession. After this period, the right to recover possession is lost.

92. (D) - A contract can only be specifically enforced if it meets the conditions outlined in Sections 14 to 21 of the Specific Relief Act. Contracts that do not fulfill these criteria cannot be specifically enforced.

93. (D) - Agreements to enter into a contract, marriage agreements, and contracts for property sales under allotment are not specifically enforceable under the law due to their inability to meet the criteria for specific performance.

94. (D) - In a suit for specific performance, defenses such as money being adequate compensation, uncertainty in contract terms, or lack of validity due to vendor's power are permissible defenses.

95. (D) - Specific performance can be denied if the plaintiff violated an essential term of the contract, acted fraudulently, or deviated from the terms of the contract.

96. (A) - Specific performance is a discretionary remedy granted by the court for enforcing civil rights, where monetary compensation is insufficient to remedy the breach of contract.

97. (C) - A suit for possession under Section 5 of the Specific Relief Act can be filed within twelve years to recover immovable property. This sets the time limit for such actions.

98. (B) - Section 13 of the Specific Relief Act does not apply when the vendor has title to the property. It only applies if the vendor lacks title or has an imperfect title.

99. (B) - Rescission is granted in cases of voidable contracts, where one party can choose to rescind due to factors like coercion, fraud, or misrepresentation.

100. (B) - A declaration under Section 34 of the Specific Relief Act can be sought by a person whose legal character or right to property is disputed, to establish their rights or status.

2015

1. (D) - The 42nd Amendment (1976) inserted "Unity and integrity of the nation" into the Preamble of the Indian Constitution, alongside "Socialist" and "Secular," making the Constitution more inclusive and reflective of national unity.

2. (A) - The Ninety-Second Amendment (2003) added Bodo, Dogri, and Maithili languages to the Eighth Schedule of the Indian Constitution, aiming to promote linguistic diversity and cultural recognition.

3. (A) - Article 74 of the Indian Constitution establishes a Council of Ministers led by the Prime Minister to advise the President, who must act according to their advice in official matters.

4. (B) - Article 14 ensures equality before the law and prohibits class legislation. It guarantees equal protection of laws, preventing arbitrary discrimination against individuals.

5. (A) - Article 12 defines "State" in India's Constitution, including the government of India, state governments, and local authorities, for the purposes of Fundamental Rights and Directive Principles.

6. (C) - The 73rd Amendment (1992) granted constitutional status to Panchayati Raj institutions, empowering local self-government in rural areas by decentralizing power.

7. (C) - In Zee Telefilms Ltd. v. Union of India, the Supreme Court ruled that the BCCI is not a "State" under Article 12, as it is not under governmental control.

8. (D) - Article 19 guarantees the right to practice any profession or engage in trade or business, ensuring individuals have equal opportunities without discrimination.

9. (B) - The right to an adequate means of livelihood, as part of the Directive Principles of State Policy, guides the government in promoting social and economic welfare.

10. (C) - Article 21-A mandates free and compulsory education for children aged 6-14 years, aiming to ensure universal access to education for all children.

11. (C) - A decree does not include an order of dismissal of a suit for default under the Code of Civil Procedure, which is not a formal adjudication of rights.

12. (A) - For partition of immovable property worth Rs.12,000, the appropriate court would be the Court of Civil Judge (Junior Division), based on the subject matter's value.

13. (C) - A second appeal cannot be filed in a case where the original suit is for recovery of money not exceeding Rs.25,000, as per Section 102 of the Code of Civil Procedure.

14. (B) - Section 11 of the Code of Civil Procedure enforces the principle of res judicata, preventing re-litigation of matters already decided in previous suits.

15. (C) - Non-joinder of necessary parties can result in the failure of a suit, as it may affect the completeness of the case's adjudication.

16. (B) - Explanation IV of Section 11 of the CPC defines constructive res judicata, stating that a matter not raised in a prior suit but related should be considered as part of that suit.

17. (C) - Amendments to pleadings are typically not allowed after the trial commences to ensure the trial focuses on the evidence and issues raised during the process.

18. (C) - A court may grant up to three adjournments during a suit's hearing, though further adjournments may be refused to prevent delays.

19. (B) - To grant a temporary injunction, the court examines the balance of inconvenience, ensuring the harm to one party outweighs any benefit to the other.

20. (A) - Section 25 of the Code of Civil Procedure allows the Supreme Court to transfer cases between High Courts to ensure impartiality and fair proceedings.

21. (C) - An FIR is not substantive evidence but may be used in trial to corroborate or contradict the informant's statements.

22. (D) - Armed forces members cannot be arrested without prior consent from the Central Government when acting in official duty, ensuring protection from arbitrary arrests.

23. (A) - Under Section 2(d) of the Cr.P.C, a "complaint" excludes a police report, focusing on a personal statement made to a magistrate regarding a crime.

24. (C) - A Judicial Magistrate can award maintenance under Section 125 of the Cr.P.C at a monthly rate deemed appropriate based on the case's circumstances.

25. (A) - A warrant case involves offenses punishable by death, life imprisonment, or imprisonment exceeding two years, as defined by Section 2(x) of the Cr.P.C.

26. (B) - The Court of Magistrate holds original jurisdiction to take cognizance of an offense, initiating legal proceedings under the Cr.P.C.

27. (D) - Multiple offenses of the same kind committed within a year can be charged together under the Cr.P.C, with no specific restriction on the number of offenses.

28. (D) - Section 482 of the Cr.P.C grants the High Court inherent powers to intervene in cases involving absurd or improbable allegations to prevent misuse of the legal process.

29. (B) - Under Section 309 of the Cr.P.C, the period of remand for an accused during trial is initially set at 15 days, with extensions subject to the Magistrate's approval.

30. (C) - Section 39 of the Cr.P.C obligates any person who knows about certain offenses to report them to the nearest Magistrate or police officer.

31. (C) - Section 113A of the Evidence Act was

inserted in 1983, allowing courts to presume that a woman's suicide was due to cruelty or harassment related to dowry.

32. (C) - Presumption determines the burden of proof, indicating which party must prove a particular fact, but does not itself serve as evidence.

33. (B) - Motive is important in circumstantial evidence cases as it helps establish the accused's intent when direct evidence is unavailable.

34. (C) - Section 9 of the Indian Evidence Act governs Test Identification Parades, which are used to identify individuals in legal proceedings.

35. (D) - The principle of best evidence in law emphasizes that the most reliable, credible, and relevant evidence must be presented in legal proceedings.

36. (D) - Section 11 of the Evidence Act addresses alibi, which is relevant when inconsistent facts contradict the accused's defense.

37. (B) - The "Expert" examines electronic evidence under the Indian Evidence Act, specializing in analyzing digital or electronic data for legal proceedings.

38. (D) - A certified copy of a Will is secondary evidence, as the original document is the primary source; certified copies are used when the original is unavailable.

39. (B) - Section 113B of the Evidence Act creates a presumption of dowry death if a woman dies within seven years of marriage and has faced cruelty related to dowry.

40. (C) - A "Hostile witness" is one who resists or contradicts the party that called them, making it difficult to rely on their testimony.

41. (D) - Under the Indian Penal Code (IPC), the "State" is not considered a "person," as it refers to the government and its legal structures, not individuals.

42. (C) - Voyeurism is punishable under Section 354C of the IPC, addressing non-consensual acts of capturing or sharing images of individuals in private situations.

43. (A) - Chapter V of the IPC deals with "Abetment," which involves instigating, aiding, or facilitating the commission of a crime.

44. (A) - Section 301 of the IPC covers the doctrine of transferred malice, holding a person liable for murder if they intend to kill one person but accidentally kill another.

45. (B) - A man making unwelcome sexual advances involving physical contact is punishable by rigorous imprisonment for three years, under the law against sexual harassment.

46. A: The right of private defense allows an individual to protect themselves, their property, or others from imminent harm or unlawful aggression, based on the natural instinct of self-preservation.

47. C: Rape involves sexual intercourse with a woman under 18 without her consent. The age of consent varies depending on the legal framework in different countries or jurisdictions.

48. B: Section 81 of the IPC exempts actions likely to cause harm if done in good faith for the benefit of the person harmed, with harm meaning injury or damage.

49. B: 'A' commits mischief under Section 426 IPC by intentionally throwing 'Z's ring into a river, causing damage to 'Z's property with wrongful intent.

50. B: 'A' commits extortion under IPC by inducing 'Z' to sign a blank cheque under the threat of harm, unlawfully obtaining property through coercion.

51. D: Execution proceedings are not governed by Section 3 of the Limitation Act, which pertains to the limitation period for filing suits, appeals, and applications.

52. C: Section 17 of the Limitation Act states the limitation period for suits based on fraud begins only after the fraud is discovered.

53. B: Section 5 of the Limitation Act allows the court to extend the period for filing an appeal if sufficient cause for the delay is shown.

54. D: A time-barred debt cannot be claimed as a set-off, counter-claim, or through a new suit once the limitation period has expired.

55. C: Section 12(2) of the Limitation Act considers the actual time taken to complete an act or procedure, focusing on the duration rather than minimum or maximum time limits.

56. B: The period of limitation for a suit to redeem or recover mortgaged immovable property is 30 years, as per Article 61 of the Limitation Act.

57. A: Section 5 of the Limitation Act grants the court the power to condone delay in filing a suit, appeal, or application if sufficient cause is shown.

58. A: When a new party is added to a suit, it is deemed to have been brought on the date of the addition, preventing the suit from being time-barred.

59. C: The limitation period for a suit relating to money lent under an agreement payable on demand is three years from the loan date, as per Article 55.

60. D: Public institutions like banks are not treated the same as private individuals or

institutions when it comes to condoning delay under Section 5 of the Limitation Act.

61. C: Standing timber is considered movable property, not immovable, as it is not permanently attached to land.

62. C: Paddy land is agricultural land that can be transferred as immovable property, though specific laws may regulate such transfers.

63. C: A covenant for pre-emption does not violate the rule against perpetuities, as it does not create future interests that may vest too remotely.

64. C: Section 13 of the Transfer of Property Act allows property transfers for the benefit of unborn persons, transferring property to individuals who are not yet born but may exist in the future.

65. C: The Doctrine of lis pendens, under Section 52 of the Transfer of Property Act, renders transfers of immovable property during pending suits void against subsequent transferees.

66. B: A vested interest refers to a property interest that takes effect immediately or on the happening of an event that must occur.

67. B: A mortgage of immovable property transfers an interest in the property, creating a security interest for the mortgagee but not transferring the title or ownership.

68. C: A suit for redemption is required to enforce the right to redeem mortgaged property, allowing the mortgagor to reclaim it by repaying the mortgage debt.

69. C: The notice period required to terminate a lease from year to year is six months, ensuring either party provides adequate notice before the lease ends.

70. A: Prior to the Transfer of Property Act, 1882, the transfer of immovable properties in India was governed by English Law and Equity principles.

71. A: Determining a reasonable time for contract performance is a question of fact, dependent on the specific circumstances of the case, including the contract's nature.

72. B: 'A' is not obligated to inform 'B' about a change in prices that could affect 'B's willingness to proceed with the contract unless there is a legal or fiduciary duty.

73. C: For a contract to be valid, it must have a lawful object, meaning the purpose must not be prohibited by law. Other key elements include free consent, competency, and lawful consideration.

74. A: A contract is enforceable when the offer is accepted, forming a promise that is legally binding once other elements of the contract,

like consideration, are satisfied.

75. A: A contract caused by a unilateral mistake regarding a matter of fact is not voidable. A mutual mistake may render a contract voidable by the affected party.

76. C: 'B' may set aside the bond obtained from 'A' under coercion, as threats or duress vitiate consent, making the agreement voidable.

77. B: In ONGC Ltd. v. Saw Pipes Ltd. (2003), the Supreme Court ruled that proof of loss is unnecessary if genuine pre-estimated loss is specified in a contract.

78. D: The agreement where Rama promises to give Shyama Rs. 10,000 without consideration is void under the Indian Contract Act.

79. D: When no time is specified for performance, the promisor must fulfill the promise within a reasonable time, determined by the circumstances of the case.

80. B: 'B' is entitled to recover the cost of repairing 'A's failure to complete repairs as agreed, ensuring the repairs conform to the contract.

81. B: Cognates refer to individuals related by blood or adoption, excluding those related only through the male line.

82. C: The Hindu Succession Act does not apply to members of Scheduled Tribes, who follow their own customary laws for succession and inheritance.

83. D: Property succession regulated by the Indian Succession Act due to Section 21 of the Special Marriage Act is excluded from the Hindu Succession Act's provisions.

84. C: The Hindu Succession Act, 1956, came into effect on June 17, 1956, bringing significant changes to Hindu law regarding succession and property devolution.

85. B: When a Hindu male dies intestate without Class I or Class II heirs, his property devolves upon the agnates, relatives connected through the male line.

86. (b) Right to possession: "Possessed" in Section 14(1) of the Hindu Succession Act refers to the right to possess property, meaning the entitlement to occupy or control it.

87. (a) Hindu Succession Amendment Act, 2005: The amendment granted daughters equal rights as sons in ancestral property, making them coparceners by birth, irrespective of marital status.

88. (c) Codicil: A codicil is a legal document that amends, explains, or adds to a will without revoking it entirely.

89. (d) All of the above: A female Hindu's property under Section 14 includes movable,

immovable property, stridhana, and maintenance/arrears.

90. (b) After a court of competent jurisdiction in India has granted probate: The rights of executors or legatees are established post-grant of probate by a competent court.

91. (b) To enforce individual civil rights: Specific relief can enforce civil rights, including compelling contract performance or preventing breaches.

92. (c) 12 years: A suit for possession under Section 5 of the Specific Relief Act must be filed within 12 years of wrongful dispossession.

93. (b) After expiry of six months: A suit for recovery of possession under Section 6 can be filed six months after dispossession.

94. (d) Winding up proceeding: Specific performance can be granted in winding up proceedings during the dissolution of a company.

95. (c) Compensation: When specific performance isn't granted, the court may award compensation for the breach of contract.

96. (b) In personam: The effect of a declaration of right over land under Section 34 is "in personam," establishing rights between the parties.

97. (a) By Injunction: An injunction is a preventive relief that orders a person to refrain from or perform a certain act.

98. (d) Both (b) and (c): Specific relief can be granted when compensation is insufficient or damages are difficult to calculate.

99. (c) Mandatory injunction: A mandatory injunction compels the defendant to perform specific actions ordered by the court.

100. (c) To restrain any person from instituting or prosecuting any proceeding in a court not subordinate: Injunction can be refused to restrain proceedings in courts outside the jurisdiction.

2016

1. (B) Government of India Act, 1935: The Government of India Act, 1935 provided the framework for India's Constitution, introducing key features such as federalism and bicameralism.

2. (B) A Union of States: India is described as "A Union of States," indicating a federation with states having their own powers, but united under a central authority.

3. (B) Article 22: Article 22 safeguards individuals against arbitrary detention, ensuring rights such as being informed of detention grounds and access to legal counsel.

4. (C) Six Months: A non-member appointed as Minister must become a member of Parliament within six months of their appointment.

5. (A) Comptroller and Auditor General: The Comptroller and Auditor General audits government finances to ensure transparency, accountability, and proper financial management.

6. (A) One month: A Proclamation of Emergency under Article 352 must be approved by Parliament within one month and can last for six months with approval.

7. (B) Ninety-first Amendment: The Ninety-first Amendment limits the number of Ministers to 15% of Lok Sabha members and aims to prevent political instability due to defections.

8. (B) Government of India Act, 1919: The Government of India Act, 1919 introduced the system of Diarchy, giving Indian ministers power over some areas while British control remained in others.

9. (D) I. R. Coelho Vs. State of Tamil Nadu: In I. R. Coelho, the Supreme Court ruled that laws in the 9th Schedule are subject to judicial review if they violate the Constitution's basic structure.

10. (A) 395 Articles and 8 Schedules: The original Constitution of India had 395 Articles and 8 Schedules, which have since been amended to include more Articles and Schedules.

11. (C) Jurisdictional error: Section 115 of the CPC allows challenges to orders based on jurisdictional error by subordinate courts.

12. (C) Pleadings should state the evidence: Pleadings must state facts, not evidence. They provide the basis for the claims or defenses in a lawsuit.

13. (B) Explanation IV, Section 11 CPC: Explanation IV of Section 11 CPC treats matters "constructively" controverted as if actually contested and decided.

14. (D) Where a defendant is added, the plaint need not be amended: Adding a defendant to a suit may require amending the plaint to include relevant allegations.

15. (B) No fresh suit will lie on the same cause of action: If a suit abates due to failure in bringing legal representatives of a deceased defendant, no fresh suit can be filed on the same cause of action.

16. (A) 15 days: A decree must be drawn up within 15 days of the judgment to ensure timely documentation and finalization.

17. (C) Mandatory: Section 80 CPC requires serving notice before filing a suit against the government or public officer, and non-compliance can result in dismissal.

18. (B) Ordinary suit: In an ordinary suit, the defendant has the right to defend the suit, presenting their case and opposing the plaintiff's claims.

19. (A) On or before settlement of issues: Documentary evidence must be produced before or at the settlement of issues during the pleading stage.

20. (B) Summons to defendant: Order V CPC governs the procedure for serving summons to the defendant, specifying methods for notifying them of the lawsuit.

21. (B) Section 2(n): Section 2(n) of the CrPC defines "offense," outlining what constitutes a criminal offense under the legal framework.

22. (C) 2 years of attachment: A proclaimed person can claim attached property or sale proceeds within two years; otherwise, it may be forfeited to the government.

23. (B) Two: A death sentence requires the confirmation of at least two High Court judges for judicial review and scrutiny.

24. (C) Taking accused by police from one state to another: Transit remand allows the police to transfer an accused from one state to another for investigation or trial.

25. (D) Section 304: Section 304 of the CrPC ensures free legal aid for the accused if they cannot afford it, guaranteeing a fair trial.

26. (C) Section 320 of Cr.P.C.: Section 320 of the Cr.P.C. categorizes offenses as compoundable or non-compoundable based on whether they can be settled through compromise.

27. (C) Section 358 of Cr.P.C.: Section 358 provides compensation to individuals who have been arrested without grounds, ensuring fairness for the wrongfully detained.

28. (D) Nagaland: Certain provisions of the CrPC, excluding specific chapters, do not apply in Nagaland.

29. (C) Recording of confession in the presence of advocate of accused: Section 164 of Cr.P.C. does not require a confession to be recorded in the presence of an advocate, though it has other procedural requirements.

30. (D) Section 298: Section 298 of the Cr.P.C. allows the court to consider the accused's prior convictions when determining punishment.

31. (A) A case: Section 101 of the Indian Evidence Act places the burden of proof on the party claiming the existence of a legal right or liability.

32. (A) It can base conviction on it without corroboration: A court may convict based on a trustworthy dying declaration, even without corroborating evidence.

33. (B) Sections 18, 19, and 20 of the Evidence Act are exceptions to the doctrine of privity: These sections allow statements made by non-parties to be admissible in evidence.

34. (C) Section 58: Section 58 of the Evidence Act requires oral evidence to be direct when proving facts in a case.

35. (A) Specific state of mind: Section 14 of the Evidence Act requires evidence to show the specific state of mind relevant to the case.

36. (B) Presumption of continuance of life: Section 107 of the Evidence Act presumes that a person is alive until proven otherwise, even if they haven't been heard from for seven years.

37. (B) Criminal cases: In criminal cases, the accused's previous good character can be considered to support the presumption of innocence.

38. (D) Both (A) and (B): Section 165 of the Evidence Act allows judges to question parties about both relevant and irrelevant facts to elicit necessary information.

39. (C) Dying Declaration: The case of Queen Empress Vs. Abdullah established the legal value of dying declarations as evidence.

40. (B) Section 74: Section 74 of the Evidence Act defines public documents, including records from government authorities and official bodies.

41. (C) Section 52: Section 52 of the IPC defines good faith as actions done with care and attention, excluding actions lacking such consideration.

42. (C) 7 years: Theft from a dwelling house under Section 380 of the IPC carries a maximum sentence of 7 years in prison.

43. (D) Section 95: Section 95 of the IPC exempts actions done in good faith with consent from being considered offenses.

44. (D) Section 228A: Section 228A of the IPC prohibits the disclosure of the identity of a rape victim to protect their privacy.

45. (C) Section 204: Section 204 of the IPC punishes the destruction of evidence, including electronic records, to prevent its production in court.

46. (D) Macaulay: Lord Thomas Babington Macaulay drafted the first Indian Penal Code (IPC) as a member of the Law Commission of India.

47. (B) Section 279: Rash and negligent driving on a public road is punishable under Section 279 of the IPC.

48. (D) Married woman: Section 497 IPC addresses adultery, where a man has sexual intercourse with another man's wife without consent.

49. (A) Fact: The question of whether provocation is sufficient to reduce an offense is a matter

of fact for the court to decide based on evidence.

50. (A) Stalking: Stalking includes monitoring a woman's electronic communication, which is an offense under Section 354D IPC.

51. (B) Limitation: The extended limitation period cannot exceed 3 years from the cessation of disability.

52. (D) Section 12: This section excludes time spent on certain legal proceedings from the limitation period for filing a suit.

53. (C) Section 6: Covers persons under legal disability and extends the limitation period for those entitled to sue or execute decrees.

54. (B) Sections 6-8: These sections provide extensions to the limitation period in cases involving legal disabilities or when the defendant is absent.

55. (B) Section 10: The principle "Once a trust, always a trust" extends limitation periods in suits by beneficiaries against trustees.

56. (C) Copyright infringement compensation has a limitation period of 3 years from the date of infringement.

57. (B) A time-barred debt is unenforceable in court, though the debt still exists.

58. (C) If two disabilities occur consecutively, the limitation period extends until both disabilities cease.

59. (A) Section 5 requires proof of sufficient cause for the exercise of discretionary jurisdiction in legal matters.

60. (B) Section 2(j) defines "period of limitation" for suits, appeals, or applications.

61. (D) Section 12 of the Transfer of Property Act does not apply to leases, only to sales, exchanges, or gifts.

62. (A) Bellamy Vs. Sabine discusses the doctrine of lis pendens, where property transfers during litigation are void against subsequent purchasers.

63. (C) Section 82: In conflicts between marshalling and contribution, marshalling prevails, determining property use to satisfy charges.

64. (C) Sections 63 and 70 cover accession to mortgaged property, addressing improvements and subsequent property additions.

65. (B) Mortis causa gifts, made in contemplation of death, are not governed by the Transfer of Property Act.

66. (C) Foreclosure is a remedy available in mortgages by conditional sale, terminating the mortgagor's rights in the property.

67. (B) The rule against double possibilities was recognized in Whitby Vs. Mitchell, applying to alternative contract performances.

68. (D) "Redeem up, foreclose down" refers to the order of redemption in multiple mortgages, based on priority.

69. (A) Section 100 defines a charge as an encumbrance on immovable property to secure payment or obligations.

70. (B) Section 10 invalidates conditions that restrain the alienation of immovable property, except in specified cases.

71. (D) Discharge of a contract can occur through performance, frustration, or novation, terminating contractual obligations.

72. (B) Hadley Vs. Baxandale established that damages are only awarded for losses that naturally arise or were in the parties' contemplation.

73. (A) The test for intention to contract is objective, focusing on how a reasonable person would interpret the parties' conduct.

74. (B) An inquiry into proposal terms doesn't constitute a counter-offer; it's part of the negotiation process.

75. (C) Section 25 Explanation 1 confirms that the absence of consideration doesn't invalidate a gift between a donor and donee.

76. (B) In contracts with alternative legal and illegal promises, the legal part can be enforced, while the illegal part is void.

77. (D) The Indian Contract Act doesn't include specific provisions for privity of contract, a common law principle.

78. (B) Section 159 defines gratuitous bailment as a bailment without consideration.

79. (C) Section 185 provides an exception to Section 25, allowing agreements made without consideration for natural love and affection.

80. (B) Section 10 requires offer and acceptance, intention to create legal relations, lawful consideration, capacity, and free consent for a valid contract.

81. (C) Section 29 deals with escheat, where property reverts to the government when someone dies without heirs or a will.

82. (C) Section 12 outlines the order of succession for agnates and cognates in the event of intestacy under the Hindu Succession Act.

83. (B) The Hindu Succession Act presumes the younger survived the elder when both die simultaneously.

84. (A) In intestate succession, heirs take property as tenants in common unless specified otherwise in the Hindu Succession Act.

85. (D) In partition, W1 and W2 get 1/8 each, while the son S from W1 gets 1/4 and the sons S1-S4 from W2 each get 1/4 share.

86. (A) Section 6 of the Hindu Succession Act

allows for notional partition, treating property as if it had been divided at the time of certain events, like the death or renunciation of a co-parcener.

87. (B) Section 2(f) of the Indian Succession Act, 1925 defines probate as the court's official validation of a will, granting the executor authority to administer the estate.

88. (C) Chapter VIII of the Indian Succession Act addresses the vesting of legacies, establishing conditions for when gifts in a will become legally effective.

89. (C) Under the Hindu Succession Act, the father is not a Class I heir, as it includes sons, daughters, and the mother; the father is a Class II heir.

90. (B) The Hindu Succession (Amendment) Act, 2005, enacted on 9th September 2005, introduced important changes to Hindu inheritance and succession laws.

91. (D) Section 7 of the Specific Relief Act applies to the right to present possession, which may be temporary or special, depending on the relief sought.

92. (B) Section 26 of the Specific Relief Act allows rectification of an instrument that doesn't reflect the true intention of the parties.

93. (C) The court has discretion under Section 28 of the Specific Relief Act to determine who bears the costs in a contract rescission case.

94. (A) Section 12(2) of the Specific Relief Act allows rescinding a contract where the unperformed part is a small proportion, based on the case's specifics.

95. (D) Section 41 of the Specific Relief Act lists situations where injunctions cannot be granted, including cases where specific performance is unenforceable.

96. (C) Section 23 of the Specific Relief Act allows specific performance despite the availability of damages as an alternative remedy.

97. (D) Section 18(a) of the Specific Relief Act involves fraud, mistake of fact, and misrepresentation, preventing the enforcement of contracts without variation or modification.

98. (B) Sections 38-42 of the Specific Relief Act contain detailed provisions on granting permanent injunctions, including requirements, conditions, and limitations.

99. (B) Under Section 6 of the Specific Relief Act, a plaintiff can recover immovable property possession without addressing the title, focusing on unlawful possession.

100. (A) In case of a breach of contract to transfer immovable property, courts presume compensation is inadequate, often favoring specific performance due to the unique nature of such property.

2017

1. (C) The Indian Constitution has a quasi-federal structure, combining both federal and unitary elements. Powers are distributed between the central and state governments, with the central government having overriding powers in certain cases, reflecting a partial unitary nature.

2. (A) The 42nd Constitutional Amendment in 1976 added the terms 'socialist' and 'secular' to the Preamble, emphasizing India's commitment to socialism and secularism as core governance principles.

3. (C) Article 16 of the Constitution guarantees equality of opportunity in public employment, prohibiting discrimination in recruitment or appointments based on factors such as religion, race, caste, sex, or place of birth.

4. (C) The President can issue an ordinance when Parliament is not in session. It has the same effect as a law but is temporary and must be approved by Parliament within a specific time to become permanent.

5. (A) In S. R. Bommai v. Union of India, the Supreme Court ruled that the Union cannot dismiss a State Government solely due to an election loss. The case set guidelines for the use of Article 356, preventing arbitrary use of President's Rule.

6. (C) The Supreme Court's original jurisdiction covers disputes between the Centre and States, allowing it to decide such cases for the first time, unlike appellate jurisdiction, which involves reviewing lower court decisions.

7. (D) The Supreme Court applied judicial review in cases such as Golaknath (1967), Bank Nationalization (1970), and Minerva Mills (1980), addressing fundamental rights, bank nationalization, and limits on parliamentary amendments.

8. (A) In Romesh Thappar v. State of Madras (1950), the Supreme Court addressed the scope of freedom of speech under Article 19(1)(a), marking a significant case in the interpretation of constitutional rights.

9. (B) In M. H. Hoskot (1978), the Supreme Court ruled that legal aid is a fundamental right under Article 21, requiring the state to provide free legal representation to indigent individuals.

10. (A) Article 243D ensures reservation of seats for Scheduled Castes and Tribes in Panchayats, promoting political representation and participation for marginalized communities at the local level.

11. (C) Mesne profit, defined in Section 2(12) of the CPC, refers to compensation for wrongful use of property during the pendency of a suit, allowing for claims related to unlawful occupation.

12. (A) Section 6 of the CPC sets the pecuniary jurisdiction, determining which court has the authority to hear civil cases based on the monetary value of the subject matter involved.

13. (D) Res judicata applies to both suits and execution proceedings, preventing re-litigation of the same issue after a final judgment has been made, even in enforcement actions.

14. (B) Section 10 of the CPC allows a court to stay proceedings if a similar matter is pending in another court, where the decision could affect the outcome of the original case.

15. (A) A suit for partition of immovable property must be filed in the court where the property is located, as jurisdiction is based on the property's physical location.

16. (D) Order 7, Rule 11 of the CPC allows a court to reject a plaint if it is barred by law, vague, frivolous, or does not disclose a cause of action.

17. (A) Order V of the CPC governs the issue and service of summons, outlining how legal notices are to be delivered to parties involved in a civil case.

18. (A) If a defendant fails to file a written statement within the specified time, the court may proceed with judgment, which is considered legal and valid.

19. (B) An application to set aside an ex parte decree should be filed before the court that issued the decree, allowing the defendant to provide reasons for their absence.

20. (B) A decree against B cannot be set aside if B was present or served with summons. However, the decree can be set aside for C and D, who were not notified.

21. (B) After an arrest, the accused must be presented before a magistrate within 24 hours, excluding travel time, as per legal requirements under the Code of Criminal Procedure.

22. (C) The Code of Criminal Procedure (Amendment) Act, 2008 introduced Sections 41A, 41B, 41C, and 41D, detailing procedures for arrest, anticipatory bail, and arrest in non-cognizable offenses.

23. (B) In Joginder Kumar v. State of UP (1994), the Supreme Court ruled that arrest requires reasonable grounds, preventing arbitrary or unlawful detentions by the police.

24. (A) A police report under Section 195(1)(a) of the CrPC is considered a complaint, initiating legal proceedings based on the alleged offense.

25. (B) A non-cognizable offense is one where the police cannot arrest without a warrant, though they may still investigate the matter based on a complaint.

26. (B) The order allowing the accused to appear via a power of attorney is illegal in criminal proceedings, as the accused must appear personally unless permitted by law.

27. (A) Section 20 of the CrPC empowers the State Government to appoint Executive Magistrates to assist in administering criminal justice within specific areas or functions.

28. (A) Section 133 of the CrPC allows a Magistrate to issue a conditional order for removing a public nuisance causing substantial harm or annoyance to the public.

29. (C) Chapter XI of the CrPC covers preventive police actions, allowing the police to take steps to prevent certain offenses and maintain public order.

30. (B) Section 157(1) of the CrPC requires police to record a rape victim's statement at her residence or preferred location, with a woman police officer present.

31. (B) Sections 17-31 of the Indian Evidence Act govern the relevancy of admissions and confessions, outlining when these can be used as evidence in court.

32. (A) Direct evidence makes motive irrelevant, as it directly proves the fact in question, rendering the need for motive less significant in establishing guilt or innocence.

33. (D) An admission can be oral, documentary, or electronic, and it refers to statements made by a party in the course of legal proceedings.

34. (B) A confession is admissible only if made by an accused and is voluntary, without inducement, threat, or promise of reward, in accordance with legal standards.

35. (C) In Kalawati v. State of HP, the Supreme Court ruled that a retracted confession could be used against the accused, not violating their constitutional protection under Article 20(3).

36. (C) Both A and B's confessions can be considered by the court. The involvement of both in the crime will be evaluated alongside other evidence to determine their culpability.

37. (A) The Mathura Case led to the introduction of Section 114A of the IPC, addressing custodial rape and ensuring stricter penalties for offenses of this nature.

38. (C) Examination-in-chief refers to the questioning of a witness by the party that called

them, aiming to gather evidence supporting their case.

39. (A) Res judicata is a principle that prevents the re-litigation of a matter that has already been decided by a competent court, ensuring finality in legal disputes.

40. (C) A document's contents can be proved through primary evidence (the original) or secondary evidence (copies or duplicates), depending on availability.

41. (B) A person who fails to rescue a drowning child is not legally liable unless there is a specific duty or relationship that mandates such action.

42. (C) Volenti non fit injuria is a legal principle stating that a person who voluntarily exposes themselves to risk cannot later claim damages for harm arising from it.

43. (C) Section 97 of the IPC grants the right to private defense, allowing individuals to use reasonable force to protect themselves and their property from certain offenses.

44. (A) A is guilty of instigating B to commit murder. Even if D recovers, A remains culpable for encouraging the crime, regardless of its outcome.

45. (A) Section 186 of the IPC penalizes the obstruction of a public servant in the performance of their duties, making it an offense to hinder their official functions.

46. (B) Section 201: A can be punished under Section 201 for helping B hide the body of Z to screen B from punishment. This section addresses the offense of hiding evidence to protect an offender.

47. (A) Death by rash and negligent act: If a doctor prescribes medicine outside their field, causing death, it is considered a rash and negligent act. The doctor's actions exceed their authorized practice.

48. (C) Section 405: Criminal Breach of Trust is defined under Section 405. It deals with the misappropriation of property entrusted to someone's care for personal use.

49. (A) Reema Agarwal v. Anupam: The Supreme Court held that Section 498A applies to cruelty cases even without a legal marriage, focusing on abuse by the husband or in-laws.

50. (A) Section 511: A is guilty under Section 511 for attempting to commit an offense, even if unsuccessful, such as trying to pickpocket without valuables.

51. (C) Section 4: Section 4 of the Limitation Act, 1963 allows for the expiration of a limitation period when courts are closed, extending the deadline to the next open day.

52. (A) Illegal: An order made after the expiration of the limitation period is illegal and unenforceable.

53. (A) No limitation applies: There is no time limit for suits seeking recovery of possession of wakf property from a deemed trustee.

54. (D) 12 years: The limitation period for executing a decree or court order, excluding mandatory injunctions, is 12 years from the decree's date.

55. (A) Mandatory: The time exclusion under Section 14 of the Limitation Act, 1963 is mandatory, counting only the time spent on good faith, diligent previous proceedings.

56. (A) Section 21: Section 21 of the Limitation Act addresses the effect of substituting or adding a new party to a suit, deeming the proceeding initiated on the substitution date.

57. (A) When the injury results: The limitation period for a compensation suit starts when the injury occurs, even if the cause of action needs a specific injury to arise.

58. (A) Civil Court: A civil court exclusively grants exemptions under Section 14 of the Limitation Act for time taken in a prior legal proceeding.

59. (C) 3 years: The limitation for a compensation suit related to copyright infringement is 3 years from the cause of action's date.

60. (B) 30 days: The limitation for applying to set aside an ex parte decree or rehear an ex parte appeal is 30 days from the decree or hearing date.

61. (A) Section 20: Section 20 of the Transfer of Property Act allows creating a contingent interest for an unborn person.

62. (A) Debt or beneficial interest: An actionable claim involves a debt or beneficial interest in movable property that can be legally enforced.

63. (A) Section 35: The doctrine of election under Section 35 allows a person to either accept or reject a transaction, binding them if accepted.

64. (B) Section 5: Section 5 of the Transfer of Property Act defines "Transfer of Property," covering both movable and immovable property.

65. (D) Mortgage by deposit of title deeds: No registration is required for a mortgage created by depositing title deeds; it remains valid and enforceable.

66. (A) Void: Provisions preventing a mortgagor from redeeming the mortgage, like a clog on redemption, are void and unenforceable.

67. (A) 15 days: A lease of immovable property can be terminated by either party with a 15-day notice.

68. (C) Subsequent mortgagee: A puisne mortgagee holds a mortgage on the same property but has lower priority than prior mortgagees.

69. (B) Right to enjoy the property: A lease transfers the right to enjoy the property, not ownership or possession, for a specified time.

70. (C) Fraudulent transfer: A transfer made to defeat creditors is fraudulent and can be annulled by the creditors.

71. (A) Part performance: Pinnel's Case allows part performance of a contract to enforce it under specific circumstances, even if all terms are not fully met.

72. (C) General offer: A general offer is addressed to the public, inviting anyone who meets conditions to accept and form a contract.

73. (B) When the telegram is received: Revocation of acceptance is complete when the revoking party's message is received by the original offeror.

74. (C) Coercion: The deed obtained by threatening suicide is invalid due to coercion, making the contract voidable under Indian law.

75. (C) Valid: Collateral transactions related to wagering agreements may still be valid even though the wagering agreement itself is void.

76. (C) The contract has become impossible: When a contract becomes impossible due to an unforeseen event, it is frustrated, and the parties are released from obligations.

77. (A) Remission: If a creditor accepts a lesser amount as full satisfaction of a debt, it is known as remission, discharging the debt.

78. (D) Contract of indemnity: Insurance contracts, other than life insurance, are considered contracts of indemnity, compensating the insured for actual losses.

79. (C) General offer: The Carlill v. Carbolic Smoke Ball case dealt with a general offer made to the public, forming a binding contract when accepted.

80. (B) Parties identified the same thing: Consensus ad idem refers to mutual understanding and agreement on the same terms in a contract.

81. (B) Equally: Property in Class II heirs under Section 11 of the Hindu Succession Act is distributed equally among them.

82. (D) None of the above: Class I heirs include son, daughter, widow, and certain descendants, as specified under Hindu law.

83. (A) A creature of Hindu law: Coparcenary is a unique form of property ownership under Hindu law, allowing joint family inheritance.

84. (B) Intestate: A person who dies without a will is considered intestate, and intestate succession rules apply for property distribution.

85. (D) Section 15: Section 15 of the Hindu Succession Act governs succession for female Hindus, outlining the order of succession for property.

86. (B) No: Under the Hindu Succession Act, 1956, a widow's property inherited from her deceased husband remains hers, regardless of her subsequent remarriage. This property remains her absolute property, unaffected by her marital status.

87. (B) Coparcener: A coparcener is someone who shares equally in the inheritance of a common ancestor's estate. This applies in joint Hindu families, where certain male members inherit an interest by birth in ancestral property.

88. (A) A full owner: Section 14 of the Hindu Succession Act, 1956, grants female Hindus full ownership rights over any property they possess, whether acquired before or after the Act's commencement.

89. (C) Section 2(b): A codicil, as defined in Section 2(b) of the Indian Succession Act, 1925, is a testamentary document that modifies or supplements an existing will, executed in the same manner as the will itself.

90. (B) Void: A will created under fraud, coercion, or undue pressure is void. Such a will cannot be legally enforced.

91. (B) As per the discretion of the court: Specific performance of a contract, under Section 10 of the Specific Relief Act, can be enforced at the court's discretion, considering factors like the contract's nature and the availability of damages.

92. (B) 3 years: The limitation period for filing a suit for specific performance of a contract is 3 years from the date of the breach.

93. (A) Section 12: Section 12 of the Specific Relief Act allows the court to enforce the specific performance of only part of a contract if deemed equitable.

94. (A) Prakash Chandra v. Angadlal: In this case, the Supreme Court ruled that if damages are an adequate remedy, specific performance may be denied, recognizing that monetary compensation might suffice for non-performance.

95. (B) Cannot recover damages: Once a contract is rescinded, the party cannot claim damages, as rescission terminates the contract and releases both parties from further obligations.

96. (C) Either in addition to or in substitution of such performance: In a suit for specific performance, the plaintiff may seek compensation either in addition to or instead of the specific performance, depending on the case circumstances.

97. (D) All of the above: A declaration under Section 34 of the Specific Relief Act is binding on all parties involved, including trustees and their beneficiaries.

98. (B) Section 37: Section 37 of the Specific Relief Act defines perpetual injunctions, which permanently prevent a person from performing a specific act or continuing an action until further court orders.

99. (D) Either (A) or (B): A suit for rectification can be filed when fraud or mistakes are discovered in an instrument such as a contract or deed.

100. (D) All of the above: Contracts for which monetary compensation is adequate, those with numerous details, or those that are inherently terminable cannot be specifically enforced and are better addressed with remedies like damages.

2018

1. (D) Kesavananda Bharati Case: The Supreme Court held that the Preamble can be amended, but its basic structure cannot be altered. The case introduced the "basic structure" doctrine, which limits Parliament's power to amend the Constitution. The Preamble is part of the basic structure but can still be modified.

2. (C) Doctrine of Repugnancy: This doctrine resolves conflicts between central and state laws on the same subject in the Concurrent List. If a state law contradicts a central law, the central law prevails and the state law becomes void to the extent of the conflict.

3. (B) Bachan Singh v. State of Punjab: The Supreme Court ruled that capital punishment does not violate Article 21. It should be applied only in "the rarest of rare" cases when life imprisonment is not an option.

4. (B) Fundamental Rights: In conflicts between Fundamental Rights and Directive Principles, Fundamental Rights take precedence. While Directive Principles are non-justiciable, Fundamental Rights are enforceable in court.

5. (C) Article 300: Article 300 of the Constitution grants legal personality to the Union and States, enabling them to sue and be sued in their own name, with rights and obligations like any legal entity.

6. (C) Mohini Jain v. State: The Supreme Court declared the collection of capitation fees by educational institutions unconstitutional. It argued that charging such fees commercializes education and violates equality and social justice principles.

7. (A) Olga Tellis Case: The Supreme Court ruled that the right to shelter is part of the fundamental right to life under Article 21. It emphasized that homelessness violates human dignity and ordered provisions for shelter.

8. (A) Certiorari: A writ of certiorari is issued to review the proceedings of an inferior court or tribunal to ensure they have not exceeded jurisdiction or violated natural justice principles.

9. (D) USSR Constitution: The concept of Fundamental Duties in the Indian Constitution was inspired by the USSR Constitution. The 42nd Amendment of 1976 introduced these duties to emphasize civic responsibility.

10. (D) Article 30: Article 30 protects the educational rights of minorities, allowing them to establish and manage their own educational institutions without discrimination.

11. (A) Summons were not duly served: An ex parte decree can be set aside if it is shown that the summons were not properly served, preventing the defendant from being aware of the proceedings.

12. (D) All of these: The CPC allows preliminary decrees in suits for dissolution of partnership, accounts, and partition. These orders define the rights and obligations of the parties before the final decree is passed.

13. (B) Substance of the matter: Jurisdiction is determined by the substance of the dispute, not merely the form of the suit. Courts focus on the true nature of the case to establish the appropriate jurisdiction.

14. (A) Dismissed: Under the doctrine of res judicata, a suit will be dismissed if it involves a matter already decided by a final judgment. This prevents the re-litigation of the same issue between the same parties.

15. (C) Either in Delhi or in Calcutta: A person can be sued in the court where they reside or conduct business. In defamation cases, the plaintiff may sue where the statement was published or where the defendant resides.

16. (C) Section 19: Section 19 of the CPC addresses suits for movable property, allowing them to be filed in the court where the property is located at the time of the suit.

17. (D) All of these: To claim a set-off, the suit must be for money recovery, the sum must be ascertainable, and it must fall within the court's pecuniary jurisdiction.

18. (A) Maintainable: A second suit based on fraud in obtaining an ex parte decree is maintainable. The fraud claim can challenge the validity of the decree.

19. (B) On substantial question of law: A second appeal under Section 100 of the CPC is allowed on a substantial question of law, which must significantly impact the case's outcome.

20. (A) Property is situated: A partition suit for immovable property must be filed in the court within the jurisdiction where the property is located.

21. (D) Section 62: Section 62 of the CrPC outlines the procedure for serving summons, specifying the methods for notifying the person against whom a complaint or charge is made.

22. (C) Y is not entitled, but her child is entitled to maintenance: Y is not entitled to maintenance due to her involvement in an illicit relationship, but her child has a right to maintenance.

23. (A) May be passed ex-parte: Under Section 144 of the CrPC, an order may be issued ex-parte in urgent situations involving potential threats or disturbances, without prior hearings.

24. (D) Ahmed Noormohammed v. State: The Supreme Court upheld the validity of Section 151 of the CrPC, which grants courts inherent powers to take necessary actions not covered by specific provisions.

25. (C) Power to arrest: A police officer investigating a non-cognizable offense under a magistrate's order cannot arrest the accused, as non-cognizable offenses require a warrant or court order for arrest.

26. (C) Section 161: Section 161 of the CrPC allows the police to examine witnesses during an investigation, recording their statements to assist in the investigation process.

27. (B) Section 164A: Section 164A of the CrPC mandates the medical examination of rape victims within a specified time after the offense to gather evidence.

28. (A) Eligible for plea bargaining: An accused person can apply for plea bargaining, where they agree to plead guilty in exchange for concessions such as reduced sentences.

29. (A) Section 428: Section 428 of the CrPC deals with set-off, allowing the period spent in detention to be deducted from the final sentence upon conviction.

30. (A) M.C. Abrahani v. State: The Supreme Court ruled that rejection of anticipatory bail does not justify arrest unless there are reasonable grounds and evidence for the need for arrest.

31. (B) Section 3 of the Indian Evidence Act defines fact in issue as a disputed fact central to the case that needs to be proven to establish the rights and liabilities of the parties.

32. (C) A court may treat a presumption as proof if it is not rebutted, thereby accepting it as valid and sufficient to establish a fact unless challenged by contrary evidence.

33. (C) The fact that A borrowed money from B is irrelevant to a murder trial unless it relates directly to the motive or circumstances of the murder, unlike other facts that may be directly related.

34. (A) Digital signature: In cases concerning digital signatures, the certifying authority's opinion is crucial in verifying the authenticity of the digital signature issued.

35. (B) Res Gestae: Res gestae are statements made spontaneously and contemporaneously with an event, considered admissible as they offer immediate context and relevance to the event.

36. (B) A statement by an accused to the police is admissible if not a confession and not made during the investigation, as confessions to the police are generally inadmissible unless they meet specific criteria.

37. (B) Presumption of genuineness of certified copies is covered under Section 79 of the Indian Evidence Act, which assumes that certified copies are genuine unless proven otherwise.

38. (B) When an accused claims insanity, the burden of proof lies with the accused to establish unsoundness of mind. The prosecution does not have to prove sanity unless this defense is raised.

39. (C) A preliminary examination is recommended for child witnesses to assess their competency and understanding of truth-telling, ensuring their testimony is reliable.

40. (C) Leading questions are allowed during cross-examination without court permission, as they help challenge a witness's credibility or recall of events.

41. (A) "Actus non facit reum nisi mens sit rea" means both a guilty mind and a wrongful act are required to establish criminal liability, underscoring the necessity of both elements in criminal law.

42. (B) If A intended to kill B but B's death occurred due to an unrelated accident, A is not liable for murder. The cause of death was too indirect to hold A accountable under criminal law.

43. (D) Sections 305, 364A, and 396 of the IPC

prescribe punishments including the death penalty for serious offenses like abetment of suicide, kidnapping for ransom, and dacoity with murder.

44. (B) Affray is an offense that does not require a common object. It involves a public disturbance caused by two or more people fighting, without needing shared intent or objective.

45. (B) By distributing phones and asking for votes in return, Mr. A has committed an offense under Section 171B of the IPC, which prohibits bribery in elections.

46. A: A doctor practicing Homoeopathy who prescribed an allopathic medicine leading to a patient's death is guilty of death by rash and negligent act. The doctor lacked the necessary qualifications to administer the medicine, constituting negligence.

47. B: Attempting suicide is punishable under Section 309 of the IPC. However, many countries emphasize mental health support over criminalization for individuals in distress.

48. C: A police officer who tortures a person to obtain a confession is guilty under Section 330 of the IPC, which criminalizes causing hurt to extort a confession.

49. A: Under Section 336 of the IPC, anyone whose rash or negligent act endangers human life or safety is punishable, addressing acts that pose a threat to others.

50. C: Section 509 of the IPC criminalizes actions aimed at insulting a woman's modesty, including exhibiting an object with intent to insult her.

51. D: Section 16 of the Limitation Act, 1963 specifies that the limitation period for a suit starts after a legal representative is entitled to pursue the case if the person entitled dies.

52. A: Section 25 of the Limitation Act, 1963 allows the acquisition of easement by prescription if the use of property continues openly for 20 years without interruption.

53. A: Section 27 of the Limitation Act, 1963 extinguishes the right itself if a suit for possession isn't filed within the prescribed period.

54. C: A suit for an account and share of profits after a partnership is dissolved must be filed within three years from the dissolution.

55. A: Section 55 of the Limitation Act, 1963 allows a mortgagor 30 years to file a suit for redemption or possession of mortgaged property.

56. B: An application to the Supreme Court for special leave to appeal after a High Court refusal must be filed within 60 days under the Limitation Act.

57. B: Section 3 of the Limitation Act, 1963 mandates that any suit filed after the limitation period shall be dismissed, regardless of whether limitation is raised as a defense.

58. A: A suit on a promissory note or bond with installment payments must be filed within three years from the due date of each installment.

59. A: A complaint filed on 15.11.1995 is within time, as it was filed within one month of the notice of dishonor under the Negotiable Instruments Act.

60. B: Dismissal of a civil appeal as time-barred does not constitute a decree, as it is a rejection due to expired limitation.

61. D: Income accumulation can be directed for the lifetime of the transferor or for 18 years from the date of transfer, whichever ends earlier, under Section 17 of the Limitation Act, 1963.

62. A: Fraudulent or erroneous transfer triggers feeding by estoppel when the transferee is led to believe in a right to the property.

63. A: A restriction on absolute alienation of property is valid when it benefits the lessor, ensuring such conditions are enforceable.

64. B: Lis pendens doctrine applies to pending litigation but does not cover collusive suits, where parties cooperate to deceive the court.

65. D: When a mortgagor appears to sell mortgaged property, it is termed a "mortgage with conditional sale," not any of the listed options.

66. C: A decree for the redemption of mortgaged property extinguishes the mortgagee's right to file for foreclosure, allowing the mortgagor to redeem the property.

67. C: In an English mortgage, the mortgaged property can be sold without court intervention, as the mortgagor transfers ownership with an agreement for return upon debt repayment.

68. C: A tenant remaining after the lease term expires is considered a tenant at sufferance, allowing the landlord to evict them legally.

69. D: A decree from a Civil Court is not considered an actionable claim, as it does not refer to a claim or debt that can be enforced.

70. C: "Donatio mortis causa" refers to gifts made in contemplation of death, which are conditional and transfer upon the donor's death.

71. C: A person with an interest in the consideration of a contract but not a party cannot enforce the contract unless explicitly intended.

72. A: Forbearance to sue the promisor in exchange for their promise is always valid consideration for a contract.

73. A: Acceptance of a contract is considered complete when it is put in transmission, beyond the acceptor's control to retract.

74. C: Coercion involves threatening acts prohibited by the IPC to induce a person into a contract against their free will, making the contract voidable.

75. B: A contract caused by a mistake of law is valid since parties are expected to know the law, though exceptions may apply in cases of fraud or misrepresentation.

76. C: A contingent contract depends on a specific event's occurrence or non-occurrence, affecting the obligations of the parties involved.

77. C: In joint promises, the promisee can recover the full amount from any one promisor, who can seek contribution from others.

78. B: When C pays Rs. 2,000 to B to settle A's claim, it discharges the entire claim, as the debt owed by A is considered satisfied.

79. C: The agent is responsible to the principal for the sub-agent's actions in a lawful appointment, as the sub-agent acts under the agent's direction.

80. B: Delay in suing B does not discharge A from suretyship unless specified by an agreement. A remains liable despite delays in suing the principal debtor.

81. B: A coparcenary includes male descendants of a joint family, including the father, sons, grandsons, and great-grandsons, forming a unit of inheritance.

82. B: Property will be distributed equally among the mother, adopted son, daughters, and natural-born sons of a deceased male Hindu as per Class I heirs.

83. A: A brother is a Class I heir under the Hindu Succession Act and has a right to inherit in the absence of higher-preference heirs.

84. A: Section 14 of the Hindu Succession Act, 1956 ensures that a female Hindu's property, regardless of when acquired, is her absolute property.

85. A: Under Section 8 of the Hindu Succession Act, the property of a male Hindu dying intestate devolves to his widow, children, and other Class I heirs.

86. (B) Section 27: Section 27 of the Indian Succession Act, 1925 ensures equal inheritance rights for both agnates (male relatives) and cognates (female relatives). Gender does not affect their inheritance entitlement under this provision.

87. (C) Testator: A Holograph Will is a will written by the testator, who is the individual making the will, expressing their wishes regarding the distribution of their property after death.

88. (B) Does not take effect: A legacy to B is contingent upon A's death before the testator. If A survives the testator, the legacy to B does not take effect.

89. (C) Probate: Probate is the legal validation of a will, granting the executor authority to administer the deceased's estate, with a certified copy of the will issued under the court's seal.

90. (B) Section 112: Section 112 of the Indian Succession Act declares that if a specified person does not exist at the testator's death, the bequest becomes void.

91. (D) 6 months: A suit for possession of immovable property under Section 6 of the Specific Relief Act must be filed within 6 months of dispossession.

92. (A) Section 7: Section 7 of the Specific Relief Act deals with the recovery of specific movable property, enabling the rightful owner to recover unlawfully detained or taken property.

93. (C) Declaration: A declaration is a court's authoritative pronouncement affirming a person's rights to property or their legal status.

94. (A) Mere declaration of rights of the parties: Section 34 allows courts to issue a declaratory judgment, affirming the rights of the parties without further enforcement action.

95. (C) Injunction: An injunction is a court order directing a party to do or refrain from doing a specified act.

96. (C) Perpetual injunction: A perpetual injunction is a permanent court order, remaining in force until further orders, unlike temporary injunctions with limited durations.

97. (B) Some future probable injury to rights or interests of a person: Qua timet addresses potential future harm to a person's rights or interests, allowing legal action to prevent it.

98. (A) Yes: The court may award compensation when specific performance of a contract becomes impossible, providing an alternative remedy.

99. (B) A mistake in the way in which that transaction has been expressed in writing: Rectification corrects mistakes in written documents that do not accurately reflect the parties' intentions.

100. (B) The promisor: Under Section 12(2) of the Specific Relief Act, the promisee can enforce part performance of a contract if they have performed or are willing to perform their obligations.

2019-2020

1. (B) Bhavani Singh - Bhavani Singh was the Special Public Prosecutor in the

Disproportionate Assets Case, where Tamil Nadu Chief Minister Jayalalithaa was convicted for four years.

2. (A) True - The Government of India Act, 1935, was a lengthy document with 321 sections and 10 schedules. It outlined the governance framework for British India before independence.

3. (A) Once - The Preamble to the Constitution of India was amended once, by the Forty-second Amendment Act, 1976, adding "Socialist" and "Secular."

4. (A) Delhi - The First Session of the Constituent Assembly of India was held in Delhi on December 9, 1946, marking the beginning of the drafting of the Indian Constitution.

5. Article 26 - Article 26 of the Constitution guarantees freedom to manage religious affairs.

6. (D) Article 24 - Article 24 prohibits the employment of children under 14 years in hazardous occupations, ensuring their right to a childhood free from labor exploitation.

7. (D) Both (A) and (B) - Amendments to rectify Golaknath's judgment were made to Articles 13 and 368 of the Constitution, clarifying Parliament's power to amend fundamental rights.

8. The number of items in the Ninth Schedule of the Constitution of India in 1951, introduced by the Constitution (First Amendment) Act, was 13.

9. (A) Sunil Batra Case - The Sunil Batra case upheld the right against solitary confinement, recognizing that prolonged solitary confinement violates Article 21 of the Constitution.

10. (A) Yes - Judicial review is part of the basic structure of the Indian Constitution, allowing the Supreme Court to examine the constitutional validity of laws and executive actions.

11. (D) Section 2(2) - Section 2(2) of the Code of Civil Procedure defines a "decree" as the formal adjudication that conclusively determines the rights of the parties involved.

12. (A) Sections - In case of inconsistency between sections and rules in the Code of Civil Procedure, the sections prevail as the substantive part of the law.

13. (C) The Parliament - The Parliament has the authority to amend the sections of the Code of Civil Procedure through legislation.

14. (A) Suit - Civil proceedings initiated by presenting a plaint are called suits, where the plaintiff outlines their claim and relief sought.

15. (A) Yes - A civil court can pass more than one order in a suit, including interim orders, directions, or final judgments on various aspects.

16. (B) 1859 - The first uniform Code of Civil Procedure in India was enacted in 1859 during British colonial rule.

17. (A) Sections - The sections of the Code of Civil Procedure define rights, liabilities, and procedures and form the core of civil law.

18. (A) Yes - It is necessary to state the amount of costs incurred in a suit, as the court determines financial obligations during the proceedings.

19. (A) Yes - The court can issue commissions for the examination of persons in prison to ensure a fair trial.

20. (A) Yes - The court must pronounce judgment on all issues raised in a suit, providing its findings and conclusions.

21. (B) Inquiry - Section 2(g) defines "inquiry," referring to the process conducted by a magistrate to ascertain facts before a trial begins.

22. In a Warrant case, the trial starts when a charge is framed under Section 240 of the CrPC.

23. (C) Does not vitiate the trial unless miscarriage of justice has been caused - Illegality in investigation doesn't automatically vitiate the trial unless it results in miscarriage of justice.

24. (C) Officer-in-charge of a Police Station - Identification of arrested persons can be ordered by the court upon request from the officer-in-charge of a police station.

25. (D) Any one of them - A summons can be served by a public servant, police officer, or officer of the court.

26. (D) All of them - A warrant may be directed to arrest an escaped convict, a proclaimed offender, or someone accused of a non-bailable offense evading arrest.

27. (A) Yes - Evidence of witnesses can be taken under oath by the Magistrate conducting an inquiry.

28. (C) Judgment is pronounced - A court may alter or add to charges before the judgment is pronounced.

29. (D) Three months - The maximum sentence for an offense in a Summary Trial is three months.

30. (A) Yes - A witness can refuse to sign the deposition if it is not read over to them.

31. (A) Direct Evidence - "Testimony" refers to direct evidence based on the witness's personal knowledge or observation.

32. (D) J. F. Stephen - The Indian Evidence Act, 1872 was drafted by J. F. Stephen.

33. (C) Weight of Evidence - The Indian Evidence Act, 1872 focuses on the relevancy and admissibility of evidence, not its weight.

34. (B) Legally pertinent - "Relevant" derives from the Latin "relevare," meaning legally pertinent or logically connected to the matter at hand.

35. (D) Plaint or written statement in a suit - A plaint or written statement is not a public document, as public documents are official records issued by authorities.

36. (B) Question of law - Relevancy is a question of law, determining whether evidence is legally admissible and relevant to the case.

37. (B) Hearsay Rule - Res gestae is an exception to the hearsay rule, admitting statements made during an event that are relevant to its circumstances.

38. (B) Probability of it having existed - Proof of a fact relies on the probability of its existence, not just the accuracy of statements.

39. (C) Not proved - A fact is considered not proved when its exact status cannot be determined.

40. (D) None of these - "Falsus in uno, falsus in omnibus" is not a reliable legal principle, as it assumes all testimony is false if one part is false.

41. (C) Common law - The principle "Actus non facit reum nisi mens sit rea" (an act does not make a person guilty unless there is a guilty mind) is of common law origin.

42. (C) Motive - Motive is not required for criminal liability; the essential elements are mens rea (guilty mind) and actus reus (guilty act).

43. (D) All of these - Attempt, abetment, and criminal conspiracy are inchoate offenses, preparatory to committing a substantive crime.

44. (B) Section 29A - Section 29A of the Indian Penal Code was added by the Information Technology Act, 2000.

45. (B) Wrongful loss - Wrongful loss refers to the unlawful loss of property to which the person losing it is entitled.

46. (B) The Information Technology Act defines "electronic record," which includes data, information, and documents stored in digital form and recognized by law.

47. (C) Under Section 153A, no court can take cognizance of the offense without prior sanction from either the Central or State Government.

48. (A) In a criminal conspiracy case, the prosecution must prove the conspiracy's existence beyond a reasonable doubt.

49. (C) The IPC does not include "transportation for life" as a punishment; the IPC lists death, forfeiture of property, and hard labor as possible punishments.

50. (B) The retribution theory, based on "eye for eye," advocates punishment proportional to the harm caused.

51. (B) Section 2(f) of the Limitation Act, 1963 defines "easement," referring to rights annexed to immovable property for enjoyment.

52. Section 2(j) of the Limitation Act defines the period of limitation for suits, appeals, or applications as prescribed in the Schedule.

53. (B) After the limitation period expires, a debt becomes unenforceable, though the debt itself remains intact.

54. Section 2(l) of the Limitation Act clarifies that "suit" excludes appeals or applications.

55. (A) A time-barred application filed beyond the limitation period is illegal, and the court cannot entertain it.

56. (A) No limitation applies for suits to recover possession of waqf property from deemed trustees.

57. (A) Limitation starts when a plaint is returned for non-compliance or other issues.

58. (A) Section 25 of the Limitation Act, 1963 deals with acquiring easement rights through prescription.

59. (C) The limitation for suits related to dissolved partnerships is three years from dissolution.

60. (C) The limitation period for suits concerning decrees and instruments is three years.

61. (C) "Inter vivos" transactions involve living persons, including both natural and juristic persons.

62. (D) Section 13 of the Transfer of Property Act allows property transfers for unborn persons under certain conditions.

63. (C) Subrogation refers to substituting one person in place of another in legal rights or claims.

64. (A) Section 82 of the Transfer of Property Act addresses co-mortgagors' rights to seek contribution for mortgage debt.

65. (C) The definition of actionable claims was amended in 1900, altering how claims are understood.

66. (D) Notice to the debtor is not required to perfect an assignment of actionable claims.

67. (D) A mortgagee can seek foreclosure only after the mortgage money is due.

68. (A) The pendency of a suit for Section 52 purposes begins when the plaint is filed.

69. (A) The doctrine of holding out involves an ostensible owner transferring property by appearing as the rightful owner.

70. (A) Section 35 of the Transfer of Property Act explains the doctrine of election, allowing

the choice between inconsistent rights.

71. (A) The Indian Contract Act, 1872 is not exhaustive and is supplemented by other legal sources.

72. (C) Coercion, as seen in Askari Mirza vs Jaikishori, invalidates a contract when force or threats are used.

73. (A) An agent does not have an inherent right to sell unless authorized by the principal.

74. (C) A guarantee obtained by silence regarding material facts is invalid due to lack of full disclosure.

75. (C) A fine is not a recognized remedy for breach of contract; damages, injunctions, and specific performance are.

76. (C) Sections 68-72 of the Indian Contract Act address quasi-contracts to prevent unjust enrichment.

77. (C) Promissory estoppel substitutes consideration by enforcing promises without it to avoid injustice.

78. (D) The Balfour vs Balfour case highlights the importance of intention to contract, especially between spouses.

79. (D) An agency can end due to revocation by the principal, renouncement by the agent, or death/insanity of either party.

80. (D) Section 170 of the Indian Contract Act defines a bailee's lien on goods for unpaid charges.

81. (A) Section 5 of the Hindu Succession Act, 1956 outlines the properties excluded from the Act's scope.

82. (A) A legacy refers to a gift of property through a will, effective upon the testator's death.

83. (B) The 2005 amendment to Section 6 of the Hindu Succession Act grants daughters equal inheritance rights.

84. (D) Section 14 of the Hindu Succession Act, 1956 applies to actual, symbolic, or constructive possession of property.

85. (A) Section 10 of the Hindu Succession Act, 1956 grants a widow one share in the deceased's property.

86. (A) The coparcenary is a narrower group within the joint Hindu family, limited to male heirs with inheritance rights.

87. (D) Section 15 of the Hindu Succession Act, 1956 governs the rules of succession for female Hindus.

88. (A) A life estate granted to a Hindu woman becomes her absolute estate upon her death.

89. (B) Agnate relationships occur when descendants are related through males only, either by blood or adoption.

90. (B) Section 14 of the Hindu Succession Act includes Stridhana property, granting female Hindus absolute ownership.

91. (A) True: Specific Relief is a legal remedy provided by the court to enforce specific performance or prevent breach of obligations when no other remedy is available.

92. (D) A regular suit establishing his title to the suit property: A person unsuccessful in a suit under Section 6 of the Specific Relief Act, 1963 can file a regular suit to establish their title to the property.

93. (A) Two: Section 36 of the Specific Relief Act, 1963 classifies injunctions into temporary and perpetual, where temporary injunctions are granted during a suit and perpetual ones as a final relief.

94. (D) Section 35: Section 35 of the Specific Relief Act, 1963 states that a declaration made by the court shall have the same effect as a decree.

95. (B) Rescission: Rescission is the remedy to cancel or terminate a contract, freeing the parties from obligations, unlike specific performance that enforces the contract.

96. (A) Yes: The court can award compensation when specific performance is impossible under Section 21 of the Specific Relief Act, 1963.

97. (C) Section 21: Section 21 of the Specific Relief Act, 1963 allows the court to award compensation in addition to or in place of specific performance.

98. (C) Both Specific Relief only and Preventive Reliefs: The Specific Relief Act, 1963 grants specific and preventive reliefs, including injunctions and declarations.

99. (B) Specific Performance: The Specific Relief Act, 1963 provides the remedy of specific performance, compelling a party to fulfill their contractual obligations.

100. (C) 9th Law Commission: The Specific Relief Act was a result of the 9th Law Commission of India, which reviews and recommends legal changes.

2021-22

1. (C) Both (i) and (ii) are true: Article 20 provides protection against self-incrimination and double jeopardy in India.

2. (D) Violation of the Constitution: The President can be removed only for misbehavior or incapacity, not for violating the Constitution.

3. (A) Shankari Prasad v. Union of India: The case confirmed Parliament's power to amend the Constitution, including fundamental rights, without limitations.

4. (D) Supreme Court and High Courts: Judicial review is vested in both the Supreme Court and High Courts under Articles 32, 226, and 227.

5. (A) 14 days: Rajya Sabha can withhold a Money Bill for a maximum of 14 days, after which it is deemed passed.

6. (A) According to Election Commission: The President acts based on the Election Commission's opinion regarding MP disqualification.

7. (C) Must have completed 35 years: Age is not a requirement for a Supreme Court judge; citizenship and judicial experience are essential.

8. (C) Parmanand Katara v. Union of India: Established the right to medical assistance under Article 21.

9. (B) Shreya Singhal v. U. O. I.: Mismatched; the case concerns internet freedom of speech, not unwed mother recognition.

10. (D) State of Bombay v. F. N. Balsara: Concerned the doctrine of pith and substance regarding the validity of laws.

11. (C) The party and pleader: Pleadings must be signed by both the party and their legal representative.

12. (C) Both (A) and (B): Section 3 of CPC defines the subordination of District and High Courts.

13. (B) A municipal councilor: Not considered a "public officer" under CPC Section 2(17).

14. (B) Order VIII Rule 6: CPC's set-off provision for counterclaims in civil suits is in Order VIII Rule 6.

15. (B) Section 13 of CPC: Governs the binding character of foreign judgments with exceptions.

16. (A) Order XL Rule 5: Allows appointing a collector as a receiver under CPC.

17. (C) Suit for dignity or honor: Such suits are not considered civil in nature.

18. (B) Power of Supreme Court to transfer suits = Section 24, CPC: Grants Supreme Court the authority to transfer suits.

19. (B) Prohibition of arrest of women in execution = Section 56, CPC: Not Section 57, which does not cover this.

20. (B) Order XXXIII: Provides for suits by indigent persons under CPC.

21. (C) Section 55A: Relates to the health and safety of an arrested person under Cr.P.C.

22. (D) All of these: Under Section 167, detention during investigation can be authorized for up to 90 days for serious offenses.

23. (C) Transit remand: Refers to taking an accused from one state to another.

24. (B) Section 154 of Cr.P.C.: Requires police to register a case for cognizable offenses upon receiving information.

25. (A) Section 273: States that all evidence in inquiry or trial must be taken in the presence of the accused.

26. (B) CJM cannot try theft cases above Rs. 3,000 in a summary way; summary trials are for less serious offenses.

27. (D) Section 438 of Cr.P.C.: Grants anticipatory bail powers to both Sessions Court and High Court.

28. (B) Section 401 Cr.P.C.: Grants High Court power to revise lower court proceedings.

29. (A) D. K. Basu v. State of West Bengal: Set guidelines for the arrest and detention of individuals.

30. (A) Plea Bargaining: Provisions under Chapter XXIA of Cr.P.C., added after Justice Verma Committee Report.

31. (C) R. M. Malkani v. State of Maharashtra: Related to "Res gestae," statements made during events closely connected to the case.

32. (B) "Witnesses are the eyes and ears of Justice": A quote attributed to Jeremy Bentham, emphasizing the importance of witnesses.

33. (C) Section 35 of Evidence Act: Relates to the admissibility of evidence for facts and their relevance.

34. (D) Section 14 of Evidence Act: Makes facts showing state of mind or bodily feelings relevant.

35. (C) Only statements (i) and (iii) are true: 'Confession' isn't defined in Evidence Act, and Lord Atkin's definition hasn't been accepted.

36. (C) Section 112 and Narendra Nath Pahari v. Ram Govind Pahari: Address the presumption of legitimacy of a child born during marriage.

37. (A) Pickard v. Sears: An English case, unlike the other Indian cases listed.

38. (A) Both Assertion and Reason are true: A judge is a competent witness in this scenario.

39. (C) Mismatched: Section 128 protects confidential communication with legal advisers, not specifically during marriage.

40. (D) Section 141 of Evidence Act: Defines leading questions, which suggest answers to the witness.

41. (C) Taking property from a dead body: Constitutes criminal misappropriation under IPC.

42. (C) K. M. Nanavati v. State of Maharashtra: Defined grave and sudden provocation as a mitigating factor for reducing murder to

culpable homicide.

43. (A) 'X' committed murder: Causing death after grave and sudden provocation by 'Z'.

44. (B) 'X' committed house trespass: Entering 'Y's bedroom at night with intent to murder.

45. (C) Mithu v. State of Punjab: Struck down Section 303 IPC as unconstitutional.

46. (A) R. v. Dudley and Stephens: A landmark case for the criminal defense of necessity in extreme situations.

47. (A) Sedition: Concerned with intent, not consequences.

48. (B) Theft committed by 'A': Theft is complete once property moves in his direction.

49. (D) Extortion committed by 'A': Obtaining Rs. 10,000 by threatening 'B' with death.

50. (D) Unlawful assembly and rioting: Use of violence by five or more people constitutes unlawful assembly.

51. (C) The Limitation Act does not prescribe a specific 120-day limitation period for filing a writ petition under Article 32 of the Constitution. This statement is false.

52. (D) Under Section 3 of the Limitation Act, the court must consider limitation suo motu, even if the defendant does not raise any objection regarding it.

53. (B) In N. Balakrishnan v. M. Krishnamurthy, the delay was not condoned, while R. B. Ramalingam v. R. B. Bhavneshwari emphasized that the test for sufficient cause is individualistic.

54. (C) Section 13 of the Limitation Act excludes time if an indigent person's application to sue or appeal is allowed and 'good faith' is required for this benefit.

55. (C) The incorrect statement is that the day from which the limitation period is reckoned should be excluded, not included.

56. (B) Section 15 of the Limitation Act applies to appeals, not suits. It excludes time spent in prosecuting another civil proceeding.

57. (C) Section 10 of the Limitation Act applies to both express and implied trusts, relating to cases where suits are stayed or neglected.

58. (C) Once time begins running, no subsequent disability can stop it. A fresh limitation period starts with each continuing breach of contract or tort.

59. (C) Section 25 of the Limitation Act concerns the acquisition of easements by prescription through continuous enjoyment.

60. (A) Section 10 of the Transfer of Property Act, 1882, restricts alienation of property, limiting the freedom of transfer by the owner.

61. (C) A claim to mesne profits is not an actionable claim, as mesne profits are damages for wrongful possession, not a legal claim.

62. (B) The term 'sale' is defined in Section 54 of the Transfer of Property Act, outlining the requirements for a valid sale of immovable property.

63. (D) Transfer by Ostensible Owner is covered under Section 41, not Section 40 of the Transfer of Property Act, which deals with transfer by authorized persons.

64. (C) Section 58(d) of the Transfer of Property Act deals with usufructuary mortgages, defining the rights and obligations of the mortgagee and mortgagor.

65. (C) A gift is void if the donee dies before accepting it, as per Section 122 of the Transfer of Property Act.

66. (A) The legal right of "C" in the scenario is determined under Section 27 of the Transfer of Property Act.

67. (C) In Alamelu v. Meenakshi, a marriage settlement designed to defraud creditors was voidable under Section 53 of the Transfer of Property Act.

68. (A) Section 20 of the Transfer of Property Act grants a vested right to an unborn person upon birth, benefiting from the transfer.

69. (B) Novation of a contract involves substituting a new contract or obligation with the consent of all parties.

70. (B) If "Y" is guilty of fraud, "X" can rescind the contract but cannot recover damages unless actual harm occurred.

71. (C) Misrepresentation occurs when a false statement is made without intent to deceive, and the person believes it to be true.

72. (B) Quasi-contractual obligations arise from unjust enrichment, imposed by law to prevent the wrongful retention of benefits.

73. (C) A life insurance contract, dependent on a future event, is a contingent contract under Section 32 of the Indian Contract Act.

74. (B) A loan agreement at a high interest rate is valid unless it violates usury laws, despite market conditions.

75. (B) A is not liable, as there was no intention to create a legally binding agreement with B.

76. (C) In Hadley v. Baxendale, damages are recoverable if they were foreseeable or communicated to both parties at contract formation.

77. (C) If no time is set for performance, the contract is not void, and it can be performed within a reasonable time.

78. (C) A brother's son is not a Class I heir under the Hindu Succession Act, 1956.

79. (B) The Hindu Succession Act disqualifies children in the womb at the time of an intestate's death from inheriting, but not those born after conversion.
80. (B) Blindness or impotence doesn't disqualify a person from inheriting under the Hindu Succession Act. Property devolves on the government if no heirs exist.
81. (C) Under the Hindu Succession Act, the widow of a predeceased son is a Class II heir.
82. (D) Section 14 of the Hindu Succession Act grants female Hindus absolute property rights.
83. (D) The Hindu Succession Act doesn't apply to members of a scheduled tribe under Article 366(25) of the Constitution.
84. (B) There is no prescribed format for drafting a will under Section 74 of the Indian Succession Act.
85. (C) The domicile of origin is determined by the father's domicile for legitimate children and by the mother's domicile for illegitimate children under the Indian Succession Act.
86. (A) Part VI of the Indian Succession Act governs "Probates, letters of administration, and administration of assets" after a person's death.
87. (D) Under Section 6 of the Specific Relief Act, orders or decrees are appealable and reviewable.
88. (A) Section 37 of the Specific Relief Act outlines the conditions under which a perpetual injunction may be granted.
89. (C) Part III of the Specific Relief Act covers "Preventive relief," which involves legal remedies to prevent violations of rights.
90. (C) Section 10 of the Specific Relief Act allows the specific enforcement of contracts to recover objects of historical value.
91. (D) Section 26 of the Specific Relief Act does not impose a time limit for discovering mistakes or fraud.
92. (B) Rescission is granted when a contract is voidable, allowing a party to void a contract for valid reasons.
93. (C) Section 37 of the Specific Relief Act allows both temporary and permanent injunctions to prevent rights violations.
94. (A) Section 31 of the Specific Relief Act deals with "Cancellation of instruments," empowering courts to cancel written instruments in certain situations.
95. (B) Section 21 of the Specific Relief Act allows compensation when specific performance is not granted.
96. (A) 'Domestic violence' under the Protection of Women from Domestic Violence Act is influenced by international frameworks like the UN Model Legislation.
97. (D) Under the Protection of Women from Domestic Violence Act, both Judicial and Metropolitan Magistrates can handle cases of domestic violence.
98. (D) Magistrates under the Protection of Women from Domestic Violence Act can issue Protection Orders, Residence Orders, and Monetary Reliefs.
99. (B) Protection Officers under the Protection of Women from Domestic Violence Act are public servants responsible for implementing the Act.
100. (A) A magistrate may pass an ex parte or interim order based on the affidavit of the aggrieved party under the Protection of Women from Domestic Violence Act.

2022-23

1. (D) Correct match: (ii) M.S.M. Sharma v. S.K. Sinha - Habeas Corpus Case, (iv) R.K Garg v. Union of India - Search light case, (iii) R.C. Cooper v. Union of India - Bank Nationalisation case, (i) A.D.M. Jabalpur - Bearer Bonds v. Shukla case.
2. (B) Article 141 declares the Supreme Court's law as binding, but the Court can reverse its own decisions.
3. (D) Under Article 370(3), the President can declare Article 370 inactive, but only with J&K Constituent Assembly's recommendation.
4. (A) The Right to Life under Article 21 includes human dignity and, by extension, the Right to Die.
5. (C) Article 20(3) protects individuals from self-incrimination, ensuring they aren't compelled to testify against themselves.
6. (A) Bijoe Emmanual v. State of Kerala, the National Anthem Case, involved students expelled for not singing the anthem for religious reasons.
7. (C) The Supreme Court in Bengal Immunity Co. Ltd v. State of Bihar affirmed that the Court's decisions are binding but not self-binding.
8. (A) State through SPE and CBI v. M. Krishna Mohan confirmed fingerprint and handwriting samples aren't protected under Article 20(3).
9. (D) Directive Principles guide governance and policy formation, providing a framework for state action.
10. (D) The sequence: (ii) Re Berubari Case, (i) Keshvananda Bharati v. State of Kerala, (iii) Excel Wear v. Union of India.
11. (B) In C. Magesh v. State of Karnataka, the FIR is not substantive evidence but can

corroborate its maker.

12. (D) Section 119 of the Indian Evidence Act allows evidence from a witness unable to speak, using writing or other means.

13. (C) Ningamma v. Chikkaiah cautioned against blood tests to establish legitimacy, highlighting sensitivity toward reputation.

14. (C) Section 11 of the Indian Evidence Act makes inconsistent facts relevant, even if otherwise irrelevant.

15. (D) Section 48 of the Indian Evidence Act details how a custom's existence can be proven by relevant opinion.

16. (D) Hearsay evidence is relevant under Section 6 of the Indian Evidence Act or when ratified by admission or included in public documents.

17. (C) A copy compared with a machine-made copy is considered secondary evidence, as per Section 63.

18. (B) Explanation II to Section 14 of the Indian Evidence Act discusses the relevance of previous convictions.

19. (A) 'Omnia praesumuntur rite esse acta' means all things are presumed to be done correctly.

20. (D) The right to private defense under IPC includes defense against harm to the body, movable property, and immovable property.

21. (B) 'Valuable security' in Section 30 of IPC refers to documents creating, transferring, or extinguishing legal rights.

22. (B) Section 149 of IPC applies to all members of an unlawful assembly, regardless of active participation.

23. (B) 'X', the doctor, is not guilty as the communication was made in good faith for the patient's benefit.

24. (D) The match: (a) Death to safeguard property - (ii) Murder, (b) Child's death - (iii) No offence, (c) Bodily injury sufficient to cause death - (ii) Murder, (d) Escaping trespasser - (i) Exception 2 to Section 300.

25. (B) Common intention requires pre-meditation and shared intent to commit an unlawful act, beyond similar intention.

26. (B) 'X' and 'Y' planning theft in 'Z's house, even without execution, constitutes criminal conspiracy under Section 120-A IPC.

27. (D) The distinction between culpable homicide and murder was elaborated in Reg v. Govinda.

28. (NV) Section 398 IPC punishes the attempt to commit robbery with deadly weapons, with imprisonment of not less than 7 years.

29. (A) Section 357-A mandates Victim Compensation Schemes formulated by state governments in coordination with the Central Government.

30. (C) In Navjot Singh Sidhu v. State of Punjab, the Court emphasized a person's duty to highlight potential consequences of not suspending a conviction.

31. (D) Section 186 of the CrPC resolves disputes between courts on jurisdiction over criminal matters under different High Courts.

32. (B) A warrant case under Section 2(x) CrPC involves offenses punishable by death, life imprisonment, or over two years' imprisonment.

33. (D) An arrested person has the right to consult a lawyer privately, without police presence, as per legal safeguards.

34. (A) Consecutive sentences in Metropolitan Magistrate trials cannot exceed twice the punishment for a single offence under Section 29 CrPC.

35. (B) Under Section 84 CrPC, claims on attached property must be filed within six months of attachment.

36. (B) Under Section 91 CrPC, a person summoned to produce documents does not become a witness and is not cross-examined.

37. (C) Property attachment objections can be raised by both parties and third parties.

38. (A) Under Order IX Rule 8 CPC, a fresh suit is barred after dismissal of a suit on the same cause of action.

39. (D) For the res subjudice principle, suits must involve the same parties, title, and directly identical issues.

40. (B) Under Order VIII, filing a written statement on time is discretionary, not mandatory for judgment pronouncement.

41. (C) Review under Section 114 CPC is permissible when no appeal is available or when appeal is not filed.

42. (A) In Dinesh Kumar v. Yusuf Ali, a second appeal is allowed only if the lower court's findings are perverse.

43. (A) Order 7 Rule 11 CPC allows the court to reject a plaint if no cause of action is disclosed or material facts are suppressed.

44. (A) The CPC Amendment Acts of 1999 and 2002 were upheld as constitutionally valid in Salem Advocate Bar Association v. Union of India.

45. (D) In Kamla Devi v. Khushal Kanwar, Section 100-A of CPC has no retrospective effect according to the 2002 Amendment.

46. (C) The shared household definition in the Protection of Women from Domestic Violence

Act, 2005, is under Section 2(s).

47. (A/C) In Satish Chander Ahuja v. Sheha Ahuja, for shared household status, it must be shown the aggrieved person resided during the domestic relationship.

48. (C) 'Violence' under the Protection of Women from Domestic Violence Act includes economic and sexual violence.

49. (C) Failure of a Protection Officer to perform duties under the Domestic Violence Act can lead to imprisonment or fine.

50. (A) Matching the Domestic Violence Act, 2005 Sections: (a) Section 6 - Protection Officers' duties, (b) Section 7 - Medical facilities' duties, (c) Section 9 - Shelter homes' duties, (d) Section 11 - Government duties.

51. (D) The Domestic Violence Act, 2005, came into force on October 26, 2006.

52. (B) The Magistrate must notify the Protection Officer of the hearing date under Section 12 of the Domestic Violence Act, 2005.

53. (D) 'Child' under the Protection of Women from Domestic Violence Act includes adopted, step, and foster children.

54. (B) Breaching a Protection Order under Sections 31 and 32 of the Domestic Violence Act is an offence that is cognizable and non-bailable.

55. (B) The Protection of Women from Domestic Violence Act, 2005, is supported by Articles 14, 15, and 21 of the Indian Constitution.

56. (C) Section 6 of the Limitation Act, 1963, does not apply to appeals.

57. (B) Section 5 of the Limitation Act, 1963, allows delay condonation based on the explanation, not the delay length.

58. (C) For term loans, the limitation period is three years from the due date of each installment.

59. (B) The fraud covered by Section 17 of the Limitation Act, 1963, refers to fraud by the defendant.

60. (D) Suits related to accounts, contracts, and declarations must be filed within three years under the law of limitation.

61. (A) Section 11 of the Limitation Act, 1908, covers suits on foreign contracts.

62. (A) A second appeal to the Central Public Information Officer must be filed within 90 days.

63. (B) A legal representative can be appointed within 90 days following the death of a defendant or respondent.

64. (B) A temporary injunction can restrain dispossession from property.

65. (B) The right to mesne profits is transferable under the Transfer of Property Act, 1882.

66. (B) Implied surrender of a lease occurs if the lessee abandons possession.

67. (B) Under the TP Act, 1882, the seller must disclose latent defects in the property.

68. (C) Under the TP Act, 1882, contract benefits can be assigned as actionable claims, except in certain cases involving personal qualifications or obligations.

69. (D) A vested interest under the Transfer of Property Act, 1882, is not defeated by the death of the transferor or transferee.

70. (B) Default interest under Sections 63 and 63A of the TP Act, 1882, is 9% per annum.

71. (C) A valid mortgage can arise after 12 years if an illegal mortgage continues in possession despite lack of registration.

72. (B) An anomalous mortgage involves a possessory mortgage with a right to sell the property if payment defaults.

73. (C) Instruments like shares and bills of exchange are excluded under Section 137 of the Transfer of Property Act, 1882.

74. (C) The Doctrine of Supervening Impossibility applies when impossibility is known at the time of contract formation.

75. (C) A proposal can be revoked under the Indian Contract Act by notice, failure to meet conditions, death/insanity of the proposer, or time lapse.

76. (B) Implied agency arises through Estoppel, Necessity, or Ratification.

77. (B) A void contract ceases to be enforceable by law.

78. (D) The correct sequence in the Indian Contract Act, 1872, is: (i) offer, (v) acceptance, (iii) promise, (iv) agreement, (ii) contract.

79. (C) Statement (I) is incorrect, but Statement (II) is correct.

80. (C) Statement (I) is correct, Statement (II) is incorrect.

81. (C) Consent under the Indian Contract Act is when parties agree on the same thing in the same sense, signifying mutual understanding.

82. (D) The Indian Contract Act, 1872, applies to "the whole of India."

83. (A) The Hindu Succession Act came into force on June 17, 1956.

84. (B) Section 9 of the Hindu Succession Act, 1956, deals with the order of succession among heirs in the Schedule.

85. (A) Section 19 of the Hindu Succession Act, 1956, governs the mode of succession among two or more heirs.

86. (A) Section 12 of the Hindu Succession

Act, 1956, outlines the order of succession among agnates and cognates.

87. (B) Section 25 of the Hindu Succession Act, 1956, disqualifies a murderer from inheritance.

88. (B) A will takes effect after the testator's death.

89. (A) A will can be revoked or altered by the maker of the will.

90. (A) The application for revocation of a succession certificate can be made by an interested person.

91. (B) An appeal lies to the High Court against the order of the District Judge under the Indian Succession Act, 1925.

92. (B) The Specific Relief Act, 1963, extends to "the whole of India."

93. (A) Specific relief is granted to enforce individual civil rights, not penal law.

94. (D) Injunctions cannot restrain criminal matters, prevent unenforceable contracts, or interfere with legislative bodies.

95. (C) Preventive relief can be granted by the Court through temporary and perpetual injunctions at its discretion.

96. (C) Specific performance of a contract is subject to Section 11(2), Section 14, and Section 16 of the Specific Relief Act, 1963.

97. (C) A contract can be rescinded by any interested party if it is unlawful or voidable due to the defendant's fault.

98. (B) Temporary injunctions are issued until a specified time or further order, regulated by the Code of Civil Procedure, 1908.

99. (B) No appeal or review is allowed for orders or decrees passed in suits under this Section.

100. (B) A plaintiff may seek rescission and cancellation of a contract if it cannot be specifically enforced.

2023-2024

1. Correct Option: B – The 42nd Amendment Act of 1976 added the terms "Socialist," "Secular," and "Integrity" to the Preamble of the Indian Constitution. The term "Sovereign" was already present in the original Preamble adopted in 1950. Therefore, the correct expressions added are "Socialist," "Secular," and "Integrity."

2. Correct Option: B – Article 324 of the Indian Constitution establishes the Election Commission of India, granting it the authority to supervise, direct, and control elections to Parliament, state legislatures, and the offices of the President and Vice-President. This ensures the conduct of free and fair elections across the country.

3. Correct Option: C – Justice Kuldip Singh of the Supreme Court of India is renowned as the "Green Judge" due to his significant contributions to environmental jurisprudence. He delivered landmark judgments promoting environmental protection and sustainable development, thereby earning this epithet.

4. Correct Option: D – Fundamental rights enshrined in the Indian Constitution cannot be waived by individuals. These rights are guaranteed to every citizen and are inalienable, ensuring the protection of individual liberties against state actions. The Supreme Court has held that individuals cannot relinquish these rights, as they are essential to the constitutional framework.

5. Correct Option: D – The Sixth Schedule of the Indian Constitution contains provisions for the administration of tribal areas in Assam, Meghalaya, Tripura, and Mizoram. Manipur is not included under this schedule. Therefore, the correct answer is Manipur.

6. Correct Option: D – Under Article 356, President's Rule can be imposed in a state for an initial period of six months. It can be extended, with parliamentary approval, up to a maximum of three years. Beyond this period, further extensions require specific conditions, such as a national emergency being in force.

7. Correct Option: C – The writ of Quo Warranto is issued to challenge the legality of a person's claim to a public office. If an appointment is made contrary to statutory provisions, this writ can be sought to question the authority by which the individual holds the office, ensuring that no one occupies a public position unlawfully.

8. Correct Option: C – The Eighth Schedule of the Indian Constitution lists the officially recognized languages.

9. Correct Option: D – The freedom to manage religious affairs does not include the right to construct religious places on government land.

10. Correct Option: A – The Union of India v. H.S. Dhillon case addressed Parliament's power to legislate on matters not enumerated in the State or Concurrent Lists.

11. Correct Option: B – Section 10 of the Civil Procedure Code (CPC) deals with the stay of proceedings in certain cases, where the court may stay a suit if a matter involving the same subject matter is pending before another court. If a party is aggrieved by a court's order under Section 10, the remedy available is revision, not appeal. An appeal is not available in this

case because Section 10 orders are not appealable as a matter of right. However, a revision can be filed under Section 115 of CPC to challenge an order that has caused injustice or exercised jurisdiction in an improper manner.

12. Correct Option: B – Section 11 of the Code of Civil Procedure, 1908, addresses the principle of res judicata, which bars the re-litigation of matters that have already been adjudicated between the same parties. This section explicitly prohibits the trial of any suit or issue that has been directly and substantially in issue in a former suit between the same parties or their representatives.

13. Correct Option: A – Order I, Rule 8 of the Civil Procedure Code provides for a "Representative Suit."

14. Correct Option: B – Order XXXIX, Rule 2 of the Civil Procedure Code deals with Temporary Injunctions.

15. Correct Option: C – Order XXXIII, Rule 18 of the Civil Procedure Code provides for "free legal services to indigent persons."

16. Correct Option: C – Res judicata is not similar to estoppel; they are distinct legal doctrines. Res judicata prevents the re-litigation of the same matter between the same parties, effectively ousting the court's jurisdiction to try the case again. Estoppel, on the other hand, prevents a party from asserting something contrary to what has been established as the truth in previous proceedings, serving as a rule of evidence.

17. Correct Option: D – A suit for restitution of conjugal rights can be filed where either the husband or wife resides.

18. Correct Option: C – Order 6, Rule 17 of the Civil Procedure Code provides for compulsory amendment of pleadings.

19. Correct Option: B – If a party does not amend their pleading within fourteen days after obtaining leave, they must seek further permission from the court.

20. Correct Option: A – Abatement of proceedings is provided for under Order 22 of the Civil Procedure Code.

21. Correct Option: B – The Bharatiya Nagrik Suraksha Sanhita 2023 received the President's assent on 25th December 2023.

22. Incorrect options. Bare reading of Part II of the Schedule -I of CrPC shows that, if the offences in the other laws are punishable with imprisonment for three years and upwards then the offences are cognizable and non bailable.

23. Correct Option: C – Statement 2 is correct: An accused shall not be released on bail if previously convicted on two or more occasions of a cognizable offense punishable with imprisonment for three years or more. Statement 3 is also correct: The necessity for identification by witnesses during investigation is not sufficient ground for rejection of bail.

24. Correct Option: C – Under Section 30 of the CrPC, a Magistrate's power to order imprisonment in default cannot exceed the Magistrate's sentencing power under Section 29 and cannot exceed one-fourth of the maximum term of imprisonment provided for the offense.

25. Correct Option: D – Section 428 of the CrPC allows the period of detention undergone by a convict to be set off against the sentence of imprisonment in the same case, but not in any other case.

26. Correct Option: A – Compounding an offense under the CrPC results in the acquittal of the accused.

27. Correct Option: D – Under Section 209 of the Code of Criminal Procedure (CrPC), when a Magistrate determines that an offense is triable exclusively by the Sessions Court, the case must be committed to the Sessions Court. This provision applies regardless of whether all accused are present, absconding, or exempted from personal appearance. Therefore, the case can be committed to the Sessions Court against all the accused, including 'A', 'B', 'C', 'D', and 'E'.

28. Correct Option: A – The Court can record the demeanor of a witness under Section 280 of the CrPC.

29. Correct Option: C – Section 389(3) of the CrPC, 1973, empowers the appellate court to suspend the sentence of an accused person and grant bail pending appeal.

30. Correct Option: C – A police report is specifically excluded from the definition of a complaint under Section 2(d) of the Code of Criminal Procedure, 1973.

31. Correct Option: A – Section 90A of the Indian Evidence Act, 1872, applies to electronic records that are at least five years old.

32. Correct Option: D – In fiduciary relationships, the burden of proving the good faith of a transaction lies on the party in whom confidence is reposed, not the one who reposes confidence.

33. Correct Option: C – Section 3 of the Indian Evidence Act defines "Facts in issue" among other terms.

34. Correct Option: A – Under Section 145 of the Indian Evidence Act, a witness may be cross-examined about previous statements

made in writing or reduced into writing.

35. Correct Option: C – In civil cases, evidence of character is generally inadmissible unless the character is directly in issue.

36. Correct Option: A – Section 32(2) of the Indian Evidence Act, 1872, addresses the admissibility of statements made by individuals who are deceased, cannot be found, or are otherwise unavailable to testify. Specifically, it states that statements made in the ordinary course of business are relevant and can be admitted as evidence.

37. Correct Option: D – A Will is a private document created by an individual to manage their property and distribute assets after death. Unlike public documents, which are maintained by public authorities or courts, a Will is not a public record unless it is probated. In contrast, documents like court judgments, police charge-sheets, and mercantile contracts are public records accessible to the public. Since a Will deals with personal matters and is not part of public documentation, it is not considered a public document under the Indian Evidence Act, 1872.

38. Correct Option: A – Section 92 of the Indian Evidence Act applies to disputes between parties to the instrument only.

39. Correct Option: C – Relevancy and admissibility under the Evidence Act are neither synonymous nor coextensive; a fact may be relevant but not admissible and vice versa.

40. Correct Option: B – The Indian Evidence Act, 1872, was drafted by Sir James Fitzjames Stephen.

41. Correct Option: C – Section 346 of the Indian Penal Code deals with wrongful confinement in secret. It addresses situations where a person is confined in such a manner that the confinement is intended to be kept unknown to those interested in the person or to public servants.

42. Correct Option: C – 'A' can be tried for culpable homicide amounting to murder if the victim dies after 'A' was convicted for voluntarily causing grievous hurt. This is because the subsequent death introduces a new element, constituting a distinct offense from the original conviction, and does not violate the principle of double jeopardy.

43. Correct Option: D – Section 388 of the Indian Penal Code addresses extortion by threat of accusation of an offense punishable with death, imprisonment for life, or imprisonment for ten years. It criminalizes extortion by threatening to accuse someone of such serious offenses.

44. Correct Option: A – 'A' commits robbery by holding 'B' down and fraudulently taking 'B's cell phone without consent. Robbery involves theft accompanied by the use of force or intimidation, which is evident in this scenario.

45. Correct Option: B – If 'A' obtains a decree against 'B' for a sum not due, and does so fraudulently, 'A' may be guilty of an offense under the IPC. Fraudulent actions to deceive the court and cause wrongful loss to another are punishable offenses.

46. Correct Option: B – Section 194 of the Indian Penal Code pertains to giving or fabricating false evidence with the intent to procure the conviction of a capital offense. It imposes stringent penalties for such actions, especially if they lead to the execution of an innocent person.

47. Wrong question / options. Section 194 of the Indian Penal Code (IPC) prescribes severe penalties for giving or fabricating false evidence with the intent to procure the conviction of a person for a capital offence. The punishment includes imprisonment for life, or rigorous imprisonment for up to ten years, and a fine. If an innocent person is wrongfully convicted and executed as a result of such false evidence, the individual responsible may face the death penalty or the previously mentioned punishments. Therefore, the options A to D, do not align with the punishments stipulated under Section 194 IPC.

48. Correct Option: A – 'A' commits dishonest misappropriation of property by picking up 'Z's lost ring and pledging it to raise a loan. This act involves dishonestly converting another's property for personal use without consent.

49. Correct Option: A – 'Z' has committed no offense. Under Section 81 of the Indian Penal Code, an act likely to cause harm, done without criminal intent and to prevent other harm, is not an offense. In this case, 'Z' acted in good faith to rescue 'A' from the tiger, knowing the risk involved.

50. Correct Option: C – 'A' is guilty of the offense of hurt. Section 330 of the Indian Penal Code criminalizes causing hurt to extort a confession. By torturing 'Z' to induce a confession, 'A' has committed this offense.

51. Correct Option: C – All three statements cover the definition of "domestic violence" under the Protection of Women from Domestic Violence Act, 2005. The Act defines domestic violence broadly, including physical, emotional, and economic harm inflicted by a family

member; any act of violence committed against a woman in her home; and any form of abuse occurring within a domestic setting.

52. Correct Option: C – The Protection of Women from Domestic Violence Act, 2005 (PWDVA) recognizes multiple forms of domestic violence, including physical and verbal abuse. Physical abuse involves any act that causes bodily harm or endangers the health or life of the aggrieved person. Verbal abuse includes insults, ridicule, humiliation, and name-calling, which can harm the mental well-being of the victim. Therefore, both physical and verbal abuse are acknowledged under the PWDVA as forms of domestic violence. Given this, the correct answer is (C) None is true, as both (A) Physical abuse and (B) Verbal abuse are recognized forms of domestic violence under the Act.

53. Correct Option: D – Section 22 of the Protection of Women from Domestic Violence Act, 2005 provides for compensation orders. It allows the Magistrate to direct the respondent to pay compensation and damages for injuries, including mental torture and emotional distress, caused by acts of domestic violence.

54. Correct Option: B – Section 31 of the Protection of Women from Domestic Violence Act, 2005 prescribes a punishment of up to one year imprisonment, or a fine of up to twenty thousand rupees, or both, for breaching a protection order by the respondent.

55. Correct Option: A – Only Statement 1 is true. The Protection of Women from Domestic Violence Act, 2005 provides for the establishment of Protection Officers to assist victims of domestic violence. However, the Act does not specifically provide for the rehabilitation of children of victims of domestic violence.

56. Correct Option: B – If the prescribed period of limitation for any application expires on a holiday, the application may be made on the day when the court reopens. Section 4 of the Limitation Act, 1963, provides that when the prescribed period expires on a day when the court is closed, the application may be made on the day the court reopens.

57. Correct Option: B – Section 5 of the Limitation Act applies to appeals and applications. It allows the extension of the prescribed period for filing an appeal or application if the appellant or applicant can prove sufficient cause for the delay.

58. Correct Option: A – Section 5 of the Limitation Act does not apply to suits. The extension of the prescribed period under Section 5 is applicable only to appeals and applications, not to the institution of suits.

59. Correct Option: C – The incorrect proposition is: "In computing the period of limitation for any suit, the day from which such period is to be reckoned shall not be excluded." According to Section 12 of the Limitation Act, in computing the period of limitation for any suit, the day from which the period is to be reckoned shall be excluded.

60. Correct Option: A – The plaintiff shall not get the benefit under Section 14 of the Limitation Act where another civil proceeding is disposed of after adjudication on merits by the competent court. Section 14 allows for the exclusion of time spent in bona fide litigation in a court lacking jurisdiction; it does not apply when the previous suit was decided on its merits by a competent court.

61. Correct Option: D – The Supreme Court in N. Balakrishnan v. M. Krishnamurthy held that the length of delay is immaterial as long as a satisfactory explanation is provided, emphasizing that condonation of delay is at the court's discretion and broadening the scope of the Limitation Act.

62. Correct Option: D – A suit for possession of immovable property based on title can be brought within 12 years from the date when the defendant's possession becomes adverse to the plaintiff.

63. Correct Option: A – If the defendant is abroad during the period of limitation, such period is excluded from the period of limitation.

64. Correct Option: D – Section 14 of the Limitation Act, 1963, allows for the exclusion of time spent in pursuing a civil proceeding with due diligence and in good faith in a court that ultimately lacks jurisdiction or faces a similar impediment. Failure to pay the requisite court fee or errors in valuing a suit are generally considered lapses on the part of the plaintiff and may indicate a lack of due diligence or good faith. Therefore, neither (A) Failure to pay the requisite court fee found deficient nor (B) Error of judgment in valuing a suit amounts to presenting civil proceedings with due diligence and in good faith within the meaning of Section 14. Thus, the correct answer is (D) Neither (A) nor (B).

65. Correct Option: D – An indemnity-holder acting within the scope of his authority is entitled to recover from the promisor all damages, costs, and sums paid under any compromise of any suit.

66. Correct Option: B – Continuing Guarantee

is defined under Section 129 of the Indian Contract Act.

67. Correct Option: D – Anson stated that an offer need not be made to an ascertained person, but no contract can arise until it has been accepted by an ascertained person.

68. Correct Option: B – Quasi-contracts emerged from indebitatus assumpsit, a common law form of action for debt recovery.

69. Correct Option: D – Novation is not a quasi-contract; it involves the substitution of a new contract or party, replacing an existing agreement.

70. Correct Option: D – The contract between 'X' and the tent house is frustrated due to the imposition of a curfew, rendering the performance of the marriage celebration impossible. Under Section 56 of the Indian Contract Act, 1872, a contract becomes void when an act becomes impossible to perform after the contract is made. Therefore, 'X' is not liable to pay the contracted charges.

71. Correct Option: B – In a joint loan agreement, all co-borrowers are jointly and severally liable for the repayment of the entire loan amount. The insolvency of 'X' does not absolve 'Y' from the obligation to repay the full loan. Therefore, 'Z' is entitled to sue 'Y' alone for the entire outstanding amount.

72. Correct Option: B – The principle that damages for breach of contract should be those that arise naturally from the breach or those that were in the contemplation of both parties at the time of contract formation was established in the case of Hadley v. Baxendale.

73. Correct Option: D – Section 73 of the Indian Contract Act, 1872, which deals with compensation for loss or damage caused by breach of contract, is based on the principles established in the case of Hadley v. Baxendale.

74. Correct Option: D – Under the Specific Relief Act, 1963, the term "settlement" refers to an instrument, including a codicil or will, whereby the destination or devolution of successive interests in movable or immovable property is disposed of or is agreed to be disposed of.

75. Correct Option: B – The Specific Relief Act, 1963, was enacted following the recommendations of the Law Commission of India's Ninth Report (1958), which reviewed the Specific Relief Act of 1877.

76. Correct Option: C – An order or decree passed in a suit under Section 6 of the Specific Relief Act is neither appealable nor reviewable. Section 6(3) explicitly states that no appeal shall lie from any order or decree passed in any suit instituted under this section, nor shall any review of any such order or decree be allowed.

77. Correct Option: B – A defendant in a suit for recovery of possession of immovable property cannot take the plea of lawful title and, in the alternative, the plea of adverse possession, as these two defenses are mutually exclusive. The two are antithetical to each other.

78. Correct Option: A – If any person is dispossessed of immovable property without his consent and otherwise than in due course of law, he may, by a suit, recover possession thereof within six months from the date of dispossession.

79. Correct Option: B – Option (B) explicitly states a contract involving continuous duty that courts cannot supervise, it matches Clause (d) of Section 14(1). Hence, Option (B) is correct.

80. Correct Option: D – According to Section 41 of the Specific Relief Act, 1963, no injunction can be granted to restrain a person from prosecuting or instituting criminal proceedings. The court cannot intervene in criminal matters by issuing a restraining order against the prosecution of a criminal case. Thus, no such injunction can be granted to prevent Mr. 'A' from pursuing criminal proceedings.

81. Correct Option: A – In Union of India v. Ibrahim (2012) 8 SCC 148, the Supreme Court addressed the maintainability of a suit seeking only a declaration of title to property without a claim for possession, particularly when the plaintiff is not in possession. The Court held that such a suit is not maintainable under Section 34 of the Specific Relief Act, 1963.

82. Correct Option: C – Injunctions cannot be granted in cases where the performance would impede infrastructure projects or where the contract performance is not subject to specific enforcement. Specifically, it cannot be granted to prevent the breach of a contract that involves services not enforceable in nature, nor can it restrain proceedings in a civil matter under specific circumstances.

83. Correct Option: B – The doctrine of 'lis pendens' in Section 52 of the Transfer of Property Act does not invalidate the transfer of immovable property during the pendency of a suit but makes it subject to the result of the litigation. This means the purchaser of property during the suit is bound by the judgment, even if they are not a party to the suit.

84. Correct Option: B – 'D's title is not affected by the rule of lis pendens because the transfer occurred during the pendency of a suit but before 'B' was made a party to the suit. Since 'B'

was not a party to the suit at the time of the transfer to 'D', the doctrine of lis pendens does not apply.

85. Correct Option: B – The correct matching of the provisions with their respective sections is: Sale: Section 54, Marshalling: Section 81, Gift: Section 122, Contingent Interest: Section 21

86. Correct Option: D – In a simple mortgage, the mortgagor retains possession and agrees to repay the loan. Here, A mortgages his house for a Rs. 5,000 loan from B. The deed states that if A fails to repay within 5 years, B can sell the property to recover the amount, and A remains liable for any shortfall, making it a simple mortgage.

87. Correct Option: B – The mortgagor's right to redeem the mortgage property arises when the mortgage money has become due, as per Section 60 of the Transfer of Property Act. The right to redeem can be exercised after the debt is due.

88. Correct Option: C – The mortgagee has the right to sue for the mortgage money under both Section 68(1)(c) and Section 68(1)(d) of the Transfer of Property Act. These provisions allow the mortgagee to sue when they are deprived of their security or when the mortgagor fails to deliver possession of the mortgaged property.

89. Correct Option: D – The correct matches are: (a) Doctrine of Subrogation is under Section 92 of the Transfer of Property Act (TPA), allowing a person who settles another's debt to claim their rights. (b) Doctrine of Consideration is under Section 61, dealing with the transfer of property for consideration. (c) Doctrine of Accumulation is under Section 17, restricting the accumulation of income from property. (d) Doctrine of lis pendens is under Section 52, which prevents the transfer of property during ongoing litigation to ensure the final decision is effective. The correct matching of the doctrines with their respective sections is: Doctrine of Subrogation: Section 92, Doctrine of Consideration: Section 17, Doctrine of Accumulation: Section 61, Doctrine of Lis Pendens: Section 52

90. Correct Option: D – The payment made by 'A' to 'B' is valid, and 'C' cannot sue 'A' for the debt. According to Section 131 of the Transfer of Property Act, a debtor is only liable to the new creditor (i.e., 'C') after being notified of the transfer. In the absence of such notice, 'A' has discharged the debt by paying 'B'. Since 'A' was not aware of the transfer, the payment to 'B' remains valid.

91. Correct Option: D – The gift of the house made by 'A' to 'B', with the condition that the gift will be forfeited if 'B' does not reside in it, is valid. A condition that involves the forfeiture of the gift if certain conditions are not met (like residence in this case) is enforceable, as long as it does not violate public policy.

92. Correct Option: B – Under Section 15(2) of the Hindu Succession Act, 1956, if a female Hindu inherits property from her father or mother, and there are no children (or children of pre-deceased children), the property will devolve not upon the heirs specified in Section 15(1) but upon the heirs of her father.

93. Correct Option: B – Section 22 of the Hindu Marriage Act, 1955, mandates that all proceedings under the Act be conducted in camera (i.e., not open to the public) and prohibits the printing or publishing of any matter related to these proceedings, except with prior permission from the court.

94. Correct Option: C – Escheat under the Hindu Succession Act occurs when an individual dies intestate (without a will) and does not leave behind an heir qualified to succeed the property. In such cases, the property devolves to the Government.

95. Correct Option: C – A codicil is an addendum to a will. It is created by the original creator of the will and can modify or add to the provisions of the will without altering its fundamental structure. It is not a separate will but an extension of the original.

96. Correct Option: D – In a coparcenary property, each coparcener can acquire an interest by partition, birth, or attaining majority. These events can alter the share and rights of each coparcener within the family property under the Mitakshara system.

97. Correct Option: B – According to the Hindu Succession Act, 1956, a father is considered a Class I heir, while a daughter's son is considered a Class II heir; therefore, the correct answer is (B) Father is placed in class I and daughter's son is placed in class II of the Schedule.

98. Correct Option: D – Under Section 26 of the Hindu Succession Act, 1956, a Hindu who converts to another religion is disqualified from inheriting the property of their Hindu relatives. Furthermore, their descendants, born after the conversion, are also disqualified from inheriting the property of any of their Hindu relatives, unless they are Hindus at the time when the succession opens.

99. Correct Option: B – In the case of Prakash v. Phulwati, the court dealt with the interpretation of Section 6 of the Hindu Succession Act, 1956, as amended by the Hindu Succession Amendment Act, 2005. This amendment granted daughters equal rights to ancestral property, making it an important judgment regarding the retrospective application of the Act.

100. Correct Option: B – The case of Vineeta Sharma v. Rakesh Sharma, 2020 dealt with the joint family system under Hindu law, particularly regarding the rights of daughters in coparcenary property under the Mitakshara law. The court's decision clarified that daughters have equal rights in the joint family property, making this case crucial in understanding the impact of the Hindu Succession Amendment Act, 2005.